Time, Memory,
and the Verbal Arts

Walter J. Ong, SJ, University Professor Emeritus of Humanities, Saint Louis University, St. Louis, Mo.

Time, Memory, and the Verbal Arts

Essays on the Thought of Walter Ong

Edited by
Dennis L. Weeks
and Jane Hoogestraat

SUP

Selinsgrove: Susquehanna University Press
London: Associated University Presses

Associated University Presses
440 Forsgate Drive
Cranbury, NJ 08512

Associated University Presses
16 Barter Street
London WC1A 2AH, England

Associated University Presses
P.O. Box 338, Port Credit
Mississauga, Ontario
Canada L5G 4L8

The paper used in this publication meets the requirements
of the American National Standard for Permanence of Paper
for Printed Library Materials Z39.48-1984.

Library of Congress Cataloging-in-Publication Data

Time, memory, and the verbal arts : essays on the thought of Walter
  Ong / edited by Dennis L. Weeks and Jane Hoogestraat.
      p.   cm.
  Includes bibliographical references and index.
  ISBN 1-57591-009-8 (alk. paper)
    1. Oral communication.   2. Written communication.   3. Ong, Walter
J.—Contributions in oral communication.   I. Weeks, Dennis L.,
1948–   .   II. Hoogestraat, Jane Susan, 1959–   .
P95.T562   1998
302.2—dc21
                                                              98-10635
                                                              CIP

Dedicated to
The Rev. Walter J. Ong, SJ, whose work spans the millennia

Contents

8 CONTENTS

Introduction

DENNIS L. WEEKS and JANE HOOGESTRAAT

EDITING A COLLECTION OF ESSAYS ON WALTER J. ONG IS A FORMIDABLE task. Ong's life covers eight decades and a varied range of topics and interests. His bibliography begins in 1939 with a poem, "Cosmologist," published in the *Fleur de Lis* at Saint Louis University. From that date on, each year is filled with contribution after contribution to studies of contemporary culture, literary interpretation and theory, the evolution of human consciousness, the interrelation of orality and literacy, rhetoric, philosophy, psychology, history of ideas, linguistics, theology, and other subjects. A rapid count of the entries in Ong's bibliography in *A Festschrift for Walter J. Ong* published in *Oral Tradition* 2, no. 1 (January 1987) shows 196 titles through 1986. This number does not include the translations of his nineteen book-length publications or the contributions that he has made to many volumes edited by others. An estimate of the translations, collections, chapters, and articles constituting Ong's work would certainly put the number around four hundred.

Time, Memory, and the Verbal Arts: Essays on the Thought of Walter Ong reflects its authors' sense, widely shared by others, that Ong's thought is not only currently well established but also likely to be important well into the future to those studying the history of verbalization and of human consciousness in diverse fields from cultural history through literary theory, philosophy, and much else. Scholars and others across the world know Ong's work on the evolution of human consciousness as verbal communication moves from orality to literacy and on to what he has styled the "secondary orality" of radio and television. The development of his thought on these matters provides the focus of the present book, *Time, Memory, and the Verbal Arts: Essays on the Thought of Walter Ong*. The first section of this book, "The Historical and Continuing Relevance of Ong's Thought," contains four essays, thematically arranged, that examine Ong's seminal work concerning orality and literacy. The second section, "Ongian Readings," has six essays arranged in chronological order, from the medieval period to the twentieth century, each essayist considering a particular literary period or author, especially in relation to Ong's treatment of oral and literate cultures.

While this collection presupposes some familiarity on the part of the reader with Ong's thinking, it does not exclude novice readers. Rather, the collection seeks to attract as wide a spectrum of readers as possible. Readers encountering Ong for the first time may find, however, two additional volumes useful. In 1991, Thomas J. Farrell published "An Overview of Walter J. Ong's Work" in the volume *Media, Consciousness, and Culture: Explorations of Walter Ong's Thought*, edited by Bruce E. Gronbeck, Thomas J. Farrell, and Paul A. Soukup. This collection as a whole presents applications of Ong's work to issues of social practices as well as to issues current in communication studies. In 1992, Michael Kleine published "Ong's Theory of Orality and Literacy: A Perspective from Which to Re-view Theories of Discourse" in *The Philosophy of Discourse: The Rhetorical Turn of Twentieth-Century Thought*, edited by Chip Sills and George H. Jensen. This collection is a two-volume work consisting of separate chapters on the work of C. S. Pierce, Richard Rorty, Theodore W. Adorno, Jürgen Habermas, Mikhail Bakhtin, Kenneth Burke, Walter Ong, Hayden White, Claude Lévi-Strauss, Jacques Lacan, Jacques Derrida, Michel Foucault, Jean-François Lyotard, Martin Heidegger, Hans-Georg Gadamer, Ernst Cassirer, and an assortment of woman writers, together with other authors in passing. Besides providing some seven interpretive explanatory chapters, Sills and Jensen have completed the best collection currently available in situating and comparing Ong's work. Kleine's essay argues the importance of Ong's work to literary theory in general and to composition theory in particular. The availability of these valuable introductions to Ong's work is evidence of his continuing importance across many disciplines.

As background for the present introduction, on 3 and 4 September 1993 Dennis Weeks conducted an informal interview with Ong, touching on Ong's own personal understanding of his work and some of its background. The conversation was as provocative and intricate as Ong himself. This introduction and its postscript have drawn on this interview and on further exchanges between Ong and Weeks.

One aspect of Ong's own intellectual life that emerged from the interview was the sense he has—and others have—about the dialogic or dialectical nature of his approach to understanding. He himself recalls a remark which Hannah Arendt made to him in a conversation when, in 1960–61, he and she were both Fellows at the Center for Advanced Studies in the Liberal Arts, Professions, and Sciences (later the Center for the Humanities) at Wesleyan University in Middletown, Connecticut. Ong no longer remembers the gist of their conversation, but he remembers clearly Arendt's apodictic statement during the conversation: "You," she remarked to Ong, "have a dialectical mind." Ong took the statement as a profound compliment, as Arendt—given her own background in phenomenology—certainly meant it to be.

Ong describes his own intellectual development through his life as coming in part initially from "a dialectic between the somewhat fictitious religious medievalism which had framed the world of much Catholic and much other thought in the early years of my life and the intellectual world of those who did not share this mind set. I had my fingers crossed on both of the worlds as being neither of them totally complete. They both had something to offer, but neither of them was telling the whole story. Nobody's ever told the story yet, and nobody ever will. Needless to say, the medievalism which framed so much of Catholic thought some few generations ago is not identical with the Catholic faith, which extends far beyond any such framing."

For Ong, "telling the whole story" is a dialogic and dialectical process. Understanding comes from examining the interrelatedness of ideas or phenomena embedded in the concreteness of historical existence. Ong stated to Weeks that he thinks of his own work as basically interpretive or hermeneutic and shies away a bit from being considered a "critic," literary or other. Although he once taught courses labeled "Practical Criticism," after the book of that title by I. A. Richards, he now finds the term "criticism" somewhat censorious. His earlier courses in "Practical Criticism" he later renamed "Practice of Interpretation." He is suspicious of monolithic "theories." His own work on orality-literacy issues, including the technologizing of verbal expression through writing, print, and electronics he regards as reportorial and interpretive and necessarily incomplete, not as an attempt to devise a comprehensive theory.

Ong is acutely aware that "total verbal explicitness is impossible" (an observation that countless students and others have heard him reiterate). He notes that this does not mean that you do not know quite what another person is saying, but that verbal communication, textual as well as oral, always occurs in a com-

munication situation involving more than words. It is a commonplace of discourse analysis that verbalized meaning is always
embodied and validated and understood in nonverbal as well as
verbal contexts—such as assumptions or unarticulated para-
digms shared by speaker (or writer) and hearer (or reader), and
so on ad infinitum. The most straightforward propositional statements always occur in nonverbal contexts. Ong illustrates the
point with the observation that the complete "content" of its
own teaching cannot be stated in a finite series of propositional
statements by the Roman Catholic Church or by anyone else.
True statements expressing central elements in the teaching can
be made, but they are always incomplete in their explicit verbal
formulations, involving the understanding of something more
than the purely verbal (or even the nonverbalizable). Earlier cre-
dal statements of the Church had to be fleshed out in the later
so-called Nicene Creed and other creeds. And, since new questions and thus the possibilities of new insights into the total
life of the Church had emerged and will continue to emerge
throughout history, further explicitation is likely to continue in-
definitely. This is a far cry from saying that we cannot know
what Christian teaching on a given matter is. Church teaching is
known both in articulated statements and also in not-yet-
conceptualized knowledge or awareness included in Church
"tradition." Tradition is in greater part nonverbal, learned simply by living in the Christian community. Thus the Church's
teaching can be subject to hermeneutic development as tradition
previously unarticulated is made subject to articulation. But all
that we know is not known articulately: we know many things
which we have never articulated or never fully articulated.

Perhaps in accord with his sense of the impossibility of reduc-
ing full knowledge and understanding to a finite series of propositional statements which invite no further explanation, Ong
stated that he is reluctant to be identified with any particular
"school" or "movement," literary, philosophical, or other. This
is evident, for example, in the case of the New Criticism, to which
Marshall McLuhan introduced him when McLuhan taught
(1937–44) at Saint Louis University. The New Criticism had con-
centrated on the work of literature as a self-contained creation,
to be evaluated on its own, uncomplicated by biographical considerations concerning the author or other considerations outside it, appropriated in terms of its own object-like consistency,
as a truth that is "solid," a self-contained unit thought of as
something perceived by touch (often backed by sight). These

emphases had been caught in the titles of Cleanth Brooks's *The Well Wrought Urn* and William K. Wimsatt's *The Verbal Icon*. In "The Jinnee in the Well Wrought Urn," first published in 1954 in *Essays in Criticism*, Ong insisted that such tactile-visualist, object-like analogies can distort our sense of what a work of literature is. For a work of literature is basically a verbal creation, precisely not like a visual and/or tactile object. It consists of words, which are basically sounds, utterances ultimately between persons. The tangible "object" of much New Criticism turns out to have something alive and vocal within it, represented here by Ong as something of itself invisible but responsive and resonant, a jinnee or jinni. Although Ong's preoccupations here show some of his deviance from doctrines of the New Criticism, he has always valued the New Criticism's emphasis on close, attentive reading of the text, which, he reiterates, always has a nontextual as well as a textual context. The dialectical movement of Ong's thought is nowhere more evident than in his handling of the dialectic of textual and nontextual relationships. Text explains the nontextual, and the nontextual explains the textual. What we know involves the interaction of the two.

Orality and Literacy: The Technologizing of the Word (1982) continues Ong's interpretation of oral cultures and textual cultures (first chirographic or writing cultures, then print cultures) elaborated in *The Presence of the Word*, the Terry Lectures which he delivered at Yale University, published in 1967. The latter work itself connects with Ong's lengthy 1958 studies, *Ramus, Method, and the Decay of Dialogue* and *Ramus and Talon Inventory*, which exposed the social and psychological effects of print on the Renaissance mind and world view. These two volumes and further publications of Ong's show that it was Peter Ramus (Pierre de la Ramée, 1515–72), rather than Descartes, who marked the beginning of the quest for a method of knowing whose primary aim was clarity and distinctness. We associate clarity and distinctness most readily with visual apprehension rather than with apprehension by sound, smell, hearing, or touch. Our fixation on written texts and, even more, on printed texts, with their visible fixity and concomitant specious "clarity," has inhibited attention to the spoken word, which is never fixed or immobile. Speech rides the flow of time. Speech is sound, which, unlike visual texts, exists only when it is going out of existence. The spoken word is alive as it passes through time. Visible texts can be made alive, can generate knowledge only when they are read, that is, when they are loosened from their fixed bondage as visible texts and reintroduced into the world of sound and of evanescent succession in time, either exteriorly by being read aloud or by being sounded in our imagination. Unless a text can be read, it is a nontext. In this sense, all text is pretext.

A written text is a material human creation, tactile as well as visual, a physical, manipulable object, an artifact, something manufactured with the use of instruments, nowadays commonly hightech instruments (few people make their own ballpoint pens). A written text—or a printed text—can be folded, stored on a shelf, torn up, or crumpled and burned. Spoken words are not like this, not artifacts, Ong insists. They leave no material residue. They perish as they come into existence. In pronouncing the word *existence*, by the time the speaker gets to the *-tence*, the *exis-* is gone.

"What about the case of the tape recorder that is spinning along here as we complete this interview?" Ong's response to this query by Weeks ties in with his preceding remarks. The taped speech is also something made, an artifact, as direct oral speech is not. The tape is an object in space which, with the help of other complex artifacts, can re-create sound. As in reading a text, so in the use of tape something silent must be processed into the sound world to convey verbalized meaning. To understand a taped text, we must *listen* to the tape, not simply *look* at it, just as, to understand a text we are reading, we must convert its visual symbols into sound, *hearing* ourselves *reading* the text (aloud or in the imagination). Only when transformed into the sound world does the technological creation yield words that we can understand directly.

However, a tape is not writing. Like radio and television, a tape is a new technological development belonging to the new world, which Ong has styled the world of "secondary orality." Like the world of "primary orality," antecedent to writing, this new world is also a world of sound. But the sounds of secondary orality are produced by technological creations which can themselves be made only by means of knowledge and skills developed through the use of writing and reading. Secondary orality is orality technologically manufactured by literates. No purely oral culture could develop radio or television or sound tapes. By contrast, primary orality is nontechnological; it requires no instruments to produce speech sounds, but only the human body itself. More recent developments in electronics have made the technologizing of the word—hardware and software—even more complicated.

"Secondary orality" affects the communications world now on all sides as never before.

How does Ong's thought relate to later schools or theories that have superseded the now old New Criticism—women's studies, for example, or structuralism, deconstruction, reader-response interpretation, the New Historicism? The answer is not easy, for in his own way Ong's work incorporates many of the perspectives of such various "schools," as the studies in the present volume illustrate. Gender issues, for example, emerge prominently in his *Fighting for Life: Contest, Sexuality, and Consciousness*, the Messenger Lectures on the Evolution of Civilization delivered at Cornell University in 1979 and published in 1981. Here and in other related publications of his, Ong reports on the ways in which orality and literacy came to be involved in the ordinarily nonlethal contest for dominance that marks the animal kingdom. The history of Latin is crucial here. Gradually displaced as vernacular by the Romance languages to which it had given birth (no longer a vernacular *anywhere* after around A.D. 700), Latin developed into a textual bastion of masculinity. It was the language used in Western Europe for all subjects, secular as well as religious, in the all-male world of literate academia through the Renaissance and after, a sex-linked, all but exclusively male language, known to no one who could not write it, never learned by progression through a baby-talk stage, never a first language to anyone who used it, normally taught outside the home to young males by older males in a totally male contest which normally, and not just incidentally, entailed severe physical punishment (caning, and so on), learned in a highly competitive educational milieu conspicuously marked virtually everywhere by the male paradigm of agonistic orality, the disputation (cf. the ritual—nonlethal—combat between males in subhuman animal species, generally more marked in species higher in the evolutionary chain). In short, in the West, from late antiquity till well after the Renaissance, Latin language study ordinarily constituted a textually based male puberty rite, toughening boys into men. Latin was not alone here: comparable, although not identical, patterns of male dominance through textuality are found in the development of Rabbinical Hebrew, Classical Arabic, Sanskrit, and Classical Chinese.

The gradual displacement of Latin at the heart of all academic curricula took place *pari passu* with the entry of females into the academy—and, among other things with the beginnings of the modern novel, a genre marked from the start by its many women authors, typically featuring not heroic external combat so much as personal introspective development. Ong remarked that orality-literacy studies need to include examination of the larger societal and other implications of patterns in feminine development which are not directly apparent in the almost exclusively male track over which for centuries the historical transit from orality to literacy had taken place. Our present knowledge of the transition from orality to literacy has, of necessity, been worked out by following the most accessible path of the complex orality-to-literacy shift, namely that of a privileged male sector of society, where the orality-literacy shift was most directly in evidence. But the shift affected society also beyond the privileged male sector. The effects of this shift on other parts of society—women and non-privileged males—need much more study than they have yet been accorded.

As for other forms of recent literary and related theory, Ong departs from deconstruction, he explained in the Weeks interview, largely over what he sees as the failure of deconstruction to engage the now massive work focused directly on the use of language in cultures without writing or even an awareness of the possibility of writing. In *High Resolution: Critical Theory and the Problem of Literacy* (New York/Oxford: Oxford University Press, 1989), Henry S. Sussman has stated (215) that "To a remarkable degree, Ong successfully extrapolates a model of orality that can stand alongside the Derridean constellation of qualities and attitudes associated with writing in its explicitness and comprehensiveness" (215). Pointing out that *Homo sapiens* has been on earth, as our best estimates suggest, probably some 150,000 years and that writing is only 5,000 to 6,000 years old, Ong believes that thinking of oral cultures before writing as though their speech were some retrojected variant of writing malforms the concept of orality and fails to do justice to what is now well known about orality from direct fieldwork and painstaking analysis, historical and linguistic. For some 150,000 years, until 5,000 to 6,000 years ago, all human cultures have been oral cultures, and, even today, most cultures are still basically or residually oral.

Ong is explicitly well aware that oral cultures are always studied through the use of texts by those who study them. Orality can develop great "wisdom," but cannot develop the closely reasoned "linear" analysis common in the academic and scientific work of writing, print, and electronic cultures. There is no oral "science" of orality itself, for there is no oral "science" of anything.

All scientific or scholarly explanation depends directly or indirectly on texts (and now more and more on electronic media, which pose special problems of their own). Ong's 1985 Wolfson College Lecture at Oxford (published 1986) is entitled "Writing Is a Technology That Restructures Thought." As the lecture itself makes clear, what is restructured is not only written texts of literates but also oral expression by literates. It is a commonplace of discourse analysis that fully literate peoples do not even converse orally in ways typical of oral peoples, although, of course, there are various degrees of literacy and various mixtures of orality and literacy in diverse cultures and settings. But the fact that literates' thinking, and even oral speech, and thus our very understanding of orality, is molded by writing does not mean that we cannot assess the consequences of our literate mentality and thought forms on our study of orality and compensate for them. Thought is not like things. A given form of thought can be reflectively aware of itself and of its own limitations—which is the next best thing to being rid of the limitations. Paradoxically, the use of texts gives us the ability to evaluate both orality as orality and text as text in their often complex relationships, noting, through fieldwork and otherwise, the striking differences as well as the resemblances between orally governed thinking and our own.

The Historical and Continuing Relevance of Ong's Thought

The essays in this volume have been grouped in two sections. In the first section of the book, Julie Stone Peters, in her essay, "Orality, Literacy, and Print Revisited," explores the reevaluation of orality-literacy theory which has drawn heavily on Ong's work and addressed the conjunction of poetics, stylistics, and epistemology that Ong developed from his own early work and the work of classicists such as Milman Parry and Eric Havelock and anthropologists such as Jack Goody. The various critiques, by literary theorists and critical anthropologists, themselves inspired principally by Derrida and Habermas, challenge Ong on the grounds that he has fallen into precisely the ethnocentric historiography of which early anthropology was guilty and which Ong in fact is at pains to avoid. While pointing out the similar historiographic and idealist fallacies of which such critiques are themselves guilty, Peters identifies the ways in which

Ong's work, reflectively utilized, might continue to serve as a foundation for explorations of orality, literacy, print, and electronic communications technologies. Ong's work is still useful as critics attempt to formulate transcultural and transhistorical vocabularies for describing the ways in which different groups use media of communication.

Jane Hoogestraat's essay, "'Discoverers of Something New': Ong, Derrida, and Postcolonial Theory," explores Ong's notion of primary and secondary orality and how these are useful terms in the ongoing engagement of literary critics with the discourses of both postcolonialism and feminism. Hoogestraat points out two ideas: Ong's work has contemporary political application in that it allows for a means of recreating the past histories of those excluded from dominant, colonial languages because they could not write those languages; those who could not write in the colonizing languages either did not speak these languages in the first place (in the case of the indigenous peoples of the Americas) or did not, prior to the seventeenth century (in the case of most European women and many men), know how to read them. She concludes that it is of crucial theoretical importance in the present that postcolonial theorists reserve a space for at least imagining and marking the absence of lost oral traditions and cultures, which existed external to the written accounts of the colonizers.

Vincent Casaregola, writing in "Orality, Literacy, and Dialogue: Looking for the Origins of the Essay," explains that the "familiar" or "personal" essay began to evolve in the late sixteenth century, at the very time during which printing was becoming a powerful force in European culture. As Montaigne and Bacon launched the first ventures into the new genre, the culture was shifting from one in which oral discourse had dominated the assumptions about the nature of language to one in which the written (especially the printed) text would become the principal paradigm of language. Taking Ong's explanation of "residual orality" as a starting point, this essay develops an important understanding of the evolution and nature of the personal essay.

Finally, John Miles Foley addresses the relationship between a traditional oral bard and his or her audience in "The Bard's Audience Is Always More Than a Fiction." In concert with his recent studies, especially *Immanent Art* (1991) and *Word Power, Performance, and Tradition* (1993), his essay extends the examination of those liminal cases in which we must confront oral tradition preserved solely in the form of manuscripts. The crucial question for Foley is what difference the face-to-face interaction between performer and audience—real or rhetorical—makes to the nature of the communication.

Ongian Readings

In the second section of the collection, Werner H. Kelber's contribution is a revised version of the Milman Parry–Albert Lord Lecture he delivered on 11 October 1993 at the University of Missouri, Columbia, under the title "Language, Memory, and Sense Perception in the Religious and Technological Culture of Antiquity and the Middle Ages." In this revised version, "Incarnations, Remembrances and Transformations of the Word," Kelber suggests that words, as fundamentally spoken, "live in the evanescent actuality of sound, and shifts from sound to silence, and from temporality to spatiality, bring about alienation and complexification of human thought"—a thesis central to Ong's life work. Kelber's essay pays tribute to Ong by demonstrating the implications of Ong's theories from ancient to medieval culture, showing the connectedness between oral and chirographic incarnations of the word and the structuring of thought.

"'Lewedly To a Lewed Man Speke': Chaucer's Defense of the Vulgar Tongue," by James R. Andreas, notes that Rousseau writes—curiously—that "Writing is nothing but the representation of speech; it is bizarre that one gives more care to the determining of the image than to the object." Not so for Chaucer, who showed a predilection for the oral, vulgar tongue over written, polite language throughout his literary career. Chaucer's works are riddled with explanations about the primacy of speech "experienced" as opposed to written texts that are "authored," and which then come to represent the "dictates" of "auctoritee." Some of the major cultural critics of the twentieth century, including Ong, have pioneered the rediscovery that *language*, as the very term itself conveys from the Latin, *lingua*, is first and foremost a *tongue*. This rediscovery owes its debt to Chaucer's "mother tongue" while simultaneously illuminating central aspects of Chaucer's use of the vernacular.

Alvin Kernan, in "What the King Saw, What the Poet Wrote: Shakespeare Plays before King James," explains that the social and psychological effects of oral culture and print culture, Ong's central interest, appear in interesting ways in a variety of historical scenes at critical points of transition. One such historical scene is the interaction of King James I, a monarch who wrote and published, with his official playwright William Shakespeare, an actor and dramatist who, nonetheless, had a Gutenberg vocabulary and style in the theater, an oral-visual medium. The complexities of this situation are tracked by Kernan in his essay as he stipulates that the simple kinds of meaning transmitted by oral performance in the theater appear in the response of the king and his court to the play. The complex and subtle meanings characteristic of print appear, especially in *Hamlet*, in the way the internal plays comment on the surrounding world of play.

In "The Beautiful and the Merely Pleasing: Love, Art, and 'The Jinnee in the Well Wrought Urn,'" Patrick Colm Hogan takes as his starting point some of Ong's observations in "The Jinnee in the Well Wrought Urn." Specifically it explores the traditional aesthetic problem of differentiating beauty from the "merely pleasing," in Kant's phrase. While Ong's observations on love and literary response indicate how this problem might be solved, they also raise questions about the degree to which reciprocation or the possibility of reciprocation is necessary for a feeling of aesthetic pleasure.

Sister Anne Denise Brennan, SC, explores the relevance of Ong's work in "Breaking the Ice: Some Highlights of the History of *Humor* and *Sense of Humor*." In her essay, Brennan asserts that present-day studies on the eighteenth and nineteenth centuries can profit from attention to change in the use of the term *humor* and to the appearance of the phrase *sense of humor* during this period, as indicated by comparative studies of various dictionaries and of usage citations in the *OED*. Ong's studies of orality, literacy, and the development of consciousness underlie Brennan's entire presentation.

Thomas J. Farrell's essay, "Faulkner and Male Agonism," describes Faulkner as a student of male agonism or contesting behavior. Farrell's study sets forth Ong's insights about how male-male contesting enables men to establish a specifically masculine sense of identity, noting how males who have developed an inadequate sense of masculine identity will tend to feel threatened by the feminine and, therefore, may become violent toward women. Arguing further, Farrell posits that Faulkner's focus on male contesting most likely grew out of Faulkner's personal situation as well as out of his reflections on the culture of the Old South and American culture in general. The essay concludes with some reflection about how the cultural conditions under which Faulkner wrote have been changed for the better as a result of the African-American civil rights movement and the women's movement, and about how men in the 1900s might appropriate the psychodynamics of contesting to rise to new levels of human flourishing

Finally, George P. Weick in "The Crucial Antithesis: Orality/Literacy Interaction in the Poetry of Dylan Thomas" argues that Thomas's poetry, in significant ways, parallels Ong's understanding of the development of human consciousness "from the individual's awakening through 'articulate language as a self engaged in participatory union with others, through the 'division and alienation' introduced by writing, to a 'higher unity' consisting of 'more conscious interaction between persons.'" Orality/literacy polarities, as explicated by Ong, thus help clarify Thomas's thematic interests, imagery, and poetic structures.

Postscript

At the end of their interview sessions, Ong and Weeks walked through the campus of Saint Louis University, stopping first at St. Francis Xavier (College) Church to admire the recently renovated interior. Ong pointed out where the old pipe organ that he used to play had once been situated as well as the altars where he had celebrated Mass for over forty years, helping out part-time, but regularly, as other university Jesuits have likewise done in ministering to the spiritual needs of several generations.

The College Church, a parish church which also serves the University community, is located at one edge of the University campus. Only two blocks away one now finds the University Computer Services—today's latest communication technology here at work in intimate geographical contact with a liturgy that incorporates into itself forms still discernibly deriving from the successive ages of orality, of manuscript and print cultures, and of the electronic present. Ong likes to think about this geographical and temporal coincidence and to invite others also to do so.

He likes to remind his fellow Catholics and other fellow Christians that the Incarnation took place on our globe in a universe which in actuality is far different from what Moses or Aristotle or Thomas Aquinas or Dante or Milton or Galileo or Newton imagined it to be. A central theological task of Christianity today, Ong urges, is to update its cosmology—a task which a few theologians have courageously begun, but only begun. Ecclesial and other documents, even of quite recent years, he recalls, in reflecting on the course of history have referred to what they gin-

gerly distance as "the wonders of modern science," sounding as
though with "modern science" the development of the universe
has lately somehow taken an astounding and unexpected turn.
Ong insists that this is no way to react. Scientific and technological developments, including computers, are no more astounding
wonders in this universe than are mountains or roses or ele-
phants. Computers are one of the things that the universe was
from the beginning set up to produce in our time. God created
a universe, Ong never tires of saying, that would ultimately generate computers—and who knows what further in ages to come?
Whatever else may be true about the universe around us, and
about the achievements and dismaying problems of the human
beings on our globe, Ong points out that the present universe,
with all its digital communications revolutions, other changes,
and its persistent mysteries, is still, for persons of faith, just as
much God's world and the subject of God's concern and love as
it has always been.

Time, Memory,
and the Verbal Arts

Section One
The Historical and Continuing Relevance of Ong's Thought

Orality, Literacy, and Print Revisited

JULIE STONE PETERS

IN DERRIDA'S FAMOUS DISCUSSION OF THE INTRODUCTION OF WRITING among the Nambikwara (in *Of Grammatology*, now over a quarter of a century old), he describes Lévi-Strauss's lament over the introduction of writing among the Nambikwara, his outcry against the evils of writing: agent of totalitarianism, social hierarchy, empire, the violence of the law.[1] In identifying the inevitable effects of writing, Lévi-Strauss is (for Derrida) perpetuating the myth in which writing is seen as a secondary supplement to speech—as a loss, a falling away from the primacy of presence.[2] The object of study (residually still the "primitive") offers us access to an earlier form of ourselves, rawer, closer to the original, closer to life itself—to pure and unadulterated presence, not yet corrupted by the material sediment of writing.[3]

In taking it for granted that the Nambikwara have no writing, Lévi-Strauss is perpetuating another aspect of the Western myth of writing: that there are peoples without it; that it developed in the West; and that Westerners now export it to oral cultures. For, as Derrida points out, the Nambikwara make "dots and zigzags on their calabashes," they "scratch," "engrave," "scribble," "scrape," "incise," "trace," "imprint" (Derrida 122–23). Phonetic writing is just one rather narrowly construed kind of writing. Just as the Chinese word *wen* signifies not only the conglomeration of marks that makes up writing but also constellations, the tracks of birds, to tattoo (as well as literature and social courtesy [Derrida 123]), so might we, less ethnocentrically, understand "writing" to be inclusive of the whole range of traces, of inscription in the world, of the play of difference.[4]

For Derrida, the distinction between "peoples without writing" and those with it poses as an anti-ethnocentrism that masks a much deeper ethnocentrism. At the heart of Lévi-Strauss's portrait of Nambikwara oral culture—its "self-presence," its "transparent proximity in the face-to-face of countenances and the immediate range of the voice," its "social authenticity" (138)—

27

at the heart of this "classic" (Rousseausitic, Platonist) "metaphysics of presence" (135, 138) is an "ethnocentrism *thinking
itself* as anti-ethnocentrism" (120).[5]

Derrida's critique of the distinction between "peoples without
writing" and those who write, between "illiteracy" and "literacy" (132), between "oral language" (125) and written, then, re-
vokes the metaphysics on which Lévi-Strauss's unconscious
ethnocentrism relies. For Derrida the anthropological analysis
of the effects that accompany "literacy" and "orality" (like the
artificial orality/literacy distinction itself) serves classic theology
and metaphysics. By effacing the conventional boundaries between the oral and the literate, he challenges traditional studies
of speech, writing, and culture.

And yet there is still, for him, a history of "writing in the
colloquial sense," a phrase he repeats frequently throughout *Of
Grammatology* (Derrida 124, 125, and so on).[6] All forms of differentiation may be writing (and everything may be differentiation),
but the question remains: what is the meaning of "writing in the
colloquial sense"? If the lines on the Nambikwara pots aren't
altogether the same as the marks Lévi-Strauss makes in his note-
pad, in what sense are they different? If they are different—if,
for instance, those practices which have been called "writing"
and "speech" are particular in that they've perpetuated the metaphysics that has protected the ethnocentric order—what are the
cultural conditions that have accompanied their introduction,
construction, and identification? If Lévi-Strauss's "writing" is
different, and if (as a collection of simultaneously material and
cognitive effects gathered under a specific terminology: "writing") it has cultural and ideological meanings and impact, how
can those within that system of writing study the ways in which
its uses have influenced and altered thinking processes, ways of
doing things, kinds of poems people make? Without assuming
relations of inherent causation between a given communication
technology and a series of cultural effects, how can we study
technologies as they interact with cultural processes? How can
we, from inside our system of naming, study the meanings and
impact of "writing," of "print," of the "gramophone," of the
"pen"? We know that a pen is never just a pen. But then, nothing
is ever just itself.

The understanding of the nature of "literacy" has, of course, a
European history that precedes anthropological work on speech
and writing. In English, the word "literate" dates back at least
to the fifteenth century, indicating a variety of things, from the

knowledge of Latin, to learning in literature, to the ability to read and write, to European identity (as opposed to "savage").[7] The word "literate" was often used to distinguish the civilized West from the rest of the world, as Chapman suggests when he refers, in *Caesar & Pompey*, to "The Ægaean sea, that doth divide Europe from Asia. (The sweet literate world From the Barbarian)."[8] "Illiteracy" is older than "literacy," identifying, most often, ignorance of "letters" (usually, of Latin), or sometimes simply general erroneousness.

The word "literacy" is a relatively recent coinage, needed (for one) in the debates about education and suffrage in the later eighteenth and nineteenth centuries, and accompanying the proliferation of state-sponsored surveys of reading and writing. By the later nineteenth century, then, it indicated the ability to read and write in the vernacular, a quality that was seen as quite measurable, though there were disagreements as to the proper measurement of it. (The issue of what constituted—or constitutes—reading and writing, even in the conventional senses, is a complex one.)[9] "Orality" was used occasionally to describe that which was spoken as opposed to written. But academic research, appropriating it as an ostensibly nonderogatory alternative to "illiteracy," gave it more frequent usage only in the twentieth century. The ethnographic and linguistic study of the effects of writing or the cultural structures common to peoples without it gave the word "orality" new associations. Reciprocally, "literacy" came sometimes to indicate not only the capacity to write, but also the cultural attributes identified with that capacity.

Both "orality" and "literacy," then, in the twentieth century, generated formal study of the cultural effects associated with reading and writing or with their absence, emerging from centuries of speculation among classicists about the composition of the Homeric poems (speculation which Walter Ong describes at the beginning of *Orality and Literacy* [18–25], and whose twentieth-century history John Miles Foley gives in some detail in *The Theory of Oral Composition*).[10]

Such speculation, as Ong recounts, culminated in the explorations of Milman Parry who, trying to understand Homer's oral style, began to study Slavic bards in the 1920s and 1930s. Parry and many of his contemporaries and near-contemporaries (classicists like Arnold van Gennep, Albert Lord, and Eric Havelock; those like Vasilii V. Radlov, Friedrich Krauss, Matija Murko, and Marcel Jousse who had been studying contemporary oral art forms for decades) tried to identify the ways in which the conditions of oral composition and reception shaped rhetorical and formal structures, and came up with a series of conclusions about the characteristics that most oral productions share: repeating formulae (for character, scene, and theme); the mnemonic use of meter and dependence of word choice on the shape of the metrical line; the use of epithets, metrically varied to provide for a variety of exigencies; the absence of exact verbatim memory (as many argued), and so on.

The Soviet linguist A. R. Luria was, also in the 1930s, doing similar kinds of field work in Uzbekistan and Kirghizia to study what he understood as oral cognitive structures, and came up with broader sociological conclusions, not just about oral-verbal art forms but about the general thinking processes of those individuals who had grown up without writing: their preference for concrete references, for situational thinking, for the contextualization of problems; their resistance to syllogistic logic as irrelevant; their sense that the self can be evaluated only by the community (Ong 49–57).

Such work was at once linguistic, psychological, literary-stylistic, and ethnographic, and led to the possibility of cross-cultural and interdisciplinary theorizing about the cognitive effects associated with orality and literacy, and with communication technologies in general. By the time Lévi-Strauss wrote the passage on writing among the Nambikwara, the Marxist oriented critique of the relationship between technology and culture, mostly identified with the Frankfurt School, had entered into the anthropological consideration of the nature of writing, extending questions about the impact of communication technologies to the history of the developed West and, in particular, to the mechanized twentieth century, identifying specific technologies with specific cultural and political meanings, and (for technologies used in the production of art) with specific formal principles. Although there was much disagreement about the impact of particular technologies and the meaning of particular forms (as debates, for instance, among Bloch and Lukacs, Benjamin and Adorno suggested), such a politically oriented critique of technology set the stage for the new field of "media studies."

Attempting to formulate a comprehensive theory of media, fed by the 1960s neo-Marxist interest in technology, as well as its embrace of the future, Marshall McLuhan was at the center of the field. In books like The Gutenberg Galaxy (1962) and Understanding Media (1964) (as well as seductive pamphlets like The Medium is the Massage [1967]), he popularized the discussion of the impact of literacy, print, and electronic media, and became the oracle of the machine, predicting the happy future of international multimedia in the "global village." McLuhan's work, as well as the larger structuralist project of identifying cross-cultural patterns in social formations, encouraged anthropologists like Jack Goody to explore in still broader historical and cross-cultural terms the ramifications of the introduction of literacy. In *Literacy in Traditional Societies* (a collection edited in 1968), *The Domestication of the Savage Mind* (1977), *The Logic of Writing and the Organization of Society* (1986), and *The Interface Between the Written and the Oral* (1987), Goody offered broad accounts of the relationships between literacy and culture.

Exploring Renaissance rhetoric, logic and print, agonistic engagement and sexuality, the hierarchization of the senses, literacy and attitudes toward the word in text-based communities, and other aspects of the relationships among technology, consciousness, and culture, Ong helped to bring together the anthropological, linguistic, philosophic, and psychoanalytic study of orality and literacy with the historical study of printing and the book. Showing the critical relations between technology and European culture from the Renaissance on in studies like *Ramus, Method, and the Decay of Dialogue* and *Rhetoric, Romance, and Technology*, underlining the intersections of multiple and more various cultures in studies like *The Presence of the Word, Interfaces of the Word*, and *Orality and Literacy*, he explored the complex relationships between written and spoken words.

By combining the study of traditions considered "Western" and other traditions, Ong brought to more conventional work in literature and culture the recognition that orality/literacy studies need not be relegated to "peoples without writing." Indeed, as he recognized, to do so was unconsciously to perpetuate the artificial split between the "primitive" and the "civilized" by casting that split anew as the "oral" and the "literate." That division masked the interaction of modes, as Ong demonstrated, for instance, in his analysis of Renaissance copia, of the visualist oral-literate interface in mass media, or of the use of formulae in written poetry (whether that of Tudor courtiers or that of Xhosa poets). As the theorist of ethnography James Clifford has observed, Ong's work shares with Derrida's "an overarching rejection of the institutionalized ways one large group of humanity has for millennia construed its world" (Clifford 10). Cross-cultural work, as Ong's showed, could be the basis for resisting the residual bifurcation of the "savage" and the "civilized" in

the bifurcation of the "oral" and the "literate," the "Western"
and the "non-Western."

Media studies, along with early studies in print history like
Febvre and Martin's important social history of the advent of
printing, The Coming of the Book (1958) (as well as studies like
Ong's Ramus [1958] and Frances Yates's The Art of Memory
[1966]) raised a number of issues for historians of printing and
the book which they had only begun to address. The central
question for historians of print—how was the printed book "a
force for change?" (as Febvre and Martin put it in their last chapter)—was, in essence, the basis for Elizabeth Eisenstein's two-
volume The Printing Press as an Agent of Change (1979).

Eisenstein's work is, in many ways, close to that of McLuhan,
Goody, and Ong in both its vastness of scope and the strength of
its thesis: that printing technology caused a cultural revolution
in early modern Europe. Bibliographers, historians, scholars of
literacy, and those working in "sociology of the book," have, since
then, been eager to explore in greater detail some of the claims
of pioneering work like that of McLuhan, Goody, Ong, and
Eisenstein, whether to append, to correct, or to confirm. A few
examples: classicists like Rosalind Thomas and William Harris
have both substantiated and challenged some of Eric Havelock's
claims about the interiorization of literacy in fifth-century
Greece; medievalists like Brian Stock and Rosamond McKitterick
have demonstrated the vast implications of literacy for law,
administration, and poetics in thirteenth-century Europe and
earlier; historians of European printing (most notably Roger
Chartier) have examined closely regional differences in the uses
of printing; Robert Darnton has explored the relationships
among pamphlet printing, the Enlightenment, and the French
Revolution; literary scholars like Alvin Kernan (in his investigation of the intersection of print with Samuel Johnson's career)
have looked at the impact of print on the intersection of the
aesthetic and the sociopolitical.

In the last decade or so, then, many scholars and field-workers,
as well as theorists, have taken issue with aspects of what Stock
has called the "strong model" of technological impact: theories
(like Ong's, McLuhan's, Goody's, and to a certain extent
Eisenstein's) that understand new technologies as the agents of
large-scale, transhistorical, cross-cultural change and that speculate on the influence that the introduction of communication
technologies has on life and thought. Stock opposes the "strong
model" to the "weak model": local-situational descriptions of

the interaction of (new) technologies with the older ones and with a given culture (Stock 6).

The most mild form of objections to the "strong model" comes from those most interested in detailed empirical research in specific areas (history of the book in Renaissance Europe, for instance, or fieldwork on literacy in the Sudan, or studies of oral narrative in Texas, to mention a few examples). These argue that strong-model theorists offer too rigid a paradigm for cultural change, one which fails to take account of the infinitude of local differences (in historical and contemporary situations) that make up the human response to technology.

Recent fieldwork in oral artforms (described most comprehensively by Ruth Finnegan in *Oral Traditions and the Verbal Arts* [1992]) alters significantly the accepted ways of thinking about oral composition: many epic poets (as Finnegan [1977] and Sherzer [1982], for instance, have shown) do, after all, have verbatim memory; even the most conventional formulae bear a great deal more artful and inventive variation than was believed; the understanding of oral composition is incomplete without an analysis of nonverbal aspects of individual performances; contexts are crucial.

What recent fieldwork shares with recent work on the introduction of literacy and on classical and medieval orality and literacy in Europe, then, is the recognition that there are many forms of oral production, many literacies, many varied conventions in oral, literate, and printed production, many ways in which each kind of form is put to use. The proposition that specific technologies cause specific cultural effects (aesthetic, cognitive) is a kind of technological or "single-factor determinism" (Goody xv), suggesting misleadingly an inevitable "if"/"then" causality. Technologies have different effects in different localities in different periods among different elements of the population.

While most historians and anthropologists view both the "strong" and "weak" models as having both advantages and disadvantages (Stock, for instance, whose work both confirms and takes issue with Ong's, Goody's, and Eisenstein's arguments), some take serious issue with the theoretical premises of the "strong" model. The anthropologist Brian Street, for instance, whose distinction (in his *Literacy in Theory and Practice* [1984]), between "autonomous" theories of literacy and "ideological" theories is comparable to Stock's distinction between "strong" and "weak" models of change (though it has a different import), argues that "autonomous" models are fundamentally ethnocentric. For Street, such models fail to take account of the particular sociopolitical contexts in which literacy (in this case) is at issue, and hence see writing as an autonomous entity, capable of abstraction from its context. "Ideological" models, on the other hand, identify technologies of communication as having no inherent power (or even existence) in themselves, but power only in the ways they are used in specific local contexts. Such models are ideological in the sense that they recognize the uses of technology as responding to specific sociopolitical conditions and, still more, to the ideologies that govern them.

The division between the ideological and the autonomous is applicable not only to anthropological studies, but also to literary studies, many of which have been deeply influenced by the post-Althusserian reading of culture as ideology (as well as by Derrida's identification of the ethnocentricity of the speech/ writing division). Some studies that emphasize their ideological content nonetheless reiterate standard claims for the split between orality (as a dominant mode of communication preceding print) and literacy (as a dominant mode of communication consequent on print). Friedrich Kittler, for instance (in *Discourse Networks 1800 /1900* [1985]), comfortably puts together that history of print with a Derridean history of phonocentrism, offering a reading of the relationship between German literary culture and systems for writing things down (a rough translation of *Aufschreibesysteme*, the title of the original German). Kittler's work springs directly from that of the historians of print:

> Only books could provide serial storage of serial data. They had been reproducible since Gutenberg, but they became material for understanding and fantasy only when alphabetization had become ingrained. Books had previously been reproducible masses of letters; now they reproduced themselves. The scholarly republican heap of books in Faust's study became a psychedelic drug for everyone. (116)

This is the background of the story of nineteenth-century phonocentrism that Kittler sets out to tell: in 1800, the "metaphysics of silent reading, whose prerequisite was the alphabetization of central Europe" (65), could make it seem that "voice, as pure as it is transcentental," was rising "from between the lines" (65), a voice that brings the reader back to a primary orality: the orality of the mother's voice. If print serves nineteenth-century phonocentrism, another technology for the mechanical reproduction of letters—the typewriter—serves the return to the material trace in 1900, when "hallucinatory sensuousness" was "abandoned to the entertainment industry and serious literature renew[ed] its commitment to the ascesis that knows only black letters on white paper" (117).

For Kittler, the history of the impact of print is comprehensible through the filter of both a Derridean history of phonocentrism and a Foucauldian history of knowledge systems (contained by the two moments of epistemic rupture—1800/1900—that mark their differences). For other literary historians, Derrida's work seriously challenges the history of the impact of print.

Timothy Murray, whose *Theatrical Legitimation* (1987) describes print and spectacle as ideology in seventeenth-century France and England,[11] at once reiterates many of the arguments of the print culture theorists about the uses of print for spatialization and authorial legitimation, and challenges others along the lines of Marxist and psychoanalytic poststructuralism. For Murray (relying as much on Jameson and Foucault as on Althusser), print is ideology, and hence (Murray quotes Althusser) "represents the imaginary relation of individuals to their real conditions of existence" (7). In discussing print, then, Murray can "deconstruct" (as he writes) "the methodology of authorship" which depends "on the playwright's trust in semiotic practices and representations" (Murray 16). A psychoanalysis of spectatorship uncovers the process of "theatrical legitimation," which "is dependent on the allegorical re-positioning or re-generation of objects and Subjects through their narration," itself the function of "a process of *allegorical transference*" (Murray 15).

Murray's arguments show that print as material history cannot be separated from print as ideological and epistemological history, and therefore that its discursive constitution (and the politics that inhere in its discourses) are as much part of its history as the bibliographic description of its effects. What Jonathan Goldberg (in *Writing Matter* [1990]) shares with Murray is a mistrust in the existence of any given technology, outside the ways people represent themselves to themselves by reference to that technology. Using as a starting point Derrida's position that writing (in the colloquial sense) has specific ideological and cultural meaning in the West, Goldberg shows the mutual constitution of the "hand," of the materials and pedagogy of handwriting, and of "the social and historical positions that these instructions and those instructed come to occupy" in Renaissance England

(Goldberg 1). Becoming less a technique (or technology) only as writing begins to be a necessary part of a gentleman's education rather than simply a craft product of a specialized labor force, writing as matter, as the practice of the new writing subject, and as ideology are inextricable. These together contribute to the constitution of the "civilizing process," the control of the body, the modern state, and finally of the bourgeois individual subject, whose signature is the mark of the self, and hence of the subject who can mark those who do not write as "other."

For Michael Warner (in *The Letters of the Republic* [1990]) it is, similarly, the uses of writing and print that give them their meaning. Indeed, for Warner, perceived uses create the "printing press," whose history (like that of writing for Goldberg) is the history of the discourses that belong to and construct it. Inspired by Habermas's arguments about the role of print in the creation of the "public sphere" (though he takes issue with them), Warner begins with the presumption that the "printing press" is not a fixed reference point, and that it has no identity autonomous from its particular history, in this case as part of the "public sphere" and the "republican" idea in eighteenth-century America.

One of Warner's central theses is that "print discourse was a cultural matrix in which the definitions of 'individual,' 'print,' 'public,' and 'reason' were readjusted in a new set of ground rules for discourse" (xi). He claims that writing itself (as well as various kinds of stamping, embossing, and marking) were long conceived of as printing (or "imprinting"), and that printing was not immediately distinguished from manuscript production. Things with different names, then ("stamping," "impressing," and "printing," for instance) may have once had similar meanings. Reciprocally, things with the same name may have rather different meanings to different people. "Writing," for instance, may have meant one thing to the literate in eighteenth-century America, and quite another to "the entirely or even partially illiterate, including almost all Native Americans and the enslaved blacks," for whom "writing and print may have appeared most clearly as technologies of power" (Warner 11).[12] For Warner, then, it is crucial to recognize the instability of discursive identity, and hence the multiplicity of any form to which we have given nominal identity.

A similar ideological orientation has brought a number of scholars to rethink the practice of anthropology, from theorists of enthography like Johannes Fabian, James Clifford, George Marcus, and George Stocking, to literary theorists and historians interested in the idea of the primitive like Marianna Torgovnick or Christopher Herbert. Recognizing that writing is not so much a reified technology or outcome as a practice with its own ideological structures, recognizing the complexity of the activity of the (ethnographic) "writer" in relation to "those who don't write," sensitive to ideologically oriented aesthetics, they have reconceived, in particular, the category "peoples without writing." Describing the constitution of the primitive in the nineteenth and twentieth centuries and the establishment of the observing "I" in relation to its cultural objects, exploring the ideological stances of ethnographic subjects, such studies project (implicitly or explicitly) a different ethnography, one that would be reflexive, conscious of the ethnographer's act of writing, conscious of its own positionality. Clifford describes such an ethnography in his introduction to *Writing Culture:*

> Ethnography is actively situated *between* powerful systems of meaning. It poses its questions at the boundaries of civilizations, cultures, classes, races, and genders. Ethnography decodes and recodes, telling the grounds of collective order and diversity, inclusion and exclusion. It describes processes of innovation and structuration, and is itself part of these processes. (2–3)

It includes "all those studies that focus on meaning systems, disputed traditions, or cultural artifacts" (3).

Ethnographic angst is not particularly new. The issues instanced by Lévi-Strauss's meditation on the introduction of writing among the Nambikwara had haunted anthropologists for decades: What happens when oral cultures attain writing? How do anthropologists change the cultures they study by writing in and of them? What is the position of the ethnographer, the status of the observation point? The irony in the title of Goody's *The Domestication of the Savage Mind* (1977) suggests the extent to which institutionalized anthropology had become self-conscious about the neocolonialist implications of its own project, even those inherent in the attempt to preserve cultures for the sake of observation.

In attempting cross-cultural work, those like Goody and Ong were attempting to avoid the fetishizing of the primitive—the treatment of the primitive as "other"—by reading the history of home cultures and more distant ones simultaneously. But, in broadening the meaning of technology as cause, in positing trans-

historical sets of cultural causes and effects, they sometimes implied an inflexible set of rules for cultural change that (so critics
argued) reinforced ethnocentric notions about culture, one that
appropriated the voices of "others" by measuring them according to the standards of the Eurocentric orality/literacy divide, one that reinforced the metaphysics that preached
invariable patterns, forms outside material and perspectival
change and flux, laws that, in their immutability, might fortify
the bases of power.[13]

Though each historian or theorist who has offered a critique
of the "strong" or "autonomous" model theorists takes a different
position, most of the theorists whose reading of orality, literacy,
and media has been influenced by various poststructuralist accounts of culture are skeptical about some or all of the following:

> Subject positions in general, hence the neutrality of the Western
> attitudes toward speech and writing, which may veer toward a posi-
> tivist overvaluation of literacy and/or a nostalgic and reactionary
> overvaluation of orality.
>
> The notion that technology alone (outside of human agency)
> causes certain effects (and a simplisitic understanding of causation
> in general, which would hold that the introduction of a technology
> causes a specific series of effects).
>
> The existence of a smoothly linear cultural history (the positivist
> narrative of evolution), of one made up of radical historical breaks
> (the old-style Marxist narrative of revolution), or of one in which
> culture follows always and everywhere a series of given patterns (a
> classical narrative updated as structuralism). The validity of cross-
> cultural or trans-historical accounts (as opposed to local accounts)
> of the impact of technology.
>
> The notion that material (technological) objects themselves can
> serve as fixed reference points, outside of their discursive
> construction.
>
> The possibility of interpretation (historical or cross-cultural) free
> of the inevitable Western imperialist appropriation of the voice of
> the "other."

A full discussion of any of these issues, as they've been raised
by contemporary theorists, would require far more detailed attention than I can offer here. But, by sketching their outlines, I
hope to indicate briefly both some of the difficulties such critiques identify in earlier studies and some of the difficulties they
themselves face, suggesting both their limitations and their util-
ity for future studies.

Most theorists committed to ideologically self-conscious criticism have objected, above all, to what they see as the celebratory Western history of writing as the origin of reason, logic, democracy—indeed the entire history of the alliance between humanism and political structures as we know them. While arguing that the uses of writing *have* indeed been complicitous with sociopolitical structures and their progenitors (imperialism, the capitalist order, weapons of mass destruction), they reject any condemnation of writing that might be linked to what they see as a nostalgic, primitivist overvaluation of speech, which relies on a naive notion of self-presence and lack of mediation.

Phonocentrism and chirocentrism, then—myths about the pure and unmediated oral life-world, on the one hand, and positivist progressivist myths underlying laudatory accounts of the progress of literacy, on the other—offer competing dangers for the Western observer, and are both blamed for the skewing of studies of orality and literacy.[14] Derrida's argument about the ethnocentrism attached to the speech/writing divide relies on his account of the overwhelming dominance of phonocentrism for the history of Western thought. But several historians have asked whether greater power has really been attributed to the voice than to inscription. The account of the ontological priority given to speech is at least debatable.

In his study of authorship in Renaissance England (*Authorizing Words*), Martin Elsky seriously questions Derrida's history of the dominance of phonocentrism. While Elsky describes the "insistence of the Renaissance humanists that language is primarily speech" (6), he also describes

> writing-dominated views of language, beginning with the spatialization of speech in the printed Renaissance book, and its coincidence with Renaissance views—Hebraicist and Cabalist—that give writing logical and historical primacy over speech, particularly in the belief that God created writing before man pronounced the written letters of God's alphabet. (6–7)

In his investigation of theories of language and speech in Restoration and early eighteenth-century England (*The Material Word*), Richard Kroll similarly challenges Derrida's history of the metaphysics of speech, showing the extent to which theorists of language in the early centuries of print recognized that "all language, whether spoken or written, is an artificial, contractual fabric of '*Materiall*' signs" (203). For Kroll, "the oral habitually loses precedence to the written, printed, the manufactured, because the gestural myth inevitably favors the materiality of the visual over the immateriality of the aural" (205). As Kroll and Elsky show, as most readers of European philosophy and literature from the medieval to the modern would recognize, the phonocentric bias and the chirographic bias constitute competing traditions, both of which are inscribed in the cultural consciousness.

Those theorists most suspicious of the inherent phonocentrism in the ethnographic myth of an oral world seem most radically both to attack the culture of literate "logocentrism" and to identify it with the history of culture in the West, with a history in which (as Goldberg writes) "the technologies of destruction are complicit with humanism" (12) and hence with the history of writing. Warner, for instance, falls into his own version of Lévi-Straussian chirophobia when he writes:

> In our society, outfitted as it is with unprecedented technologies of discipline, the forms of coercion are innumerable. The supreme means of deriving force over the will of others, however, is to win the appeal to a written text. (Warner 97)

Goldberg (acknowledging his debt to Lévi-Strauss and his discomfort with some of the political and historical implications of Derrida's reading [4–6])[15] similarly falls into a version of the history of writing as the violence at the center of bourgeois individuation, imperialist coercion, and the modern state. Indeed, Derrida himself (as Goldberg points out) has a Lévi-Straussian oration on "writing in the colloquial sense" (which, while Derrida reminds us that this is the history of a complicitous collection of myths, not a history of cause and effect, somehow loses its ironic intent in its polemical power): "All clergies, exercising political power or not, were constituted at the same time as writing and by disposition of graphic power," writes Derrida:

> Strategy, ballistics, diplomacy, agriculture, fiscality, and penal law are linked in their history and in their structure to the constitution of writing; . . . it communicated in a complex but regulated manner with the distribution of political power as with familial structure; . . . the possibility of capitalization and of politico-administrative organization had always passed through the hands of scribes who laid down the terms of many wars; . . . there could be no law without . . . notation in the narrow sense. (Derrida 92–93; qtd Goldberg 19–20)

If, for some theorists, "the supreme means of deriving force over the will of others is to win the appeal to a written text," that does not necessarily mean that, for them, writing itself (as technology or as material effect) causes the use of force. This is one of the central arguments of theorists critical of the account of communication technologies as the cause of specific effects. For such theorists, technological matter does not have a life of its own, but is invented and used by human beings with some combination of individual and collective agency. Hence, technology causes nothing. People cause things by using technology: pens, printing presses, voices.

But the danger of "technological determinism" is not merely an oversimplification of causation that attributes it solely to machines. In fact, for the critics of technological determinism, it is made up of at least three fallacies: it implies that causation is mechanical; it posits material things as somehow independent of the subjects who perceive and hence constitute them (ignoring the fact that object and subject formation is a simultaneous and mutual process); and its assumptions about historical change rely on a model of linear history, in which technology comes first and cultural effects inevitably follow.

Some theorists insist that no overarching historical model could be sufficiently elastic to account for local historical differences, and that such models consume the voices of difference, then, in sameness. Those with historiographic objections suggest that "strong" models are, on the one hand, ahistorical in attributing a transhistorical power to technology and, on the other, mistaken in their radical historicity when they claim that a technological innovation has caused a sudden, revolutionary change.[16] Extending their challenges not only to transhistorical theorizing, but also to cross-cultural theorizing, many such theorists argue that "strong" models are inevitably blind to the specificity of each local (historical, regional, cultural) version of technology and its accompanying epistemic and institutional structures. Those troubled, for instance, by the early-anthropological connection of writing with "rationality" (cross-culturally) argue that the historian-subjects of such overarching models are blinded by their own positionality, their own assumptions, for instance, about the boundaries that define speech and writing, literacy and illiteracy.

If the historian eliminates overarching historical models, it becomes more difficult to talk about the cross-cultural implications of "speech," "writing," and "print," for these suddenly look

like culture-specific referents, phenomena whose meanings and
boundaries make sense only to a limited number of European
and Eurocentric cultures. If one describes cultures only in local
terms, if one describes only the uses of technologies within a
given culture, then the terms with which technologies and media
are identified—defined and understood by a given culture—do
not extend past the groups in which they have become part of
the language. Technological entities (material forms) can belong
only to the local discursive constructions that form them. There
can be no identity over time and space of a particular technology
(no translatability, for instance, between "writing" and "print"
in sixteenth-century Europe and the things the Chinese or
Uighur Turks were doing with the mechanical reproduction of
visual-linguistic systems somewhat earlier, nor, for that matter,
between printing in the northeastern corner of the American
continent in the eighteenth century and anything that might look
similar in the Southeast, or Britain, or elsewhere, or earlier or
later).

In order to understand the nature of a technology, then, one
must look at the discursive construction of that technology in
the precise historical moment. It is impossible to understand the
impact of print on culture, for instance, for such a phrase implies
that "print" is a stable entity, an ahistorical point of reference.
Both media technologies (indeed material objects in general) and
concepts that ostensibly accompany them (logic, democracy, a
public sphere) are construed in local contexts. New technologies
are "people representing artifacts to themselves in new ways."

We are back to Derrida: "writing in the conventional sense"
is not a cross cultural concept; to presume that our definition of
"writing" is applicable cross culturally or transhistorically is
to be egregiously ethnocentric, to be drawn into a dangerous
metaphysics. But there is a difficulty. Those who insist on the
discursive construction of media categories (writing, print,
voice), and who therefore must eliminate from the story material
identity over time and space, can fall into precisely the metaphysics they so assiduously resist by attempting, finally, to see
beyond their own historicity. For they must project a vocabulary
onto history that transcends not only the history of contemporary discourse, but all the discursive history that led up to assumptions of translatability, that allowed the English language,
for instance, to call by the name of "writing" (and thereby lend
the idea of continuity) to thousands of years of practices. It has
surely been noted before, for instance, that in projecting a

super–metaphoric "writing" (one that transcends the ways in which "writing" has been used), Derrida appropriates the advance task of conceptualization which is metaphor's job, and, in so doing, unintentionally implies access to systems that transcend the contemporary-discursive, that is, unintentionally creates his personal metaphysics.

The insistence on discursive construction, in turning traditional materialism on its head (while attempting to keep some of the materialist focus on the socioeconomic implications of the production and use of material forms) has other difficulties. Those who (resisting the old Marxist narrative of materialist agency) identify only people as agents (as creators of change, as creators of objects through their discursive construction), leave out the other half of the story. Artifacts do resist and change people's representations of them; machines do disrupt our refiguring of them (unless Hiroshima and Chernobyl were merely instances of people representing nuclear power to themselves in new ways). Human beings don't control everything they cause, as the older theories of media impact recognized when they acknowledged the power of objects to shape those things over which human beings think they have most control. We need both sides of the story: our refiguration of things, but also, their refiguration of us.

To question conventional Western discursive categories (and with them the notion that technologies have force outside their particular constitution in a given community) does not, in itself, guarantee the absence of ethnocentricity in one's account. Someone like Warner, who is painfully conscious of the situation in which writers on cultural difference find themselves by attempting to make the "other" accessible, suggests some of the difficulties in such an attempt when he describes the difference between the notion of "writing" held by "illiterate" Native Americans or black slaves in eighteenth-century America and that held by "literate" Americans of European descent. Such a description requires the historian to identify subjects with a single, fixed subject position or another. But, as Warner knows, the boundaries among forms of identity are inevitably nebulous.

Warner argues, for instance, that black colonial writers like Jupiter Hammon and Phyllis Wheatley "define their public voices as white, even if only proleptically," and so cannot give us access to "what colonial blacks thought about print." He uses the slave narrative of Olaudah Equiano, "who was brought to America and the Western world of letters in the late 1750s," as the only example of "a vivid record of a nonliterate black's perception of books as a technology of power" (11). "I had a great curiosity to talk to the books, as I thought they did," writes Equiano,

> and so to learn how all things had a beginning: for that purpose I have often taken up a book, and have talked to it, and then put my ears to it, when alone, in hopes it would answer me; and I have been very much concerned when I found it remained silent. (qtd Warner 11)

But is this Equiano? What gives Equiano, in his relation to writing, an ineradicably different subject position from that of, say, Benjamin Franklin, one more different than Benjamin Franklin's might be from Phyllis Wheatley's? To sustain his position, Warner must narrow his frame into a self-proving tautology: What makes the "print"/"public sphere" discourse particular to the eighteenth-century northeastern American colonies? The fact that eighteenth-century northeastern American colonists are articulating it. What about those in the eighteenth-century colonies who aren't articulating it, or those earlier or later or elsewhere who are? Well, they don't, then, belong to *that* discourse.

Warner knows (without making this explicit) that the writing of those ostensibly alienated from the medium's base of power is already translated, inevitably, in such a way that we may understand it: either through a literacy acquired later (and hence, Warner would hold, a new subject-position for Equiano, one that makes him closer to Wheatley); or through the notation-systems of those already inside hegemonic writing (the white translators of "oral" narrative, early versions of the twentieth-century ethnographers). If we attempt to avoid relying on writing-in-the-conventional-sense as the basis for our knowledge of others (recognizing that such writing gives us voices that have already been appropriated by "the [hegemonic] frame"), choosing instead to rely on writing-in-the-extended-sense (nonscripted artifacts, texts of the broadest kind: physical objects, practices, customs), then we become simply another version of the fetishizing ethnographers.

Those critiques which resist models of large-scale history (linear evolutionary history; the history of culture as a series of epistemic ruptures; and the history of culture as a series of universal fixed structures) have a related problem. Without any larger-scale model, the object of study must be treated as if it were temporally and physically isolated from any larger history or geography. Yet any such treatment requires the historian to overlook the difficulty in identifying a cultural entity as discrete (for there is, of course, no such thing as an isolated culture), to overlook the fact that the local isn't always a clearer referent than the larger-scale, and to overlook the fact that even a dialectic between the local and the large-scale (of the kind which all history writing finally uses) requires some kind of large-scale model.

As most writers on culture are forced to recognize, it is almost impossible to stick to the local, even if one's official historiography requires one to historicize as radically as possible, even more radically, that is, than did the previous generation of Marxist-influenced historians. Warner's contrast of the noncapitalist organization of "the emergence of printing" among the Chinese and the Uighur Turks with its emergence elsewhere (Warner 9) relies on the assumption that these are the same technologies. In arguing that historically local writing practices serve as the origin of modern bourgeois individualism (although fifteenth-through seventeenth-century England is not so very local), Goldberg seems similarly to undermine his explicit political agenda: to take away power from the master narratives (whether bourgeois or old-style-Marxist) and to allow the story to be many stories, to allow "writing" to be many instances of writing.

To generalize at all about the other (historical or cultural) is to belie difference. But where is one, then, to find the smallest unit (temporal, local, conceptual) about which one can say something? Surely not in the individual, which is, after all, simply made up of a compilation of subject positions. In the subject position, then? But what could *a* subject position be? Hermeneutic anxiety about our access to alterity is a necessary part of methodological choice. But if we yield to the full implications of such anxiety, we end up, finally, with the inescapable sense that we can read only ourselves.

As most theorists implicitly acknowledge (in underlining the ideological import of their histories, in emphasizing their suspicion of the ostensible "objectivity" of historians who ignore their own positionality as subjects), sensitive narratives of alterity are no greater fictions than sensitive narratives of the self, just as the fictions of historical continuity and cross-cultural resemblances are no greater than that of the isolated, local instance. For we do inevitably make up histories, insofar as we are mimetic-poetic animals with an impulse to record memory. Our superimposition of the present on the past is not so much blind teleology as a recognition of the uses of those histories.

Most of those attempting, in the 1930s and after, to discover the inherent logical principles in orality and literacy never imagined that they could transcend their own discursive constructs; they never imagined that they could choose to re-direct the conceptual-metaphoric structures built deeply into their language. But they did feel that they could make a genuine effort to highlight the legitimacy already discreetly built into other forms of recording to which they might have access. With a bit more of the history of twentieth-century ethnocentrism at the forefront of discourse, it might well be after all that a genuine attempt to understand forms of inscription (or differentiation) that have traditionally in the "West" been discounted as lesser than the differentiations of "writing" is a less ethnocentric project than some ideologically self-conscious theorists have felt.

It might well be, too, that we have moved beyond a poststructuralist fear of talking about sameness and can now return to cross-cultural work in a new way. It might well be possible to have faith that we have some access to alterity, both past and present. Although technological categories are neither essential nor eternal nor transhistorical, that there is translatability over time and space seems an indubitable a priori for any kind of historical work ("work" understood as process, not as product). It has not, finally, been the fallacy of the accessibility of others— of their translatability into our realm—that has been the most dangerous, but the fallacy that others are entirely other to us.

This is not by any means to imply that we should (or could) recapitulate earlier histories of speech and writing. The ethnography and historiography of the local has suggested the limitations of narratives that either trace the growth of writing and print as a linear move toward high European culture, understand the introduction of print as a revolutionary innovation with a centrifugal force in the heart of Europe, or posit a universal cognitive and behavioral orality/literacy dualism. It has suggested the directions in which alternative histories of the interactions of speech and writing (of the necessary interplay between "phonocentrism" and "chirocentrism") might move. It has suggested both the dangers and the importance of remaking, with different kinds of insight, our stories about inscription.

Notes

1. Derrida quotes Lévi-Strauss: "The struggle against illiteracy is thus indistinguishable from the increased powers exerted over the individual citizen

by the central authority. . . . Writing may not have sufficed to consolidate human knowledge, but it may well have been indispensable to the consolidation of dominions. . . . All this moved rapidly from the national to the international level, thanks to the mutual complicity which sprang up between new-born states . . . and an international society of peoples long privileged." When "nations whose knowledge of the written word has not, as yet, empowered them to think in formulae which can be modified at will" are "first given the freedom of the library shelves they are perilously vulnerable to the ever more deliberately mendacious effects of the printed word." Writing, finally, "seems to favor rather the exploitation than the enlightenment of mankind" (qtd Derrida 101, 131–33).

2. "Only an innocent community," writes Derrida, describing Lévi-Strauss's position,

> only a micro-society of non-violence and freedom, all the members of which can by rights remain within range of an immediate and transparent, a "crystalline" address, fully self-present in its living speech, only such a community can suffer, as the surprise of an aggression coming from without, the insinuation of writing, the infiltration of its "ruse" and its "perfidy." Only such a community can import *from abroad* "the exploitation of man by man." (Derrida 119)

3. This Rousseauistic constitution of "the other as a model of original and natural goodness," and the narrative of the violence of the intrusion of writing among those as yet unadulterated, offers anthropology a founding myth. By "accusing and humiliating oneself," one creates the "remorse that produces anthropology" (Derrida 114).

4. "If writing is no longer understood in the narrow sense of linear and phonetic notation, it should be possible to say that all societies capable . . . of bringing classificatory difference into play, practice writing in general. No reality of concept would therefore correspond to the expression 'society without writing.' This expression is dependent on ethnocentric oneirism, upon the vulgar, that is to say ethnocentric, misconception of writing" (Derrida 109).

5. Lévi-Strauss's narrow understanding of writing (like Saussure's or Rousseau's) involves

> an ethnocentrism *thinking itself* as anti-ethnocentrism, an ethnocentrism in the consciousness of a liberating progressivism. By radically separating language from writing, by placing the latter below and outside, . . . by giving oneself the illusion of liberating linguistics from all involvement with written evidence, one thinks in fact to restore the status of authentic language, human and fully signifying language, to all languages practiced by *peoples whom one nevertheless continues to describe as "without writing"*. (120)

6. Derrida uses a variety of phrases for this concept: "writing in the colloquial sense," "'writing' in the usual sense" (127–28), "writing in the narrow sense" (128).

7. I've relied, here, both on my own random collection of phrases in the syntactic fields belonging to "literate" and "oral," and on the *Oxford English Dictionary.*

8. V.i.; qtd *Oxford English Dictionary.*

9. Those studying the history of literacy disagree not only on standards for its measurement but also on its definition. Is it the ability to read, the ability to read and write, the ability to sign one's name? Cressy shows, for Tudor and Stuart England, a high correlation between the ability to sign one's name and

the ability to read and write, which are (not surprisingly) related to economic factors. Goldberg (for fifteenth- through seventeenth-century England) and Furet and Ozouf (for seventeenth- through nineteenth-century France) both show that reading, writing, and signing one's name do not always go together and are often divided along gender and occupational lines. Where Cressy argues that economic factors are the primary determinant of literacy, Goldberg and Furet and Ozouf argue that social factors are its primary determinant. The differences here reflect not so much different patterns of literacy (or interpretive error) as the use of different kinds of sources and different methodological and theoretical assumptions.

10. See the excellent accounts of orality and literacy studies in Ong (1982), Foley (1988), and Finnegan (1992) (whose handbook on research practices may be used as a full annotated bibliography of studies of oral production, offering both a guide for researchers and a lucid account of the theoretical issues at stake in work on orality). I am not attempting here to offer another such account or anything like a comprehensive bibliography, but merely to sketch, from the particular perspective of "literary" history, some of the crucial issues at stake in current work on orality and literacy, both historical and contemporary.

11. Murray frames his purpose clearly in his introduction: "In a series of ideological/epistemological analyses, [Theatrical Legitimation] comments on performative aspects of theatricality underlying the narrative re-presentation of seventeenth-century French and English theatre: the relation between ideology and theatrical representation, the display of authority, the rhetorical structures of ideological performance, and the complex discourse of the antitheatrical prejudice poised against both the theatre and the psychology of the spectator" (6).

12. "Both print and writing could only be alien to the entirely or even partially illiterate, including almost all Native Americans and the enslaved blacks. And saying that letters were 'alien' to the illiterate is more than a tautology, since it is to these groups that writing and print may have appeared most clearly as technologies of power" (Warner 11).

13. Most of the complaints about "strong-model" theorists are, of course, a cartoon versions of scholars who, in varying degrees, rework their theoretical models in the face of local evidence. One only has to examine differences between Eisenstein's exploratory and hypothetical article and her book a decade or so later, or to see Ong's discussions of disagreement among scholars of orality and literacy, or to read Goody's methodological prefaces, for instance that in The Logic of Writing, in which he comments on various models for the study of writing and culture: the analysis of particular local contexts, the analysis of developmental change, and the analysis of a single issue transhistorically and cross culturally.

> Each [type of enquiry] has its costs and gains. . . . Choosing a topic to investigate means not only that one runs the danger of inflating its importance but, worse, of being seen as believing that human affairs are determined by a single factor. Some writers even appear to assume that what is meant by "causal relations" are those determined in just this way—that is, situations that have one cause, everywhere, all the time. . . . That some readers . . . interpret the argument as unidirectional while others recognize the two-way, multi-factored influences may be due to . . . a willingness to suspend not one's disbelief but one's "beliefs", one's ideological commitments, one's predetermined categories of the understanding. (Logic xiv–xvi)

14. Goldberg, for instance, writes that, on the one hand, Ong and Goody "wish to preserve the pristine oral culture as the place of face-to-face encounters, an unalienated and virtually Edenic embodiment; on the other hand, however wary they are of writing . . . they also see it as the instrument of rationality, science, objectivity, subjectivity, history—in short, as the bringer of culture and civilization. These are the two sides of logocentrism" (17).

15. In taking up Derrida's hint that an interesting history of Western writing might be written, Goldberg has some difficulty with the fact that Derrida's implicit politics don't align very well with Goldberg's political intentions. Goldberg's perspective (he writes in his introduction) comes from both "the postmodern, postmarxist Marxism of Ernesto Laclau and Chantal Mouffe's *Hegemony and Socialist Strategy*" and Donna Haraway's "Manifesto for Cyborgs" in which "Haraway's 'we' includes as its exemplary instance 'women of color' and 'people living with AIDS'" (Goldberg 11–12).

16. Warner, for instance, implicitly attacks the ahistoricism of earlier accounts when he identifies as his major task: "to analyze the historical transformation in print discourse as fully historical—to analyze it without attributing its significance to an ahistorical point of reference, such as the intrinsic nature of individuals, reason, or technology" (xi). He implicitly attacks the radical historicity of arguments (like Eisenstein's) that there was a print revolution when he argues that "printing was initially another way of reproducing in quantity books that were already being reproduced in quantity," and it was only gradually that "printing came to be specially defined as publication, now *in opposition* to manuscript circulation."

Early printers, for instance, in no way distinguished their work from hand-produced documents. From a modern perspective, that seems to show how little they understood the latent "logic" of their medium. But that interpretation of the meaning of print is governed from the outset by a presupposed modern ideological definition of print. (Warner 8)

Works Cited

Clifford, James and Marcus, George E., ed. *Writing Culture: The Poetics and Politics of Ethnography*. Berkeley, Los Angeles, and London: University of California Press, 1986.

Cressy, David. *Literacy and the Social Order: Reading and Writing in Tudor and Stuart England*. Cambridge: Cambridge University Press, 1980.

Derrida, Jacques. *Of Grammatology*. Translated by Gayatri Chakravorty Spivak. Baltimore and London: Johns Hopkins University Press, 1974.

Eisenstein, Elizabeth. *The Printing Press as an Agent of Change*. 2 vols. Cambridge: Cambridge University Press, 1979.

Elsky, Martin. *Authorizing Words*. New York: Columbia University Press, 1988.

Finnegan, Ruth. *Oral Traditions and the Verbal Arts: A Guide to Research Practices*. London and New York: Routledge, 1992.

Foley, John Miles. *The Theory of Oral Composition: History and Methodology*. Bloomington and Indianapolis: Indiana University Press, 1988.

Furet, François and Jacques Ozouf. *Reading and Writing: Literacy in France from Calvin to Jules Ferry*. Cambridge: Cambridge University Press, 1982.

Goldberg, Jonathan. *Writing Matter: From the Hands of the English Renaissance*. Stanford: Stanford University Press, 1990.

Goody, Jack. *The Logic of Writing and the Organization of Society*. Cambridge: Cambridge University Press, 1986.

Kittler, Friedrich A. *Discourse Networks 1800/1900*. Translated by Michael Metteer, with Chris Cullens. Foreward by David E. Wellbery. Stanford: Stanford University Press, 1990.

Kroll, Richard W. F. *The Material Word: Literate Culture in the Restoration and Early Eighteenth Century*. Baltimore and London: The Johns Hopkins University Press, 1991.

Murray, Timothy. *Theatrical Legitimation: Allegories of Genius in Seventeenth-Century England and France*. New York: Oxford University Press, 1987.

Ong, Walter J. *Orality and Literacy: The Technologizing of the Word*. London and New York: Methuen, 1982.

———. *Ramus, Method and The Decay of Dialog*. Cambridge: Harvard University Press, 1983.

Stock, Brian. *Listening for the Text: On the Uses of the Past*. Baltimore and London: Johns Hopkins University Press, 1990.

Street, Brian V. *Literacy in Theory and Practice*. Cambridge: Cambridge University Press, 1984.

Warner, Michael. *The Letters of the Republic: Publication and the Public Sphere in Eighteenth-Century America*. Cambridge, MA and London: Harvard University Press, 1990.

"Discoverers of Something New": Ong, Derrida, and Postcolonial Theory

JANE HOOGESTRAAT

My PURPOSE IN THIS ESSAY IS TO ARGUE THAT WALTER J. ONG'S NO-
tions of primary and secondary orality, if read critically and
imaginatively, serve as useful terms in the ongoing engagement
of literary critics with the discourses of both postcolonialism
and feminism. Ong's work on primary and secondary orality has
contemporary political application because it allows for a means
of recreating the past histories of those excluded from dominant,
colonial languages because they could not write these languages;
those who could not write in the colonizing languages (including Latin as well as English, French, Portuguese, and Spanish)
either did not speak these languages in the first place (in the
case of the indigenous peoples of the Americas) or did not, before
the seventeenth century (in the case of most European women
and many men), know how to read them. It is of crucial theoretical importance in the present that postcolonial theorists reserve
a space for at least imagining and marking the absence of lost oral
traditions and cultures, for what existed external to the written
accounts of the colonizers.

Ong's work holds so much promise precisely because it acknowledges the category of orality: not necessarily as a pure or
immediate speech of the kind Derrida has taught us does not
exist, but rather as a category for imagining the language and
culture of others whose language is either very different than
our own or whose language has not survived, often because of
the oppression that English and other European languages made
possible. In this area, especially in terms of the politics of otherness, Ong and Derrida are not actually that far apart. To be
sure, Ong's stress in *Orality and Literacy* on the existence of
"primary orality," i.e., "the orality of a culture totally untouched
by any knowledge of writing or print," does appear to run
counter to Derrida's emphasis that no speech can be privileged

51

as original or even originary (11). Ong's notion that literacy can be used to recover a pre-literate past would also seem to display the nostalgia for presence or origin that Derrida cautions against. Ong claims, "Literacy can be used to reconstruct for ourselves the pristine human consciousness which was not literate at all— at least to reconstruct this consciousness pretty well, though not perfectly" (15).

Derrida appears to discredit any attempt to recover evidence of a pre-literate past of primary orality, choosing instead to stress, especially in *Of Grammatology*, the centrality of writing: "By a slow movement whose necessity is hardly perceptible, every-thing that for at least some twenty centuries tended toward and finally succeeded in being gathered under the name of language is beginning to let itself be transferred to, or at least summarized under, the name of writing" (6). What has not been noticed often enough, however, is that Derrida's point is not only to subsume all language under the category of writing, but to do so to the end of restoring credit to the speech of peoples who otherwise, in Derrida's view, were seen, particularly by Lévi-Strauss but also by others, not only as not having had writing, but essentially as not having had speech. Objecting specifically to Lévi-Strauss, Derrida argues: "To say that a people do not know how to write because one can translate the word which they use to designate the act of inscribing as 'drawing lines,' is that not as if one should refuse them 'speech' by translating the equivalent word by 'to cry,' 'to sing,' 'to sigh?'" (123). When Derrida attributes writing to the people involved here, he means something more than the technological fact of establishing written records, what Ong would refer to as the advent of literacy. Derrida intends, I think, to problematize the passage from orality to literacy, to argue dif-ferent, more complex boundaries and openings between the two than Lévi-Strauss would allow for.

Derrida's objection to Lévi-Strauss' model is not only that it vilifies writing but also that it discredits or marks as naive the prior speech, in this case of indigenous peoples, that it in effect denies the existence of that speech. According to Derrida, Lévi-Strauss wrongly: "consider[s] the passage from speech to writing as a leap as the instantaneous crossing of a line of discontinuity; passage from a fully oral language, pure of all writing—pure, innocent—to a language appending to itself its graphic 'repre-sentation' as an accessory signifier of a new type, opening a tech-nique of oppression" (120). It is for this problem, which occurs when two cultures with different languages come into conflict, always characterized by some level of violence or violation, that a notion of orality similar to Ong's, I will be arguing, becomes not only relevant but crucial.

In certain forms of ethnography, as Stephen Tyler has pointed out, a record of an almost purely oral culture survives only as an absence in the written record of an ethnographer. It requires, and I believe Tyler's essay centers on this point, both an understanding of what Ong means by "orality" and what Derrida means by "absence" to understand the clash between an oral and a written culture.[1] Tyler writes of the inevitable loss that occurs because an ethnographer must privilege his or her written, "scientific" accounts of field experience:

> This self-aggrandizement was paid for later in the coin of self-deception, not only in the sense of a repressed rhetoric of power and political domination, but more importantly in the suppression of another rhetoric which could not be tolerated by that political rhetoric nor accommodated to the need for a dominating scientific authorial voice. I speak here of the suppression of the voice of the native, of the dark twin of Socrates, of 'she who does not speak' in the ethnography, the trace of whose voice is only its absence. (98)

That Tyler chooses the pronoun "she" for the silenced native voice is probably appropriate, and not only because ethnographers until quite recently were most likely to be men. His choice is also appropriate because for so many centuries literacy was the privilege of some men and almost no women, so that the voice the ethnographer suppresses finds infinite echoes in other voices, often those of women, suppressed by official histories and accounts.

For Tyler, Ongian "primary orality" and Derridean "absence" converge so that they become almost identical terms. The ground of ethnography, the oral voice of natives, becomes the absent center around which the text revolves and without which it would not exist:

> the native is muted, or speaks only through the voice of the ethnographer in 'language,' in the form of a grammar, or in a translated tale or myth relegated to the appendix. But, even this trace, this faint and garbled whisper of the native's voice is only a means of hiding the fact that ethnographers spend more time talking and writing than in strict observation unmediated by talk. Yet this talk, which is the enabling condition for observing, is nowhere reported because it would contaminate the image of pure, unmediated, objective obser-

vation as the ground of description. It would jeopardize the scientific
status of the description by complicating its vision with the merely
oral and auditory. (98)

Tyler refers to a situation where the ethnographer presumably
understands at least aspects of the oral language that he or she
reports on. But his analysis also applies, I think, to the even
more dramatic situation that occurs when a culture that has a
well-established technological system for writing encounters,
usually by force, another culture with a different language system that the conquering culture does not understand and cannot
translate. It is this situation, most notable in modern history with
the arrival of European explorers on the shores of the Americas
to encounter indigenous people, that has recently attracted the
attention of literary theorists, particularly new historicists, and
to which, I think, a line began in the work of Ong lends a particular urgency.

Both Eric Cheyfitz in *The Poetics of Imperialism* and Stephen
Greenblatt in *Marvelous Possessions* focus on the language that
explorers and colonialists used upon arrival in the new world
to justify their endeavors to themselves and to their own cultures.
For Chefitz and Greenblatt, evidence of the indigenous cultures
that were destroyed, some but not all characterized by "primary
orality," still survives in the written accounts, often in very
strange and convoluted form, of the explorers. For both critics,
the language that allowed for colonial structures of massive oppression is the same language that might dismantle those structures, and indeed, after Derrida, might already be seen to be
continually dismantling itself. That language remains haunted
by the voices that it once suppressed, often by denying that the
voices spoke intelligible language.

Cheyfitz is explicitly concerned to study the clash between
one type of European literacy and one variety of Native American
orality that occurred in "the violent politics through or within
which Western European writing translated Native American
oral cultures" (23). For Cheyfitz, the difference between Native
American oral cultures and European writing made any recon-
ciliation impossible not only because languages clashed but because two different, incompatible views of property were
represented in those languages:

The development of the language of diplomacy in the written tradition is party of the history of class in the West, wherein languages

became alienated from themselves in various specialized jargons, forms of power of the upper classes over the lower; whereas in the American Indian oral tradition, which developed in societies with rank but without class, this kind of alienation cannot take place. The translation of these two languages into each other is impossible because one of these forms of eloquence, the written, is based on the proper and property—on, that is, a system of decorum (which, as we have read, is inseparable from a class system) and on the alienation of land in individual title that is also inseparable from that system. The oral form of eloquence, however, is based on an inalienable notion of land grounded in a kinship economy. Each one of these languages utterly rejects the other. (140)

While Cheyfitz's categories are not identical to the lengthy list of features that Ong attributes (in *Orality and Literacy*) to the "psychodynamics of primary oral cultures," there are some important intersections (31–77). The specific intersections include Ong's stress on oral cultures being "close[r] to the human life world," (42–43), that is, more dependent on kinship structures; "situational rather than abstract" and therefore much more dependent on a communal structure (49–57); and much more dependent on unity between an audience and a speaker because no written text exists as a back-up (74–75).

The indigenous oral cultures, as Cheyfitz represented them above, did partake of something like Derrida's notion of *L'ècriture* in a broad sense of the term. That is, Native American peoples did have a language that structured the familial and political lines of their culture. Derrida marks the emergence of *L'ècriture* or writing as identical with the emergence of culture or government:

access to the written sign assures the sacred power of keeping existence operative within the trace and of knowing the general structure of the universe; that all clergies, exercising political power or not, were constituted at the same time as writing and by the disposition of graphic power; that strategy, ballistics, diplomacy, agriculture, fiscality, and penal law are linked in their history and in their structure to the constitution of writing; that the origin assigned to writing had been—according to the chains and mythemes—always analogous in the most diverse cultures and that it communicated in a complex but regulated manner with the distribution of political power as with the familial structure. (92)

The indigenous cultures of the Americas did not, by Derrida's definition, lack writing. What they lacked, as both Cheyfitz and

Greenblatt note, is a system identifiable to the European explorers as writing. What happened then, according to Cheyfitz, is that "the Europeans need[ed] to feel that the Old World languages were superior to those of the New. Europeans needed to feel, that is, that New World languages were virtually a lack of language" (164).

The differences between and among cultures during that history was not entirely an oral or written difference: it was also a difference based on conflicting views of property and a difference based on different technologies of writing. Greenblatt notes that for the explorers, specifically for Columbus: "The narcissism that probably always attaches to one's own speech was intensified by the possession of a technology of preservation and reproduction" (9). Greenblatt's most striking (and now well-known) anecdote originates in a letter that Columbus wrote in which he noted: "'And there I found very many islands filled with people innumerable, and of them all I have taken possession for their highnesses, by proclamation made and with the royal standard unfurled, and no opposition was offered to me'" (52). Later, Greenblatt notes that the phrase "no opposition was offered" can also be translated into the stronger "and I was not contradicted"; he speculates on what Columbus might possibly have thought he was doing when he made a claim to possession in a language the Native Americans present could not possibly have understood (57–59). Of this particular moment, Greenblatt notes: "A distinction between peoples who have writing and peoples who do not will . . . become crucial in the discourse of the New World, but in the initial moments with which we are concerned Columbus does not know enough about those he has encountered to make such a distinction" (57). As Greenblatt goes on to explain, Columbus's claim to possession actually follows a written formula—it mimics the official formula and is spoken aloud so that it might be written down.

Even if this exchange had been in mutually understandable language, even if translators had been present, the distinction between an oral culture and a literate one would most likely have interfered, as it did so often in treaties made years after Columbus's landing. Ong, in a different context, speculates on the differences in conversational exchange between literate and oral cultures: "promising, responding, greeting, asserting, threatening, commanding, protesting and other illocutionary acts do not mean quite the same thing in an oral culture that they mean in a literate culture. Many literate persons with experience of highly oral cultures feel that they do not: they regard oral peoples, for example, as dishonest in fulfillment of promises or in responses to queries" (170). That formulation, however, is not immediately relevant to Columbus's proclamation, because Columbus does not have to worry about whether he is being understood. Greenblatt continues: "The formalism of Columbus' proclamation derives not only from the fact that it represents the scrupulous observance of a preconceived form . . . but also from its complete indifference to the consciousness of the other" (59). For Europeans arriving after Columbus, who presumably did have to think about whether they were being understood, Greenblatt identifies a: "recurrent failure to comprehend the resistant cultural otherness of New World peoples. On the one hand, there is a tendency to imagine the Indians as virtual blanks, wild unformed creatures, as naked in culture as they are in body. On the other hand, there is a tendency to imagine the Indians as virtual doubles, fully conversant with the language and culture of the Europeans. . . . One moment the Indians have no culture; the next moment they have ours" (95). While Greenblatt refers to historically particular situations, he also recognizes the resonance of this formulation, of the innumerable times this move has been replicated.

In *The Muse Learns to Write*, Eric Havelock argues that the coexistence of oral and written art forms in a portion of Greek culture for an extended period marks a point of origin, but a point of origin that became important only when historians and literary critics began to wonder about the implications of the clash between European languages and English on the one hand and the indigenous languages of the Americas and elsewhere on the other hand. For Havelock, the clues to understanding that clash may still exist somewhere in the period when Greek prehistory was emerging into the Greek classical tradition:

The "orality question," then, from its inception in modern times, has been entangled with the "Greek question." Somewhere there, back in classical antiquity, sometimes in the first millennium B.C., answers might lurk which would go beyond what can be inferred from "primitive" or "backward" cultures, whether American Indian or Polynesian, or more recently, Yugoslavian and African. But even this backward glance at Greece was originally provoked by experience of a cultural clash born of modernity as it encountered what seemed to be its past, still surviving beyond the Atlantic. (37)

Havelock would be the first to acknowledge that his analysis is grounded in art, in textual artifacts that carry traces of an oral language, of a different way of being in the world. In the work of Havelock, as in the work of Ong, the text is often the only point of access to the oral. While for Havelock the clash between a written and an oral culture has repeated throughout history, there may be a significant, almost originary difference, between the Greek situation and subsequent ones:

> The effect in the Greek case, which is particularly to be noticed and emphasized, is the total social control retained by the Greeks themselves, both over their own oral life and over their alphabetic life. . . . they suffered no pressure to adopt other writing systems as practiced by their neighbors. . . . [the alphabet] would present no immediate threat to the time-honored linguistic technology of oral storage commanded by the professional bards. It offered no threat to the organized performance socially central to the culture. (87)

All the implications that I've considered here of Ong's work, of a clash between the oral and the written, depend on art as much as on history; they depend on imaginative recovery when the historical record is missing. Ong's work remains important, then, in the contemporary stress on recovering a fuller history of colonialism because it expands, via the stress on the importance of orality the range of what it is possible to imagine. Perhaps in a very real sense there was never a time when language, in any form, was not used also as a tool of oppression, always and already along lines of gender, race, and class. But Cheyfitz suggests that there was another kind of language in the Americas, one based on kinship and not on property; Greenblatt marvels at the unbelievable illogic of the claims of the conquerors; and Havelock suggests a possible historical moment when the transition from orality to literacy came from within a culture and not because of an external, conquering power. For Tyler, as well as for the others working in the line of Ong, it remains possible, and imperative, to imagine and to recognize the voices—absent, other, and largely oral—that haunt the official languages that we still speak and write.

As a coda, I wish to suggest that Ong's text *Orality and Literacy* is itself haunted by the limited acknowledgment it makes of the missing voices of women; their absence haunts Ong's accounts of medieval and renaissance education for men, so central to Ong's notion of "secondary orality." Oddly, Ong is much more careful in acknowledging the role of women in a primary oral culture, as for example when he notes: "Knowledge is hard to come by and precious, and society regards highly those wise old men and women who specialize in conserving it, who know and can tell the stories of the days of old. By storing knowledge outside the mind, writing and, even more, print downgrade the figures of the wise old man and the wise old woman, repeaters of the past, in favor of younger discoverers of something new" (41). Historically, as Ong, Cheyfitz, and Greenblatt all make clear, the "discoverers" were males, privileged by that fact and by virtue of literacy.

Ong does acknowledge what it would not be possible to deny: that the scholastic system until very recently was open to men and not to women. In both *Orality and Literacy* and *Fighting For Life*, he repeatedly calls for greater study of the consequences of the increasing number of women, beginning in the seventeenth century, who were educated. Interestingly, what Ong stresses given this historical situation is the training that educated men, beginning in the late medieval period, received in rhetoric, a training which Ong seems to include under the rubric of "secondary orality." Ong discusses at some length the implication that a training in combative rhetoric had on the formation of the modern university and the changes that followed upon the admission of a large number of women into universities. I believe Ong's work is marked by a candor that will be increasingly necessary in a culture sorting out enormous changes in gender roles. However, I will be arguing below that an application of Ong's work in orality and literacy to feminism must begin with a critique.[2]

Ong fails to address at all, as far as I can tell, the power structures, based largely on political standards of literacy, that have allowed most men the dominant, and often oppressive position over most women. (Ong fails to acknowledge, for example, the problem of escalating violence against women, a particularly unfortunate lack because so much of *Fighting For Life* addresses the biopsychological origins of male aggression.) Further, more work needs to be done with the fact that women's culture, in eras when women could not read and write, would of necessity have been an oral culture, situated at midpoint between primary and secondary orality as soon as women were aware of the tools they were prohibited from using. Exploring the implications and remnants of oral women's culture during the historical era Ong concerns himself with might take place alongside an ongoing discussion of orality in Renaissance education for men. In fact, an exploration of women's oral culture is crucial if women, in Ong's position, are to be allowed a language at all. According to Ong, education conducted in Latin for men had a strongly oral component because of its backward link to classical rhetoric: "Paradoxically, the textuality that kept Latin rooted in classical antiquity thereby kept it rooted also in orality, for the classical ideal of education had been to produce not the effective writer but the *rhetor*, the *orator*, the public speaker" (113). Ong occasionally uses the word "oratorical" for this education, but he is more likely to use the word "oral." Ong's terminology effectively denies any language, written or oral, to women: Because women could not write in Latin, they also lacked access to the oral/oratorical tradition.

That Ong often uses oral when he means classical and male oratorical is even more apparent in his chapter "Some Present Issues" in *Fighting For Life* when he argues, very convincingly, the oratorical and male basis of institutions including "spectator sports, politics, business, and Christian life and worship" (149–83). In the same book, Ong has a telling passage when he discusses the technology that allowed women to, quite recently, become public speakers: "A woman's scream can carry a great distance, but intelligibly articulated speech is another problem. Women frequently narrate folktales with great skill and effect for smaller groups in oral cultures. But for large crowds, conspicuous public display of what many philosophers considered the human race's most distinctively human activity, speech, was almost exclusively the business of postpubertal males" (141). Even in a historical account where Ong appears to be attempting to be scrupulously fair, his rhetoric betrays him: he essentially denies articulate speech to women; he privileges the public, individual oration over the communal tale; and he naturalizes, although I believe unintentionally, the philosophy that privileged male speech. But that Ong's text, like those of colonial explorers and discoverers, is haunted by what it denies does not mean, finally, that Ong's notion of orality is anything less than crucial for both postcolonial and feminist theorists.

Notes

1. For other discussions of the distinctions and similarities between Ong and Derrida, see Kleine, Sussman, and Wesling. For Ong's direct response to Derrida, see *Orality and Literacy*, 75–77, and 166–71.

2. For a passing reference to a feminist critique of Ong's thought, see Gilbert and Gubar, 252. For theorists who treat Ong more sympathetically from a feminist point of view, see both Saffar and Swearingen. For positive accounts in the popular press of Ong's work in *Fighting for Life*, see Neilsen, and especially Toolan. In my opinion, *Fighting for Life* deserves more attention from feminist theorists, both critically and affirmatively, than it has heretofore received.

Works Cited

Cheyfitz, Eric. *The Poetics of Imperialism: Translation and Colonization from The Tempest to Tarzan.* New York: Oxford University Press, 1991.

Gilbert, Sandra M., and Susan Gubar. *No Man's Land: The Place of the Woman Writer in the Twentieth Century.* Vol. 1. *The War of the Words.* New Haven: Yale University Press, 1988.

Greenblatt, Stephen. *Marvelous Possessions: The Wonder of the New World.* Chicago: University of Chicago Press, 1991.

Havelock, Eric A. *The Muse Learns to Write: Reflections on Orality and Literacy from Antiquity to the Present.* New Haven: Yale University Press, 1986.

Kleine, Michael. "Ong's Theory of Orality and Literacy: A Perspective from Which to Re-View Theories of Discourse." In *The Philosophy of Discourse: The Rhetorical Turn in Twentieth-Century Thought,* Vol. 1. Edited by Chip Sills and George H. Jensen. 229–242. Portsmouth, N.H.: Boynton/Cook/Heinemann, 1992.

Neilsen, Mark. "A Bridge Builder: Walter J. Ong at 80." *America* 21 November 1992, 404 + 4.

Ong, Walter J. *Orality and Literacy: The Technologizing of the Word.* New York: Methuen, 1982.

———. *Fighting for Life: Contest, Sexuality, and Consciousness.* Ithaca: Cornell University Press, 1981.

Saffar, Ruth E. "The Body's Place: Language, Identity, Consciousness." In *Media, Consciousness, and Culture: Explorations of Walter Ong's Thought,* edited by Bruce E. Gronbeck, Thomas J. Farrell, and Paul A. Soukup, 182–93. Newbury Park: Sage Publications, 1991.

Sussman, Henry. "The Expanding Castle: The Literature of Literacy." In *High Resolution: Critical Theory and the Problem of Literacy,* 197–228. New York: Oxford University Press, 1989.

Swearingen, C. Jan. "Discourse, Difference, and Gender: Walter J. Ong's Contributions to Feminist Language Studies." In *Media, Consciousness, and Culture: Explorations of Walter Ong's Thought,* edited by Bruce E. Gronbeck, Thomas J. Farrell, and Paul A. Soukup, 210–22. Newbury Park: Sage Publications, 1991.

Toolan, David. "The Male Agony According to Walter J. Ong." *Commonweal* 20 November 1992, 13–18.

Tyler, Stephen. "The Unspeakable: Discourse, Dialogue, and Rhetoric in the Postmodern World." In *The Unspeakable: Discourse, Dialogue, and Rhetoric in the Postmodern World.* 89–103. Madison: University of Wisconsin Press, 1987.

Wesling, Donald. "Difficulties of the Bardic: Literature and the Human Voice." *Critical Inquiry* 8(1981), 69–81.

Orality, Literacy, and Dialogue: Looking for the Origins of the Essay

VINCENT CASAREGOLA

Dialogue and the Precedents of the Essay

THE "FAMILIAR" OR "PERSONAL" ESSAY BEGAN TO EVOLVE IN THE LATE sixteenth century, at the very time during which printing was becoming a powerful force in European culture. As Montaigne and Bacon launched the first ventures into the new genre, the culture was shifting from one in which oral discourse had often dominated the assumptions about the nature of language to one in which the written (and especially the printed) text would become the principal paradigm of language. Walter Ong has studied this period carefully, and he has argued that the shift of linguistic consciousness revealed itself in many new styles of writing. As Ong has demonstrated, the oratorical tradition of discourse had for centuries influenced the style of written prose.[1] From the ancient Greeks to the Renaissance (and in some cases, beyond that), prose took its structural patterns, stylistic features, and rhetorical assumptions from the oratorical forms that were the basis of traditional language education. Indeed, many individuals still experienced written texts as the spoken word, since these texts would often be read aloud in groups, as must necessarily be the case in the relatively "text-poor" world of a chirographic (i.e., manuscript) culture.

During the more than 2,000 years between the development of the ancient Greek alphabet and the invention of printing, one of the most prominent prose forms was the dialogue. Derived from oral traditions of deliberation and debate, the dialogue was favored by a wide variety of writers, from Plato in Greece and Cicero in Rome, all the way to Castiglione in Renaissance Italy. Implicit in the written dialogue is the assumption that the interchange of ideas exists not as a closed, rule-governed system but as a pattern of interpersonal interaction through acts of discourse, much as in a private conversation or a public forum. Of course, the written dialogue is not merely a transcription of oral discourse but a form of writing in which orality and textuality are effectively balanced with respect to the linguistic values, behaviors, and assumptions of a chirographic culture. As a form, the dialogue tends to resist systematizing, and so it suggests that our patterns of intellectual development, and our philosophical or ideological constructions, grow out of our social context and interpersonal discourse. In the world of dialogue, knowledge is never fully reducible to a set of abstract relationships because it is always embedded in the practical context of rhetorical processes and the variable patterns of enacted human relationships. Thus the written dialogue is not a simple allegory of intellectual processes nor a "psychomachia" in which mental faculties are personified; rather, it reflects an awareness that the making of knowledge involves action as well as thought, interaction through discourse as well as reflection on experience. During the time in which Western Europe, the Mediterranean, and the Middle East existed primarily as chirographic cultures, the dialogue offered perhaps the most revealing sense of the "noetic economies" and cultural consciousness of the various civilizations which thrived in these areas of the world.[2]

In *Ramus, Method, and the Decay of Dialogue*, Ong reveals how both the evolution of printing and spread of Ramism contributed to the decline of dialogue as an aspect of both rhetoric and dialectic. Yet even as the dialogue lost influence, the essay was emerging as an experimental form offering a new balance between orality and textuality, a balance that reflected the assumptions of an increasingly print-based culture. I believe that the literary essay as we know it began to evolve from the altered and intensified interaction between oral and written discourse, which was brought about by the development of printing. More precisely, I would argue that the ancient written genre of the dialogue, which had long reflected the balance between orality and textuality in chirographic cultures, and which had continued to be influential even in the early Renaissance, may have provided the immediate precedent for the development of the essay.

Like the dialogue, the essay exists as a means of exploring ideas and experiences that complement and/or challenge each other. Since its inception, the essay has resisted easy formulation (outside the imposed formulae of certain institutional settings; e.g., academe), in keeping with the open-ended and exploratory tradition favored by the first of essayists, Michel de Montaigne. As its name suggests, the essay is an "attempt" or a "trying out." Rather than presenting the results of an already concluded process of intellectual examination (as in the treatise), the essay offers a textual and cultural space in and through which such processes may begin, accelerate, and continue, reaching greater or lesser closure as the circumstances and the individual writer decide (Hoagland 362–64). In this way the essay reflects the implicit open-endedness of the dialogue. Though the dialogue often moves toward closure (quite significantly in some cases), the experience of the dialogue form suggests that such closure itself may be temporal, limited, and problematic. While the ideas discussed in the dialogue may attempt to move toward definitiveness and finality, its form suggests that those ideas exist in a rhetorical moment of human interaction through discourse (a feature which creates the subtle instability and dynamic tension found in some of the Platonic dialogues). As Eric Havelock, Ong, and others have noted, the development of writing revolutionized the ancient world, particularly in Greece, bringing about dramatic developments in philosophy, politics, rhetoric, and many other areas of culture (ca. 600 to 300 B.C.).[3] As the move toward philosophical abstraction interacted with rhetorical traditions of constructing knowledge through discourse, the dialogue form came to represent a balance between these two distinctive ways of knowing. When the rise of printing once again shifted the noetic economies of the Western world, the dialogue could no longer effectively maintain that balance, and so it gradually fell into disuse. However, the same cultural environment gave rise to experiments with many new forms of writing, one of which was the essay. It was this new genre, I believe, that would inherit the role of achieving and maintaining the balance between orality and textuality in the modern world, the balance between philosophy (which would become increasingly abstract, systematic, and "scientific") and rhetoric (which would grow increasingly idiosyncratic).[4]

The Essay: A Genre but Not a Form

The essay is a genre defined more by the process of its development than by standard, formal, structural features. Long viewed as reflecting "the mind at work," the essay has from its origins been linked with a process of "working things out," both conceptually and linguistically. The very word *essay* (from the French verb *essayer,* meaning "to attempt" or "to try out") was adopted by Montaigne to suggest the tentative and experimental nature of this personal project that subsequently evolved into a genre (Klaus, Anderson, and Faery 2–7). In the hands of Montaigne, this new kind of writing sought to "assay" the potential truth of both inherited intellectual traditions and direct personal experiences (Screech xv). Montaigne freely intertwined these elements in his development of the genre, as have the numerous inheritors of his tradition.

Because it can be so easily traced to the late Renaissance, many view the essay as an archaic form, suggesting a time when educated gentlemen retired to the studies of country estates and, like Montaigne, could engage in somewhat detached and/or ironic commentaries upon the affairs of their fellow humans. Even modern essayists sometimes deliberately characterize the essayist as a literary amateur and man of leisure, as does E. B. White in "The Essayist and the Essay" (728–29). However, despite the cachet of antiquity, the essay is the youngest of literary genres, and it is the only one which we can easily describe in historical terms.[5] We know its original practitioners, and we have relatively detailed knowledge of the world in and through which they began their experiments with this lively new form. The other literary genres, drama, poetry, and prose fiction, all have their origins in the relatively distant past, and in forms that were originally part of a primary oral culture. That the earliest human societies enacted ritual drama, sang songs of various kinds, and told stories can be confirmed from both ancient archeological records and more recent anthropological/ethnographic studies of oral cultures that continued to exist in the modern world (cf. work of Milman Parry, Alfred Lord, and Eric Havelock, as well as that of Walter Ong).[6] But the essay is a form that develops only later. It is true that in the ancient world there were many forms of nonfiction prose, for all variety of purposes, from philosophical treatises to letters, from legal briefs to public oratory. But "essay" is not merely a new term for the continued evolution of an earlier form; rather, it is a form unique to its development in a culture where printing had finally made written language the dominant form of artistic and intellectual discourse, and where the form of printed texts had begun to shape the fundamental assumptions about the nature of all discourse.

What is more, the essay reflects a new "noetic economy" of a print-based culture, because it represents new assumptions about consciousness and the fundamental intellectual processes we collectively label as "thought." Since the development of efficient alphabetic writing in ancient Greece, the Western intellectual tradition has evolved as a dynamic balance between the urge to represent thought spatially, visually, and quantitatively, and the contrasting desire to represent thought through patterns of enacted human relationships, especially as discourse.[7] Again, we might describe this as the balance between philosophy and rhetoric. While philosophy attempts to understand and explain experience systematically, seeking a knowledge that is stable and universal, rhetoric attempts to understand and explain human experience performatively, as an immediate, dynamic process that is rooted in the variables of the local situations and individual personalities. In short, philosophy seeks transcendent knowledge while rhetoric seeks immanent knowledge.

The chirographic cultures that existed in the Western world from about 600 B.C. to about A.D. 1500 achieved a balance between these competing patterns of understanding, and I would argue that the dialogue form was perhaps the most focused realization of that balance. But the advent of printing changed all this, providing the impetus for the vast cultural project of systematizing thought, first in Ramism and then in subsequent movements such as the "Mixts" and the "Systematics," whose overall influence is so carefully established by Ong (1958, 299ff). This shifted the long-standing balance between philosophy and rhetoric that had been achieved in the dialogue. Into this destabilized cultural context, the essay emerged as a new means of exploring the alternative pattern of thought—the open-ended, exploratory, and performative pattern that sought knowledge in social and interpersonal contexts. As the intellectual assumptions of print-based culture evolved rapidly into the philosophical precedents of the Enlightenment, the essay evolved in parallel, as a cultural space where the unfinalized and less systematic aspects of thought and experience could be explored and shared. In this new setting the balance between the systematic and communal, between philosophy and rhetoric, was achieved by the culture's acceptance of a greater separation between both. Since Ong's foundational work on Ramism, we have recognized that this intellectual-pedagogical movement, along with its cultural descendants, helped to speed the decline of dialogue in the age of print. At the same time, the Ramist tradition may have left open the cultural space necessary for a new form to emerge and establish itself, and that form was the essay.

The essay, from its earliest stages to its contemporary realization at the hands of writers such as Didion, Walker, Hoagland,
and so many others, has remained consistently difficult to formalize. One of its most distinctive features is its resistance to
form, at least if we think of form in visual, diagrammatic, and/
or architectonic terms.[8] Rather, the form of the essay grows from
the patterns of reflection and reverie which exist in contrast to
the rule-governed structures of systematic thought and discourse. These are difficult areas to explore and analyze critically
or theoretically, since just what enters into reflection and reverie
seems so indefinite. For this reason, the essay becomes a genre
that people use frequently, yet one which they feel uncomfort-
able discussing in great depth. On the other hand, these very
same qualities may make it the vital, evolving, and exciting genre
that draws so many dynamic and inspiring writers into its domain. Carl Klaus, in analyzing the structural patterns of the essay,
has gone so far as to label it an "anti-genre," reflecting the difficulty of establishing a definitive form for the essay (160). Essayist
Edward Hoagland has embraced the essay's resistance to form,
seeing the genre as a performative balance between the poles of
"what I think" and "what I am" (362–63). In addition, Hoagland
describes the essay as being "like the human voice talking, its
order the mind's natural flow, instead of the systematized outline
of ideas" (362). Both as a practitioner of this art and one who
has taken the time to analyze its form, Hoagland has recognized
that the essay is implicitly oral in its texture, evoking the spoken
voice more so than other genres, and likewise he has recognized
the unfinalized, unsystematic quality that keeps the essay an
open form. That does not mean that the essay is bereft of ideas,
but that it approaches ideas in the context of enacted discourse,
revealing ideas as immanent in the rhetoric of human interaction. As Hoagland notes, "Though more wayward and informal
than an article or treatise, somewhere it contains a point which
is its real center, even if the point couldn't be uttered in fewer
words than the essayist has used" (362). For the essay and the
essayist, thought is not abstracted into a rule-governed system;
rather, it is understood in the context of human relationships
and discourse.

Orality, Textuality, and Dialogue

The cultural theory of Walter Ong, along with the literary and
discourse theory of Mikhail Bakhtin, may offer us the most effec-

tive means of addressing the essay, understanding its form, and exploring its origins. Let us first consider Ong, who has made a life's work of examining the subtle but dynamic relationship between language, discourse, media, and culture. Summarizing that work, even in a whole volume, would be a difficult task. However, one consistent feature found throughout Ong's cultural theories is the acknowledgment that our understanding and use of language, as well as our conceptualization of ourselves and our culture, are fundamentally linked to the dominant media through which we experience language.[9] Prior to the advent of writing (and especially before the advent of the kind of versatile, alphabetic writing developed in Greece during the eighth century BC) not only is language use fundamentally different from that in cultures with writing, but the very patterns of thought and self-construction are different.[10] These are what Ong refers to as "noetic economies," and they affect all aspects of human understanding and relating in any culture.[11] Only with writing can the systematic nature of language begin to achieve some measure of separation and independence from speech acts (see Ong, *Orality and Literacy*, chap. 2–4; Havelock, *The Muse Learns to Write*, chap. 8–10).[12] As it does so, writing gradually supplants the behavioral, customary, communal patterns of an oral culture, altering the fundamental aspects of discourse. Though charged with direct meaning, these patterns lack the intensive rule-governed and more highly closed elements of abstract systems. Writing creates a culture of manuscripts as well as of speech, where for the first time knowledge can sometimes be considered as essentially separate from human relationships.

Of course, even in a primary oral culture, language has systematic and rule-governed qualities, patterns of sound and structure without which it could not be meaningful. But such cultures do not view their use of language systematically, experiencing meaningful linguistic patterns only as they are embedded in what Ong calls "the human lifeworld" (Ong, 1982, 42–43).[13] Primary oral cultures use languages which possess syntactic and semantic structures, but the individuals and groups of those cultures do not study syntax and semantics as abstract, rule-governed systems, distinct from actual linguistic behavior (42–43). In primary oral cultures the system of language is always fully integrated into the patterns of communal behavior, unifying the systematic and social construction of knowledge (81–83). All this changes with the intervention of media that "technologize the word," first writing, and then much later printing, and finally the telecommunications, broadcast, and computer technologies which have become common during the last century. In a primary oral culture, all acts of language require the actual presence of the people involved, for individuals in those cultures can neither speak to nor hear one another unless they are together in one place.[14] However, with the intervention of media technology, starting with the scribe's stylus, acts of language can be created as objects, suspended in time and potentially separate from both their originators and those who receive them. Ong understands that this separation, though highly beneficial in expanding the range of cultural experience and understanding, still produces some degree of alienation:

> Yet it would appear that the technological inventions of writing, print and electronic verbalization, in their historical effects, are connected with and have helped bring about a certain kind of alienation within the human lifeworld. This is not to say that these inventions have been simply destructive, but rather that they have restructured consciousness, affecting men's and women's presence to the world and to themselves and creating new interior distances within the psyche. (1977, 17)

Despite the revolutionary cultural changes wrought by the development of alphabetic writing, the linguistic patterns and cultural assumptions of primary oral cultures continued to shape the lives of the vast populations of nonliterate people, whether or not they lived in cultures that possessed the technology of writing (Ong 1971, 23–47; also see *Orality and Literacy* 115–16). Though instrumental in shaping chirographic cultures from ancient Greece through the middle ages, literacy was shared, in most instances, by only a relatively small educated elite. Additionally, the writing produced in these cultures often demonstrated a heavy influence from the language patterns of preceding oral cultures. Thus, the *Iliad* and *Odyssey* as written texts are still shaped largely by the conventions and formulae of the preliterate Homeric world (1971, 23–47). Ong describes these qualities as "oral residue"—the retention in a chirographic culture of the patterns of language use and social interaction common to oral cultures (23–47).

> By oral residue I mean the habits of thought and expression tracing back to preliterate situations or practice, or deriving from the dominance of the oral as a medium in a given culture, or indicating a reluctance or inability to dissociate the written medium from the

spoken. Such residue is not especially contrived and is seldom conscious at all. (25–26)

Ong shows us that a basic aspect of all chirographic cultures,
those literate cultures that existed before printing, is a relatively
high degree of oral residue in their written discourse. In chirographic cultures, the artistic and intellectual discourse, both
written and spoken, reflects a balance between the highly systematic qualities of language that become most evident in writing
and the more customary and behavioral qualities of language
that become evident in common speech.

It was in the dynamic interaction between early writing and
traditional, communal orality that one of the most influential
forms of discourse evolved—the dialogue—a form that may offer
important clues to the development of the essay.[15] In the dialogue, the interplay of concepts, the struggle of one idea with
another, and the attempt to discern, in different views, the presence of truth and authority are all brought out in a dramatic
interaction of human voices. Unlike works written for stage
performance, however, the dialogue attempts to present not a
dramatized story but the struggle of ideas, opinions, and points
of view. It is a written form that adapted itself to a wide variety
of intellectual discourse, from philosophy to literary and cultural
criticism. Yet, rather than working out a position in a systematic
fashion (though systematic positions could be offered and extended through the course of the dialogue), the dialogue as a
whole offers the more problematic setting of a conversation or
debate, with its attendant digressions and potential open-
endedness. This could all be used to reach fairly systematic results, as was often the case in Platonic dialogues, but even in
Plato one finds that the rhapsodic digression, or the brief or
extended metaphorical flight of fancy, can add much to the experience of the text. As George Kennedy has noted, "No dialogue
of Plato is untouched by rhetoric" (42). Of course, Plato used the
rhetorical arts in dialogues which often voiced great dismay at
the negative effects of rhetoric on the public discourse of politics,
justice, and philosophical inquiry (Ong 1982, 79–81; Kennedy,
41ff). Yet, regardless of his attitude toward the practices of the
sophists and rhetoricians who were his contemporaries, Plato
still found the dialogue form, with all its rhetorical potential,
the preferred vehicle for his philosophical discourse.

In the hands of other writers, the dialogue could prove somewhat less systematic in its presentation, and so closer to the

actual experience of a discussion. The dialogue, however, is not the representation of the actual occasions of public debate or interpersonal conversation. Nor is dialogue a form that provides merely a manuscript for an earlier pattern of discourse for which we can see evidence in primary oral cultures.[16] Instead, the dialogue is a hybrid form, evolving not merely from a chirographic culture's transcription of oral precedents, but from the dynamic tension and interplay that develop as patterns of traditional oral discourse and new textuality become more fully interactive (Ong 1982, 79–81; 115–16). Perhaps it is that very feature that most concerned Plato with the problematic relationship between speech and writing (Ong 1982, 79–81; Kennedy 41ff). The dialogue is a fictionalized reality, a reconstruction of that which has never genuinely happened but which gives opportunity for ideas, concepts, and opinions to be explored, to interact, and finally, to be tested and evaluated by the writer and reader alike (Ong 1982, chap. 4; esp. 79–81, 93–96, 103–8, and 177; also see Ong 1977, chap. 2). Yet the dialogue brings with it a strong sense of the communal and social aspects of making meaning, suggesting through its very form how much of our conceptual structure and systematic thought is rooted in social interaction. That the rhetorical arts played so powerful a role in the ancient Greco-Roman world further testifies to the underlying assumption that meaning grows from social engagement and interaction before it submits to systematic development.[17] It is true that, in contrast to this "dialogic" tradition of making meaning, there existed an equally powerful (and sometimes more influential) tradition of systematic thought, even present in the work of those who wrote dialogues. Certainly the Platonic dialogues represent the interaction of contrasting patterns of systematic and performative discourse, and yet, they remain dialogues. In the cultures of the ancient Greco-Roman world, as well as their cultural descendants in Medieval and early Renaissance Europe, the systematic and the dialogic were maintained in relative balance, with the hybrid form of the dialogue reflecting this balance.

Plato is still the most well-known practitioner of the dialogue form, but several centuries later, Cicero would use the same form to defend the arts so disparaged by Plato. Cicero's De Oratore stands as one of the greatest individual realizations of the dialogue form, exerting a powerful influence from Cicero's time even into the seventeenth century (Kennedy 90–100). Though he wrote several works on rhetoric, it is in De Oratore that Cicero offers his most comprehensive foundation for the central cultural

importance of oratory and the orator, whom he casts as the primary cultural hero. He puts the greatest praise of the orator into
the words of Crassus:

> For what is so marvelous as that, out of the innumerable company
> of mankind, a single being should arise, who either alone or with a
> few others can make effective a faculty bestowed upon every man?
> Or what so pleasing to the understanding and the ear as a speech
> adorned and polished with wise reflections and dignified language?
> Or what achievement so mighty and glorious as that the impulses of
> the crowd, the consciences of the judges, the austerity of the Senate,
> should suffer transformation through the eloquence of one man? (I.
> viii.31–2; vol. 1: 23–25)

That Cicero uses the rhetorical arts in the defense of rhetoric
and Plato uses those same arts to attack rhetoric provide an interesting commentary on the pervasive influence of rhetoric, and
its strong oral tradition, throughout the ancient Greco-Roman
world. But what is far more interesting, for our purposes at least,
is that both writers choose the dialogue form to present what
they consider to be their most significant contributions to the
discourse of their cultures. The philosopher who was so doubtful
of the value of rhetoric, and the rhetorician who wished to raise
his art to the cultural significance of philosophy, both found the
dialogue to be the form most conducive to their efforts. This
underlines how the dialogue served as a balancing point between
the two often conflicting worlds of rhetoric and philosophy. In
particular, Cicero's choice of the dialogue is revealing, for as
the most prominent Latin prose stylist of his own age (and any
subsequent age, for that matter), Cicero was known for both his
orations and his letters, and yet he focused on the dialogue as
the form for what many consider his most foundational work.

As noted above, Cicero considers the orator to be the central
figure of his culture, and by presenting the defense of oratory in
the context of the written dialogue he reveals that the "orator"
must achieve a balance between the spoken and written word.
This is especially true considering the comprehensive learning
that Cicero demands of the orator, a kind of learning available
only to a literate individual. Likewise, in presenting the orator
as the subject of a dialogue, Cicero suggests that oratory itself is
more than single-voiced discourse, reflecting the "polyphonic"
dynamics of the academic, legislative, and judicial settings in
which ancient oratory was practiced.[18] Examining Crassus'
praise of the orator, we find that the orator achieves his lofty

status through fulfillment of a social mission. Furthermore, it is in his interaction with the minds of judges, the Senate, and the people at large that the orator is able to accomplish his admirable goals and so fulfill the potential of his art. Therefore, De Oratore presents the orator in the interactive context of the dialogue form itself, while also demonstrating the essentially social and dialogic nature of the art of oratory. As presented by Cicero, oratory is essentially dialogic because its significance derives from the shared meaning constructed through public speech. That so influential a cultural figure as Cicero would choose the dialogue as the form for his De Oratore further reveals the central importance of the form for achieving a balance between speech and writing, and between rhetoric and philosophy, in the chirographic cultures of ancient Greece and Rome. Regardless of their assessments of rhetoric, we can see that both Plato and Cicero could share the common ground of the dialogue, and it may also be argued that the dialogue provided the common ground of both rhetoric and philosophy for more than 2,000 years.

During the period just discussed, civilizations in the Middle East, the Mediterranean, and Europe existed as chirographic cultures, where the features of textuality and orality interacted throughout all artistic and intellectual discourse. But the next revolution came with the development of printing from alphabetic type and its extensive influence throughout Europe (and eventually, throughout the rest of the world).[19] Printing made written texts inexpensive and ubiquitous, encouraging the spread of literacy and the further spread of textuality. The eventual result, as Ong has demonstrated, was the transformation of a manuscript culture into a mass culture.[20] Ong has devoted much of his work to describing the intricacies of the print revolution and its fundamental effects on Western culture. In his first major work on the subject, Ramus, Method, and the Decay of Dialogue, he examines how the advent of print encouraged the development of Ramistic thought, contributing to the gradual decline of dialogue.[21] Though I will not attempt to review these arguments here, Ong has demonstrated convincingly that printing made the written form of discourse dominant over spoken forms, at least in terms of artistic experience and intellectual authority. The balance between textuality and orality shifted, so that discourse came to be considered much more systematic, diagrammatic, and arhetorical.[22] In this environment, the dialogue form could no longer maintain the middle ground between textual and oral discourse. Though it never completely disappears, for nothing ever seems to disappear completely from the cultural stage once it has entered, the dialogue becomes a subsidiary and relatively neglected form from the late sixteenth century until well into the twentieth century. (It is difficult to know if, in the rhetorically charged and unstable conditions of the late twentieth century, the dialogue is experiencing a renaissance of sorts, perhaps in new forms.)[23]

Ong theorizes about the decay of dialogue in the wake of the developing print culture of the later Renaissance. He also theorizes, in a number of his works, about the subtle, dynamic, and fundamental relationships between oral and written forms of discourse, and also about the gradual evolution of hybrid discourse forms which reflect the changing balance between orality and textuality as new media (e.g., writing, printing, broadcast technologies, and so on) begin to dominate the presentation of discourse.[24] The essay, which first emerged in the midst of the print revolution and which has re-emerged with new vigor in the latter twentieth century, may be understood as another hybrid form that, like the dialogue, reflects a changing balance between oral and written discourse. As noted above, the essay may have developed as the unacknowledged literary descendent of the dialogue in a print-based culture. However, before we can fully explore such claims, we must examine both the essay and the dialogue in light of Bakhtin's theory of "dialogic" discourse.

Bakhtin and the "Dialogics" of Dialogue[25]

The theoretical work of Mikhail Bakhtin is important for a full understanding of both the dialogue form and the essay genre because he, along with Ong, shows a profound interest in the relationships between the spoken and written word.[26] In today's theoretical climate, where the paradigm of textuality rules and interest in the spoken word is often decried as a naive "phonologism," both Ong and Bakhtin offer a refreshingly distinctive respect for the oral/aural experience of language. Bakhtinian theory is most often associated with his analyses of the novel, which he finds to be the pre-eminent literary form of the modern age, and through which he most fully explores the ramifications of his approach to language, discourse, and culture. He is also noted for his interest in the "carnivalesque" elements in literature, the focus of his work on Rabelais. But perhaps the most relevant features of his theory, with regard to discourse in general and the essay in particular, are revealed in his concepts of the "dialogic" and "unfinalizable" nature of discourse.[27]

At the core of Bakhtin's complex and challenging collection of works is his opposition to what he considered two extreme views of human experience—systematic dogmatism and relativism.[28] He sought to resist the effects of intellectual dogmatism, which he associated with some aspects of the Russian formalism and its parallels in the structuralist tradition (Morson and Emerson 27–32). Bakhtin felt that formalist and structuralist assumptions, that language could be understood completely in systematic terms, belied the authentic experience of dialogue with all its variables of circumstance and personality. Yet he also avoided the opposite, relativistic view (favored in some communities of post-structuralist theory) that discourse was so indeterminate as to be without recognizable meaning, leaving participants in acts of discourse without any sense of personal or social responsibility (Morson and Emerson 27–32). He realized that both views presented a false dichotomy, viewing language either as totally systematic, closed, and rule-governed, or as essentially arbitrary and indeterminate.

Bakhtin countered these extremes with the view of language as essentially "dialogic," assuming that the "utterance" (as opposed to the sentence) is the basic unit of language (Bakhtin, *Speech Genres and Other Essays*, 61–102). Focusing on utterance places the core of meaning in the actual event and situation, and so into identifiable acts of speech, writing, or reading. This concentration on the "eventness" of language corresponds with Ong's insistence that words are "events" rather than "signs" (See *The Presence of the Word*, 111ff; *Interfaces of the Word*, 21; *Orality and Literacy* 75–77). For both Ong and Bakhtin, meaning and knowledge are thus fundamentally integrated into active human relationships as opposed to being governed by abstract, rule-governed systems. Bakhtin believes that meaning is embedded in language, but not language as either a closed system or an infinitely variable sea of indeterminate signs. Rather, meaning is embedded in language as a human activity and interaction, as a pattern of relationships between human beings.[29] This pattern of relationships constitutes the dialogic nature of all discourse and, indeed, of human consciousness itself, as Bakhtin indicates:

> The dialogic nature of consciousness. The dialogic nature of human life itself. The single adequate form for *verbally expressing* authentic human life is the open-ended *dialogue*. Life is by its very nature

dialogic. To live means to participate in dialogue: to ask questions, to heed, to agree, and so forth. In this dialogue, a person participates wholly and throughout his whole life: with his eyes, lips, hands, soul, spirit, with his whole body and deeds. He invests his entire self in discourse, and this discourse enters into the dialogic fabric of human life, into the world symposium. (Bakhtin qtd. in Morson and Emerson, 59–60)

Bakhtin also believed in the "unfinalizability" of human discourse, meaning that each act of language was never fully controlled or predictable. Because dialogue is not a static occasion but a dynamic event within the context of interactive personalities and processes, no act of discourse is ever complete or final (Morson and Emerson 36–62). This makes all discourse both liberating and unstable, providing a degree of freedom to act and yet never allowing full control of outcomes. As Bakhtin argues in *Problems in Dostoyevsky's Poetics:*

Nothing conclusive has yet taken place in the world, the ultimate word of the world and about the world has not yet been spoken, the world is open and free, everything is still in the future and will always be in the future. (59)

Likewise, since considerable variables are involved in each circumstance of dialogue, no one can fully predict or control its direction and interpretation—its meaning. Despite these assumptions, Bakhtin still claimed that meaning was understandable and sharable through dialogue and that the individuals involved, though not in complete control, were still responsible for their acts of discourse. As Morson and Emerson note in summary from one of Bakhtin's then still untranslated works:

In "Toward a Philosophy of the Act," he [Bakhtin] argues that each self is unique because each aggregate of the related and unrelated is different. There can be no formula for integrity, no substitute for each person's own project of selfhood, no escape from the ethical obligations of every situation at every moment. Or, as Bakhtin sums up the point: "There is no alibi for being." (see Morson and Emerson, 31)

Thus, even though we cannot fully control or "own" the dialogue in which we participate, we must still "own up for" our acts of discourse through which we create that dialogue (Morson and Emerson 176–79). In other words, Bakhtinian theory recognizes that even though language never fully submits to systematizing and predictability, it still presents the potential for order and meaning (36–62). Likewise, it acknowledges that even though human beings experience language, and so both their self-consciousness and their relationships, as not fully controllable, they still have a range of potential choice and essential responsibility within any particular context of discourse and action.

The dialogue form, balanced between systematic realm of the written word and the behavioral realm of speech, effectively demonstrates the dialogic and unfinalizable nature of discourse as described by Bakhtin. Though in describing the dialogic nature of discourse, Bakhtin himself tended to dismiss Socratic form as merely the surface of dialogue, and though his explanation of dialogic discourse derived principally from his study of the novel, we can still see how the dialogue form, in its long, multifaceted tradition, actually achieves parallel kinds of dialogic and unfinalizable discourse to that found in the novel (Morson and Emerson 60–62). The dialogue also demonstrates the effects of media on the structure and use of language that have been explored by Ong. For, as noted above, the dialogue is a form that exists as a result of the interaction between textuality and orality in the ancient world. I would argue further that because of its hybrid nature, the dialogue can sometimes come closest to representing the compositional connections between both speech and writing. It can represent the text as an evolving and unfinished process, a blending of action and suspended action, of movement and stasis, of listening (or observing) and responding. In these qualities it most fully realizes the dialogic nature of discourse as described by Bakhtin, and it most fully balances the elements of orality and literacy as explained by Ong, Havelock, and others during the manuscript ages of Western culture.

The Essay as the Inheritor of Dialogue

The development of printing from alphabetic type, along with the intellectual movements it encouraged (e.g., Ramism), fundamentally altered the existing balance between orality and textuality that had existed from about 600 B.C. to A.D. 1500 (see *The Muse Learns to Write; Orality and Literacy*, 79–81). The dialogue, which had represented that previous balance, thus fell into gradual decline and decay, though it did not disappear without a trace (see *Rhetoric, Romance, and Technology* 23–47; 227–83; also *Orality and Literacy* 115–16). A new kind of balance was necessary to reflect the emergent noetic economies of a print-based culture. As Ong has noted, as a new medium emerges, there follows a period during which all forms of linguistic activity are temporarily accelerated, even those representing the cultural assumptions that had existed prior to the advent of the particular new medium (see *Rhetoric, Romance, and Technology* 23–47; 277–83; also *Orality* 115–16). In addition, many experimental forms of discourse come into existence as the culture explores the possibilities of the new medium, seeking to renew the balance between various forms of expression (e.g., oral and written).[30] Thus, in sixteenth-century Europe, one of the many results of the development of printing was the proliferation of handbooks for training students in a traditional, highly oral form of rhetoric (see *Rhetoric, Romance, and Technology*, chap. 2 and 3). Likewise, many new forms of discourse, both oral and written, emerged and even flourished at this time, often evolving from or combining earlier forms.[31] In such a linguistically and rhetorically charged atmosphere, experimental forms had a greater chance of gaining a foothold on the cultural stage, and the essay was one such form. In addition, the essay offered in a new kind of balance between the oral and written experience of language, allowing it to enter the cultural vacuum created by the decline of the dialogue. The essay would inherit and eventually dominate that problematic middle ground of discourse that had so long been the province of dialogue.[32] Even as printed texts were multiplying across sixteenth-century Europe, and Ramism, with its revised vision of dialectic, was beginning to spread its lasting influence throughout educational institutions of the late Renaissance, Michel de Montaigne was committing himself to the solitude wherein he might begin "assaying" both his cultural inheritance and his personal vision (see Screech, xv).

Let us consider some of the similarities between these two forms that would allow the essay to inherit the role of dialogue. Like the dialogue, the essay reflects a high degree of "oral residue" because it is defined less by its structure and more by its suggestion of personality and interpersonal relatedness, which we might call "voice" (Hoagland qtd in Klaus, Anderson, and Faery, 362–64). With its exploratory motives, the essay reflects the asystematic patterns of Bakhtinian "unfinalizability" which the dialogue also suggests (more subtly perhaps) through its presentation of competing ideas as interactive characters. Likewise, while the dialogue foregrounds the dialogic and polyphonic nature of its discourse through the literal conversation of its participants, the essay suggests Bakhtinian dialogism and polyphony through its often recursive patterns of development, patterns which reflect the self-interrogatory nature of the genre.[33] The essayist often expresses one idea or position, merely to question it or compare it with its contrary, ultimately suggesting a balance and perhaps a conclusion, but not the complete end of future dialogue.[34]

We often witness this pattern in Montaigne's work, as he reveals the complex, sometimes conflicting, and always dynamic interactions of his own mind. For example, in an essay such as "How We Weep and Laugh at the Same Thing," he focuses on the mental processes that allow us to view the same events from contrary perspectives. Toward the essay's end he quotes Lucretius:

> Nothing can be seen to match the rapidity of the thoughts which the mind produces and initiates. The mind is swifter than anything which the nature of our eyes allows them to see. (262–65)

Montaigne himself comments on this observation from Lucretius: "That is why we deceive ourselves if we want to make this neverending succession into one continuous whole" (262–65). The "neverending succession" is the process of thought, which is itself a kind of interior dialogue. This interior dialogue is expressed and represented through the essay, suggesting both its unfinished and multi-voiced qualities. The statement could well serve as the underlying conviction of any who practice the essay genre, for it expresses the unfinalized and dialogic nature of human mental processes that the essay attempts to engage, reflect, and represent.

At times, the dialogic and polyphonic also emerge through the explicit intertextuality expressed through quotations, references, and various "cultural fragments."[35] This technique can be found not only in the work of early essayists such as Montaigne, but in the work of contemporary writers such as Joan Didion (who achieves a distinctly postmodern realization of the form).[36] In Montaigne, however, we find it to be a consistent pattern. His expression of almost every idea is contextualized by references to literature and history, so much so that many of his essays proceed through a series of interactive vignettes, accompanied with commentary and reflection.[37] Additionally, Montaigne will make use of quotations, often untranslated, to highlight the poly-phonic nature of his work by bringing in not only other voices but other tongues as well. This dialogic quality is enhanced fur-ther, in a more subtle fashion, through Montaigne's own editorial process; his additions and revision, over several editions, thus contain the voices of several different "Montaignes" (see Screech, "Introduction" and "Explanation of the Symbols"). Interwoven in the texture of his essays are the threads of personal memory and reflection, current speculation, quoted fragments of cultural authority, and reconstructed patterns of customary action, all in dialogue with one another.

In other cases, where the essayist expresses more specific posi-tions, one idea is presented and allowed development through a series of amplifications and refinements. These presentations are distinctively aphoristic in tone, reflecting the oral common-places so much a part of traditional rhetoric. Along with Mon-taigne, Bacon also uses this technique, and he specifically alludes to this educational tradition in essays such as "Of Bold-ness," where he begins:

> It is a trivial grammar-school text, but yet worthy a wise man's con-sideration. Question was asked of Demosthenes, *what was the chief part of an orator?* he answered, *action:* what next? *action:* what next again? *action.* (35–36)

Here Bacon reminds readers of educational practice not only by citing a text and situating it in its "grammar-school" context but also by recreating the question-response pattern indicative of the orality and dialogue of the classroom, and by extension, of the culture itself. Bacon deftly draws our attention to the common, polyphonic discourse in and through which an essayist creates new work which maintains a dialogue with its precedents, and by highlighting this additional "oral residue," he reinforces the oral precedents associated with the dialogue. Though this pat-tern of essay development is rooted in the work of Bacon and Montaigne, all essayists engage in a similar process, implying that the "event" of the essay may not be limited to the expressions of the essayist but may include an invitation for the reader to add his or her own distinctive, and perhaps digressive, patterns of amplification.

The development patterns noted in these limited samples from Montaigne and Bacon illustrate common features of the essay in its points of cultural origin, as well as in its ongoing practice.

Through these patterns, the essay implicitly encourages the reader to continue the process initiated by the essayist. In the first case, the essayist invites the reader to continue to offer ideas and their contraries, so that the dialectic pattern might continue; in the second, the essayist emphasizes the dialogic pattern by use of interactive quotations, narratives, and fragments; in the last instance, he invites the reader to continue the pattern of amplifications, based on his or her own cultural reference points, even if these might contrast with the original amplifications of the essayist. These are but a few of the possible reference points in the work of Montaigne and Bacon that illustrate the essay's fundamental parallels with the dialogue form. It would be another project, indeed another volume, even to begin a thorough interpretation of the stylistic patterns of these two foundational writers. What should be of interest to us, however, are the consistently unfinalized, dialogic, and polyphonic qualities of the genre in its early stages, identifying it as consistent with the dialogue tradition.

Whatever the technique and whoever the writer, the dialogic nature of the essay emerges through its presentation of mental processes, suggesting that the reader is allowed to hear, with acknowledgment, the writer "thinking aloud." In this way the essayist frequently presents thoughts as possibilities or probabilities, not as definitive theses which may be used deductively or systematically. Both the polyphonic and dialogic qualities of the essay imply that it exists as unfinalized discourse, discourse in which the reader is consistently invited to be more than a passive observer or auditor. The reader is invited, explicitly at times, to respond to and continue the processes of thought, and perhaps of writing, that the essayist has either originated or continued. Thus the ultimate goal of the essayist is to foreground not thought as an abstract entity but thinking as a process embedded in the social context of dialogue. Implied in every essay is a special relationship with the reader(s) which dominates the discourse. That is why the essay is so resistant to both form and closure, because it exists as an encouragement to further discourse, not as an end to a rule-governed and systematic process. Unlike the didactic orator or writer, the essayist never wins if the result of reading is silence.

Thus, we can see in the essay a further realization of the dialogic, unfinalized, and polyphonic qualities found in the dialogue. Likewise, we can see that the essay displays much of the same emphases on voice and on the relationship with the reader

that are to be found in the dialogue tradition. Of course, while
the dialogue explicitly reveals the interactive and potentially
conflicting aspects of thought in the persons of its characters,
the essay foregrounds a sense of unity by focusing on the specific
voice of the essayist. However, just as the dialogue often masks
unifying gestures beneath its interactive text, allowing unity to
emerge more by implication, so the essayist, though speaking
with "one voice" on the textual surface, often implies a polyphony of distinctive voices interacting just below that surface.
The essayist allows this instability to surface in many ways: quotations, fragmentary images, shifts in time and location (especially from the writer's present to his or her past, as noted above),
recursive patterns of expressed introspection and self-
interrogation, and even paradox or apparent contradiction.
While the dialogue is an obvious chorus that often seeks a unifying harmony, the essayist is a solo singer who, in the course of
a cyclic song, takes different parts and voices. Even though the
essay and dialogue move discourse in two different directions
(choral vs. solo), both forms achieve realizations of the dialogic,
interactive, and unfinalized elements of discourse.

Thus far, we have observed how the traditional dialogue and
the more modern essay genre share many features. We have also
noted how the decline of the dialogue and the emergence of the
essay coincided during the late sixteenth and early seventeenth
centuries, the time when printing began to exert itself as a dominant medium of language in Western Europe. Yet we must still
examine by what possible mechanism the declining dialogue
could possibly evolve into or relate to the emergent essay. I would
argue that the concept of "interiorization" is at work here, a
concept that Ong discusses, either directly or by implication, in
a number of different contexts (*Interfaces of the Word* 45–47ff;
also *Rhetoric, Romance and Technology* 23–27). Essentially, it
refers to the manner in which language and media effect changes
in human consciousness, both at an individual level and at the
level of general cultural evolution. Particularly, Ong is concerned
with how changes in the language media can fundamentally alter
the conditions of human consciousness, sometimes in ways that
we tend not to acknowledge fully. As Ong describes this process
relative to the effects of media, particularly the computer:

> The mind does not enter into the alphabet or the printed book or
> the computer so much as the alphabet or print or the computer enters
> the mind, producing new states of awareness there. Relieving the

mind of its onus of conscious but routine operations (such as computing, sorting, matching patterns, and so on), the computer, for example, actually releases more energy for new kinds of exploratory operations by the human mind itself, in which the unconscious is deeply involved and which the computer, lacking an unconscious, cannot carry forward. Earlier, writing and print had effected comparable energy releases. (1977, 47)

Thus, "interiorization" has to do with a process of gradual changes in consciousness brought about by the new linguistic behaviors fostered by cultural changes, particularly those relating to media technologies.

As Ong and Havelock have shown, the Platonic dialogues grew from an interiorization of the linguistic habits of writing in the developing chirographic culture of ancient Greece (see *Orality and Literacy*, chap. 4 and *The Muse Learns to Write*, chap. 10). In this setting, the noetics of traditional oral culture and the new patterns of literacy interacted and gradually achieved a balance that was reflected in the dialogue form. The dialogue was an expression of the interiorized balance between orality and literacy that came into existence in chirographic cultures. Later, as print altered the consciousness of Western European culture in the sixteenth century, the dialogue lost influence, since it no longer reflected the emergent "textual" consciousness of this new print culture. Still, the interactive, dialogic, and unfinalized qualities of the dialogue were retained in that cultural consciousness, though they could no longer be expressed in the form of the dialogue. The evolving consciousness did foster the development of a new form of expression, the essay. As we have already seen, the essay could be used to express the same dialogic and unfinalized qualities as the dialogue, while also reflecting the new balance between orality and literacy in an age of printed texts. Where the dialogue offers explicit voices in conflict, the essay offers exploratory statements and questions in contrast; where the dialogue represents both conflict and consensus between competing personalities, the essay expresses the experience of a mind weighing competing patterns of thought and experience. However, whereas the dialogue represented a chirographic culture with a much higher level of oral residue and its attendant social context of language, the essay reflects the emergent print culture. That culture, as Ong has demonstrated, allowed for and encouraged a much greater sense of individual alienation, psychological privacy, and introspective discourse

(Ong 1982, 152ff). As a result, the essay constructs itself from what we might call an "internal dialogue," a conversation that the essayist is having with him or herself. Perhaps more accurately, we find the essayist offering the polyphonic discourse deriving from the interaction of different patterns of thought and reflection, often in variations on so intimate a voice that the reader feels drawn into a conversation with the writer. Therefore, just as the dialogue invites us to be listeners and, by extension, eventual participants in the discourse of ideas, so the essay implicitly invites the reader into the intimate conversations of thought and reflection, as listener, as suggested interlocutor, and as another practitioner of the same reflective patterns witnessed in the essay.

During the late sixteenth century, writers such as Michel de Montaigne and Francis Bacon, both unusually polymath intellects, found the essay a congenial form for expressing the wide range of their speculations and reflections. Each sought in the essay the kind of personal and cultural space that would allow for free exploration of new ideas. Both writers have since taken on mythic status as originators of the essay, much as we associate various ancient writers with the birth of earlier genres (e.g., Aeschylus and Sophocles with tragic drama). Certainly the voluminous work of Montaigne, along with the considerable offerings of Bacon, provided an excellent start for this new genre. In Montaigne, many of the patterns of culture, especially drawn from his extensive reading and from the commonplace tradition that was still embedded in Renaissance education, are interwoven with the questions, speculations, and often ironic or melancholy reflections of one of the most dynamic minds of the era. In Bacon, the orderly voice of the legal authority can be heard in counterpoint to the speculative voice of the revisionist philosopher, and the pragmatic but exploratory voice of the proto-scientist. As the genre emerged in the hands of these two writers who provided its name, the essay was first seen as the open-ended, speculative, and exploratory form we now assume it to be.

Later generations of essayists would continue this dynamic process of development, from Addison and Steele in the eighteenth century, all the way to E. B. White and Virginia Woolf in the twentieth (and today, Bailey White and Tobias Wolff, to name only two).[38] The submerged patterns of dialogue frequently surface in the sometimes playful, sometimes conflicted voices of individual essayists who have sought to reveal "the mind at work." Even today, as inheritors of the essay tradition, and thus of the dialogue as well, essayists see their art as uncertain and indeterminate, and yet they also find it all the more inviting because of these qualities. In one sense, the essay has become our intellectual "commons," the space reserved for unfinalized and liberating discourse. In another sense, it has become the private garden, the sacred space of meditation and intimate reflection, but always in the company of the invited, companionable reader. In still another, it has become the space of game and amusement, where no idea is free from childlike scrutiny and playful irony. These are but a few of the ongoing traditions of the essay, which is a genre that thrives in many different contexts. On the editorial page and in the small literary journal, in the glossy national magazine and in the obscure periodical, the essay is found to be equally at home, and that is looking only at the medium of print.

New media have evolved in the past century, creating a cultural revolution as profound as that which came in the wake of the printing press. Perhaps "revolutions" is more accurate, for in the late nineteenth century came telecommunications, then in the early to mid-twentieth century came electronic broadcasting. Now, fast upon the changes wrought by radio and television come interactive computing and multi-media technology. What of the essay in this new context? Will it decline as did its ancestor, the dialogue? Or will it find an even more dynamic rebirth through the opportunities offered by new multi-media settings? These questions cannot be answered yet, since we are still in the midst of the accelerating change in our own "noetic economies." But for now the essay seems to be thriving, gaining even greater exposure and influence with each passing decade. However, we are best equipped to speculate on its current condition, as well as its future progress, if first we understand its origins and evolution.

I have attempted to argue here that the essay, a relatively young and still problematic genre, is actually the descendent of a great cultural and rhetorical tradition, the dialogue. Further, I have argued that both the ancient dialogue and the modern essay have shared the role of balancing orality and literacy during their respective chirographic and print stages of cultural development. What happens next to that balance is quite difficult to predict, especially given the complex interactions of all current forms of cultural expression. However, in the work of theorists such as Walter Ong and Mikhail Bakhtin, we can find the balanced and wide-ranging vision that will guide us in further explorations of the essay, and of all other cultural expressions as well. Likewise, if we wish to understand more fully the dynamic balance between orality and literacy as it will exist in the coming century, both Ong and Bakhtin will provide us with important tools. Finally, if we seek an accurate barometer for the interactive development of media, consciousness, and culture, we would do well to focus our study on the essay genre, whose experimental and exploratory traditions keep it at the forward edge of cultural developments. Of course it may take willingness to understand the essay in new ways, realized through new media—oral, visual, mixed, and so on.

Considering the richness of the essay tradition, its current wide influence, and its potential for continued growth, I am surprised that more academic literary study has not been devoted to the genre. But whatever the past omissions, the current conflicted and unfinalized state of academic literary studies may find in the essay not only material for examination but also the vehicle for achieving balance in its own troubled house. So, in the tradition of both the dialogue and the essay, let me close with an invitation into the study of this genre, in all its contexts. There is much to assay, and there is space to resonate with many voices.

Notes

1. See any number of works by Walter Ong, esp. *Ramus, Method, and the Decay of Dialogue* (Cambridge, MA: Harvard University Press, 1958, 1983); *Rhetoric, Romance, and Technology*, (Ithaca, N.Y.: Cornell University Press, 1971); *Interfaces of the Word* (Ithaca, N.Y.: Cornell University Press, 1977), and *Orality and Literacy* (London: Methuen, 1982).

2. See Ong, *Interfaces of the Word*, 44–47, for a discussion of "noetic economies"; the concept is discussed frequently throughout the work.

3. See Eric Havelock's *Preface to Plato* (Cambridge, MA: Harvard University Press, 1963) and *The Muse Learns to Write* (New Haven, CT: Yale University Press, 1983).

4. I am using the term "rhetoric" in its most traditional sense that includes the category of "poetic," thus including what we would consider all forms of literary work.

5. Some might argue that the novel is an equally recent form, but it is much more difficult to establish its origins as clearly. Prose fiction narratives have an ancient pedigree, though all prose fiction need not be considered as examples of "the novel." Suffice it to say that the novel is also a relatively young literary genre, but one whose evolution is more difficult to analyze.

6. Primary work on the nature of ancient oral art forms that form the precedents for various forms of later, written discourse, was pursued by scholars such as Milman Parry and Alfred Lord. Both Ong and Havelock rely on Parry and Lord, among others, as sources for the works cited in notes 1 and 4. For

further discussion of these issues, see Ong's *Orality and Literacy*, chap. 2; *Rhetoric, Romance, and Technology*, 33–38; and Havelock's *The Muse Learns to Write*, chap. 3.

7. See *Orality and Literacy*, chap. 4, and *The Muse Learns to Write*, chap. 10.

8. I offer a more extended explanation of the variable form of the essay genre in "The Literature of the Essay and the Discourse of Values," in *Values and Public Life: An Interdisciplinary Study for Religion and Society*, ed. Gerard Magill (Lanham, MD: University Press of America, 1995), 57–88.

9. Ong deals with these issues throughout his body of work, but perhaps his most succinct development of them is in *Orality and Literacy*.

10. See *Orality and Literacy*, chap. 2 through 4, and *The Muse Learns to Write*, chap. 8 through 10.

11. See Ong, *Interfaces of the Word*, 44–47; Ong refers to this concept through this work.

12. The remainder of this paragraph derives from these sources, but obviously I am summarizing the concepts with extreme brevity.

13. Ong refers to the concept of the "human lifeworld" and its relationship to primary oral cultures in a variety of contexts and in several of his works.

14. The concept of "presence" can cause a great deal of confusion, especially considering the level of complexity involved in discussions of contemporary literary theory. However, the "illusion" of presence, criticized in much post-structuralist theory, refers to the presence of conceptual realities (essentially, ideas) that are signified by various linguistic signifiers. But when Ong and others discuss the nature of primary oral cultures, they are talking about the necessary physical presence of speaker(s) and listener(s) to each other, shared in time and space, so that the spoken words can be heard. In a primary oral culture, meaning may be differed (it is a debatable question), but in such contexts, speaking and hearing cannot be differed. For more discussion of this issue, see Ong, *The Presence of the Word* (New Haven, CT: Yale University Press, 1967; Minneapolis: University of Minnesota Press, 1981), chap. 3. Also see Ong, *Orality and Literacy*, 165–70. Colin Falck has discussed this issue from a slightly different but also useful perspective in *Myth, Truth, and Literature* (Cambridge: Cambridge University Press, 1989), chap. 4.

15. See the discussion of Socratic and Platonic dialogues in George Kennedy, *Classical Rhetoric and Its Christian and Secular Tradition from Ancient to Modern Times* (Chapel Hill: The University of North Carolina Press, 1980), 41ff. Also see Ong, *Orality and Literacy*, 79–81.

16. See Havelock, *The Muse Learns to Write*, chap. 1. He discusses the relationship between primary oral precedents and the existing texts of Homer and Hesiod, suggesting that the texts reflect the patterns of primary orality but also reflect the assumptions of an emergent manuscript culture. See also Ong, *Orality and Literacy*, 79–81.

17. The entirety of Kennedy's *Classical Rhetoric, etc.* confirms the influence of the rhetorical arts in the ancient world, but a useful focal passage on the conflict between rhetoric and philosophy appears on 89–90. Also see Ong, *Orality and Literacy*, chap. 4.

18. "Polyphony" is a concept taken from Mikhail Bakhtin's theories of the novel. See part 3 of this article, and also see the notes for that section below.

19. Ong, *Orality and Literacy*, chap. 5, as well as in other of his works, including *Rhetoric, Romance, and Technology* and *Interfaces of the Word*.

20. Ong, *Orality and Literacy.* For a focal passage on printing and "mass culture," *Interfaces of the Word,* 40–41.

21. Along with Ong's 1958 work on Ramus, see *Rhetoric, Romance, and Technology,* chap. 6.

22. See note 19.

23. See note 21 on Ramism, printing, and the decline of the dialogue. Concerning the development of new "dialogue" in the twentieth century, see Ong's work on "secondary orality" in *Rhetoric, Romance, and Technology,* chap. 12, and *Interfaces of the Word,* chap. 11.

24. See note 19.

25. See note 8 for a discussion of the "dialogics" of the essay. For another application of Bakhtin to the essay, but in a pedagogical context, see Thomas Recchio, "A Dialogic Approach to the Essay," *Essays on the Essay,* ed. Alexander J. Butrym (Athens: University of Georgia Press, 1989), 271–88.

26. Mikhail Bakhtin (1895–1975), a Russian literary and cultural theorist, suffered internal exile and persecution at the hands of early Soviet governments. Only in the 1960s was he fully accepted back into the Soviet intellectual community. During the past twenty years or so, several of Bakhtin's major works have been translated into English, among them: *The Dialogic Imagination,* ed., Michael Holquist, trans. Caryl Emerson and Michael Holquist (Austin: University of Texas Press, 1981); *Problems in Dostoyevsky's Poetics,* trans. and ed., Caryl Emerson (Minneapolis: University of Minnesota Press, 1984); and *Speech Genres and Other Essays,* trans. Vern W. McGee, eds., Caryl Emerson and Michael Holquist (Austin: University of Texas Press, 1986). The community of translators and interpreters of this body of work (and of other, still untranslated texts) has grown rapidly. There is much dispute over some of the early texts attributed to Bakhtin but officially authored by his colleagues, and on the accurate attribution of such texts depends much on how we view Bakhtin's theories. I am adopting the views and interpretations provided in one of the most recent and authoritative studies of Bakhtin's work: Gary Morson and Caryl Emerson, *Mikhail Bakhtin: Creation of a Prosaics* (Stanford, CA: Stanford University Press, 1990). The Morson and Emerson text makes use of a vast array of primary source material, including important theoretical works by Bakhtin that have yet to be translated into English. For this reason, I use it as a "primary" interpretative source for Bakhtinian theory.

27. The concepts of the "dialogic" and "unfinalizability" are addressed in *Problems in Dostoyevsky's Poetics,* as well as in other works. For a summary discussion of these concepts, see Morson and Emerson, 36–62.

28. Much of Bakhtin's discussion of these issues comes in "Toward a Philosophy of the Act" (still untranslated at the time of Morson and Emerson's text). For a description and explanation of the importance of this work, see Morson and Emerson, 27–32.

29. See Morson and Emerson, 49–62. Also see Ong, *Interfaces of the Word,* chap. 5.

30. In my dissertation, "Inventions for Voice: Humanist Rhetoric and the Experiments of Elizabethan Prose Fiction" (University of Iowa, 1989), I discuss how this atmosphere of experimentation affected the development of prose fiction.

31. Though later than the essay, the novel also achieves the balance between orality and literacy in a print-based culture. It is the focus of Bakhtin's study

because it so fully realizes his concepts of the polyphony, the dialogic, and unfinalizability.

32. Despite the vast cultural influence and monumental status of the novel, I would still argue that it is the essay which is the most central inheritor of the dialogue tradition, for the novel is still essentially a narrative genre, while the essay more fully realizes the interactive qualities of the dialogue.

33. For a lengthy discussion of Bakhtin's concept of Polyphony, see Morson and Emerson, 231–68. Morson and Emerson see this concept as an integral component of what they call the "global concept" of "dialogue." It is true that, in one context, Bakhtin sees Dostoyevsky as the "inventor" of the polyphonic qualities of the novel, and that this is a feature usually associated with fiction from the nineteenth and twentieth centuries. However, I am using the term "polyphony" in its more general and philosophical sense in relationship to the "dialogic" quality of truth, which requires a "plurality of consciousnesses" (cf. Morson and Emerson, 234–41). It is also true that Bakhtin expands his concept of polyphony to include not only features in texts but a theory of the creative process. Therefore, I feel justified in applying the concept in reading the origins of the essay and its relationship with the dialogue. I believe that this application is a valid one, consistent with the concept as developed by Bakhtin.

34. We can see in both early essayists, Montaigne and Bacon, many features which are associated with the dialogue. It is not possible, in an article of this scope, to engage in a lengthy interpretation of multiple essays from these writers; however, I believe that their work generally represents the features I have described, and that later essayists, in the context of their own eras, continued to use similar techniques and create similar features in their work. For a more extended discussion of these features see references in note 8 and Klaus, 160.

35. This is true in both Montaigne and Bacon, but it seems that Montaigne allows the apparent discontinuity of fragments to surface more readily. Often the effect of reading Montaigne is the experience of a cultural collage, developed from an exploratory intellect's dialogue with his own culture's "commonplace" tradition.

36. I am thinking of essays by Didion such as "On the Mall" and "On Keeping a Notebook." See "On Keeping a Notebook," in *Slouching Towards Bethlehem* (New York: Simon, 1968; Washington Square, 1981) 135–44. Also see "On the Mall" in *The White Album* (New York: Simon, 1979), 180–86. In essays such as this, the fragments of memory, personal collection, cultural representation, and random occurrence are all brought together in the same kind of cultural collage achieved by Montaigne. Didion is by no means the only essayist whose work creates this effect, but I find it unusually amplified in her case, as I do in the case of Montaigne.

37. See notes 34 and 35.

38. There are a vast number of essayists available to read and study, both contemporary and from early periods. I would recommend the Klaus anthology, frequently cited here, as a useful starting point for exploring a variety of essayists. As of yet, there is no journal devoted exclusively to the study of the literary essay. In passing, I mention two relatively recent essayists: Bailey White and Tobias Wolff. Bailey White's first book is *Mama Makes Up Her Mind* (New York: Addison-Wesley, 1993)—a compilation of essays read as commentaries on National Public Radio. Tobias Wolff's memoir, which I would classify as one form of the essay, is *This Boy's Life* (New York: Atlantic Monthly Press, 1989), and it was recently produced as a film. I cite them not only because

their names echo the early two essayists (White and Woolf) but also because they each have brought about the intersection of the essay with twentieth-century media, broadcasting and film.

Works Cited

Bacon, Francis. *Essays*. London: J. M. Dent & Sons Ltd., Everyman Edition, 1973.

Bakhtin, Mikhail. *The Dialogic Imagination*. Edited by Michael Holquist. Translated by Caryl Emerson and Michael Holquist. Austin: University of Texas Press, 1981.

———. *Problems in Dostoyevsky's Poetics*. Translated and edited by Caryl Emerson. Minneapolis: University of Minnesota, 1984.

———. *Speech Genres and Other Essays*. Translated by Vern W. McGee. Edited by Caryl Emerson and Michael Holquist. Austin: University of Texas Press, 1986.

Casaregola, Vincent. "The Literature of the Essay and the Discourse of Values." In *Values and Public Life: An Interdisciplinary Study for Religion and Society*. Edited by Gerard MaGill and Marie Hoff. Lanham, MD: University Press of America, 1995.

———. "Inventions for Voice: Humanist Rhetoric and the Experiments of Elizabethan Prose Fiction." Dissertation. Iowa City: The University of Iowa, 1989.

Cicero, Marcus Tullius. *De Oratore*. 2 Vols. Translated by E. W. Sutton and H. Rackham. Cambridge, MA: Harvard University Press, 1942.

Didion, Joan. *Slouching Towards Bethlehem*. New York: Simon & Schuster, 1968; Washington Square Press, 1981.

———. *The White Album*. New York: Simon & Schuster, 1979.

Falck, Colin. *Myth, Truth, and Literature*. Cambridge: Cambridge University Press, 1989.

Havelock, Eric. *Preface to Plato*. Cambridge, MA: Harvard University Press, 1963.

———. *The Muse Learns to Write*. New Haven, CT: Yale University Press, 1983.

Hoagland, Edward. "What I Think, What I Am." In *In Depth: Essayists for Our Time*, edited by Carl Klaus, Chris Anderson, and Rebecca Faery, 1st ed. 362–64. San Diego, CA: Harcourt, 1990.

Kennedy, George. *Classical Rhetoric and Its Christian and Secular Tradition from Ancient to Modern Times*. Chapel Hill: The University of North Carolina Press, 1980.

Klaus, Carl. "Essayists on the Essay." In *Literary Nonfiction: Theory, Criticism, Pedagogy*, edited by Chris Anderson, 155–75. Carbondale: Southern Illinois University Press, 1989.

Klaus, Carl, Chris Anderson, and Rebecca Faery. "Introduction: On the Essay." In *In Depth: Essayists for Our Time*. 2d ed. 2–7. Fort Worth, TX: Harcourt, 1993.

de Montaigne, Michel. *The Essays of Michel de Montaigne*. Translated and edited by M. A. Screech. London: Allen Lane, Penguin, 1991.

Morson, Gary Saul, and Caryl Emerson. *Mikhail Bakhtin: Creation of a Prosaics*. Stanford, CA: Stanford University Press, 1990.

Ong, Walter J. *Interfaces of the Word: Studies in the Evolution of Consciousness and Culture.* Ithaca, NY: Cornell University Press, 1977.

———. *Orality and Literacy: The Technologizing of the Word.* London: Methuen, 1982.

———. *The Presence of the Word: Some Prolegomena for Cultural and Religious History.* New Haven, CT: Yale University Press, 1967; Minneapolis: University of Minnesota Press, 1981.

———. *Ramus, Method, and the Decay of Dialogue: From the Art of Discourse to the Art of Reason.* 1958; Cambridge, MA: Harvard University Press, 1983.

———. *Rhetoric, Romance, and Technology: Studies in the Interaction of Expression and Culture.* Ithaca, NY: Cornell University Press, 1971.

Recchio, Thomas. "A Dialogic Approach to the Essay." In *Essays on the Essay,* edited by Alexander J. Butrym, 271–88. Athens: University of Georgia Press, 1989.

Screech, M. A. "Introduction." In *The Essays of Michel de Montaigne.* Translated and edited by M. A. Screech, xiii–xlviii. London: Allen Lane, Penguin, 1991.

White, Bailey. *Mama Makes Up Her Mind.* New York: Addison-Wesley, 1993.

White, E. B. "The Essayist and the Essay." In *In Depth: Essayists for Our Time,* edited by Carl Klaus, Chris Anderson, and Rebecca Faery. 1st ed. 362–64. San Diego, CA: Harcourt, 1990.

Wolff, Tobias. *This Boy's Life.* New York: Atlantic Monthly Press, 1989.

The Bard's Audience Is Always More Than a Fiction

JOHN MILES FOLEY

Pour mon amie française—Frances Foley Kelly (1907–1993)

IN HIS LANDMARK ESSAY, "THE WRITER'S AUDIENCE IS ALWAYS A FIC-
tion," originally published in 1975 and winner of the William
Riley Parker Award as the best contribution to *PMLA* for that
year, Walter Ong explained what he meant by his title in terms
of a writer's and reader's communicative responsibilities:

> First, that the writer must construct in his imagination, clearly or
> vaguely, an audience cast in some sort of role—entertainment
> seekers, reflective sharers of experience (as those who listen to Con-
> rad's Marlow), inhabitants of a lost and remembered world of prepu-
> bertal latency (readers of Tolkien's hobbit stories), and so on. Second,
> we mean that the audience must correspondingly fictionalize itself.
> A reader has to play the role in which the author has cast him, which
> seldom coincides with his role in the rest of actual life. (60–61)

Driven by a partnership with an audience of his or her own
making, the author establishes an imagined "fixed foot" that
makes the arc of the narrative circle "just," an audience and a
matched mode of expression that anchor the ongoing transaction
at the same time that they imbue it with meaning.[1] Indeed, Ong
observes, "even an oral narrator calls on his audience to fiction-
alize itself to some extent. The invocation to the Muse is a signal
to the audience to put on the epic-listener's cap" ("The Writer's
Audience" 69).

Bards: Performance, Transcription, Text

The purpose of the present essay is to take this nugget of Ongian wisdom and to examine how it may apply to the kind of

verbal artists I will be subsuming under the label *bard*.[2] By this term I designate not only the (highly romanticized) epic poet in oral performance, most frequently of course the "Homer" figure we nostalgically place at the fount of Western literary tradition, but a much larger and more heterogeneous cadré of artists, living and dead. Included are performers of epic among present-day cultures but also their fellow wordsmiths around the world who work in myriad other genres as well. Some of these genres boast established relatives or outright progeny in the written traditions we know best, and are therefore familiar (lyric, folktale, ballad, and so forth), while many others are not readily assimilable to canonical Western expressive forms, and are thus unfamiliar, non-privileged, or even unknown (praise poetry, genealogy, stylized invective, and so on). Within the bounds of this essay, "bard" names all of these traditional oral performers, regardless of gender, age, genre, or culture.

The second way in which the more usual concept of bard will be expanded is to include two additional varieties of works that, strictly speaking, do not constitute oral tradition per se. One is the category of performances transcribed into written records, a group itself extremely heterogeneous in its population. Numerous Native American stories written down in the early part of this century, before the advent of tape recorders, fall into this category, as do the rich and various European collections of folktales and other narratives taken down from dictation during the widespread search for nationalistic and ethnic origins in the nineteenth century. We are as certain as latter-day readers can be that the collectors involved did in fact transcribe real oral performances, and that they did so according to their best convictions about how the process should be carried out, but we are nonetheless left only with written cenotaphs, mere libretti that, as folklorists and anthropologists have shown repeatedly, preserve only a single dimension of the experience of performance (Fine; Foley, "Folk Literature"). Such transcriptions—which still involve a bard's performance, notwithstanding the semiotic distance between event and inevitably reduced record—will present a challenge for our consideration of the bard's audience.

Perhaps even more of a challenge will arise when we confront authored texts that are, to varying degrees of certainty, not simply transcriptions but free-standing compositions in writing that, paradoxically, reveal deep roots in oral tradition. The classical and medieval European poems, as well as many Chinese and Indian works, for example, seem to amount to what early theo-

rists declared impossible: authored, literate productions that use
the expressive idiom of oral tradition.[3] Herein lies the core of
the problem. If we simplistically assign such intermediate works
to the canon of "literature" without considering the ways in
which their very constitution is indebted to oral tradition, as
many have done in order to preserve a manufactured distinction
between "oral" and "written," then we in effect exclude a crucially important dimension of their poetics. What is more, the
loss is permanent: having assimilated these works of art to our
own system of categories, and having made them culturally ours,
they can never again speak except in the foreign language we
have denominated. To preview the argument to follow, the challenge with such texts will consist of learning something of their
"mother tongue," that is, essentially of making ourselves a better audience.

Traditional, Whether "Oral" or Not

The history of studies in what we call "oral tradition," in
which Walter Ong's scholarship has been so foundational, has
suffered greatly, perhaps inevitably, from the relative weighting
given each of the two composite terms. Because the idea of composition without writing seemed so distinctive and so unlike the
kind of artistic process in which we imagine Chaucer, Shakespeare, or Spenser to have engaged,[4] *oral* appeared to be the decisive quality of this phenomenon, what linguists would identify
as the "marked" item in the pair written/oral.[5] Nor should we
underestimate the role of the nineteenth-century search for origins, mentioned above, or the influence of the Cambridge anthropologists of the 1920s and their evolutionary theory of culture;
early and oral were not seldom opposed to later and written,
against all evidence from the world outside the Western hegemony. On the other hand, Milman Parry's ground-breaking investigation of Homer and South Slavic oral epic, which with Albert
Lord's comparative emphasis has produced an enormous and
vibrant area of investigation,[6] began not with orality but with
tradition. Parry's initial move was to explain the recurrent features of Homeric style through reconceptualizing the *Iliad* and
Odyssey as the bequest of tradition—at least as much the inheritance of centuries of verse-making as the masterful creation of a
single individual. Only after he became aware of examples of
other traditional poetries that were also oral did Parry then con-

sider the possibility that Homer was an oral poet (Foley, *Theory*, chap. 2).

The skewed weighting of "oral" and "traditional" can be illustrated clearly by reference to the analytic regimen that overtook classical and medieval poetries in Parry's wake. Methods were developed to count the number of repeated phrases (formulas) in a poem and, after a percentage density was determined, the poem under scrutiny—for which only a text remained extant—was pronounced oral or written.[7] This procedure was interwoven with a minimalist poetics that saw formulas and typical scenes as primarily "useful," constituting a language that relieved the composing poet of decisions that he or she could not hope to make in the unrelenting heat of performance. Not incidentally, of course, as many critics pointed out, the same explanation also relieved the poems of artistic quality. This was perhaps the most serious consequence of setting up an oral/written typology and forging a poetics to support its reductionism.

No more helpful has been the universalist projection of an "oral culture," a hypothetically pristine society that carries on all of its verbal business face to face without any recourse to technologies of literacy or print. While some such cultures still do exist, the vast majority of those that maintain oral traditions also deal in scripts and/or typographies, even in books, once again upsetting the applecart of the Great Divide thesis of exclusive orality or literacy (especially Finnegan, *Oral Poetry*; *Literacy and Orality*). I can attest firsthand to the reality of this kind of media-mix among living cultures: our research team encountered many people in the Šumadijan region of central Serbia who practiced some sort of oral tradition, and few of them were entirely illiterate ("Field Research"). The clue to what they did and how they accomplished it was compartmentalization; they might have been able to read and write well enough to communicate with their children serving as "guest-workers" in Germany or Switzerland, but it would never occur to them to use this task-based technology to write out their tales, magical spells, genealogies, or the like. Within a culture that was, and remains, both oral and literate, people utilized the whole repertoire of communicative strategies in socially determined ways.[8] To reduce this natural heterogeneity of expression to a monolith would be to misrepresent the vibrant multivalency of the culture.

The reality of the situation, as derived from evidence submitted from societies worldwide, is that oral traditions are often practiced by functionally literate people who somehow can man-

age a variety of verbal activities, and that the idioms that constitute oral traditions are in fact "carried over" to transcriptions
and to authored texts.

If "oral" usually fails to describe the culture in its total expressive repertoire, and if, further, it fails to encompass those textual
witnesses that paradoxically use an idiom that arises as an oral
medium, then we must cease insisting on orality as the distinguishing feature of this kind of verbal art. Let us instead try the
trajectory offered by tradition, in the sense of a shared ecology of
discourse that involves a continuing responsibility for performer/
author and audience. Of course, tradition is a notoriously slippery concept, one that in folklore studies alone has been defined
in many different ways (Ben-Amos), and some care will be
needed if it is to be employed without confusion. But with the
concept of orality relegated at this point to a heuristic, we must
seek elsewhere for the definitive feature of "oral tradition" that
will allow us to account for its tremendous variety of expressive
forms while still maintaining some grasp on their shared potential for conveying meaning.

In the sense it is to be used in this essay, tradition denotes
"variation within limits," an equilibrium of discourse style not
unlike Ong's concept of homeostasis (*Orality and Literacy* 46–
49). That is, the term does not designate a fossilized or even
highly conservative mode of organization, any more than it echoes the usage in "literary tradition," wherein authors respond to
authors, texts to texts, and so forth. In order to persevere over
time, to escape the brittleness of edited texts for example, traditions need to be able to change organically and systemically.
Scholars do not often note, for instance, that relatively few of
Homer's formulaic phrases are absolutely fixed; beyond the
noun-epithet combinations that provided Parry a locus classicus
for his demonstrations lies a wealth of malleable forms, and Homer is by all accounts the most conservative "oral poet" yet encountered.[9] Ancient Greek and other poetries also exhibit great
innate adaptability—potential for change—at the level of narrative organization: the typical scenes of battle or assembly and
the story-pattern of Return, to take well-attested and studied examples from epic,[10] demonstrate how crucial the role of multi-
formity is to an ongoing tradition. Without change, rule-governed
change that is built into the very genetic code of an idiom, tradition can have no chance of maintaining itself over time.

Register, Performance Arena, Communicative Economy

In concert with developments in anthropological linguistics, I name this kind of traditional idiom—in which systemic change and recurrent patterning interact—a *register* of language, that is, one of those "major speech styles associated with recurrent types of situations" (Hymes, "Ways" 440). This distinction stems ultimately from the linguistic theories of M. A. K. Halliday, who conceived of register in terms of three controlling variables: field of discourse ("the area of operation of the language activity" [*Linguistic Sciences* 90]), mode of discourse (spoken or written, with many more layers of taxonomy possible), and style or tenor of discourse ("the relations among the participants" [92]).

Whether as originators of discourse or as its audience, we all command a number of registers in our everyday expressive (and perceptual) repertoire, and each one is to an extent a singular channel for communication. Most of us code-switch among different varieties of language when speaking to children, writing essays, composing memoranda, or "talking shop," for example, and we do so largely without conscious awareness of the adaptation we are making to the given situation. Selecting the appropriate channel is a skill we learn from participating in the culture (and subculture) of which we are part, as is the reciprocal adjustment we make when someone chooses a new register in which to begin a verbal transaction with us. An unidiomatic response—selecting the wrong register or channel—can be off-putting or humorous or simply unfathomable, not because the words themselves are necessarily harsh or comical or mysterious, but because the choice of idiom was badly made.[11] I remember with some embarrassment an inappropriate choice I once made in responding to a Serbian colleague's query concerning the whereabouts of a child's toy in my Belgrade apartment: look out on the *čardak*, I told him, not fully aware that this register-specific, now obsolete term for an Ottoman-era "porch," complete with beys, pashas, and like, was an ill-chosen label for a three-foot-square concrete extension six floors up in a modern housing complex.

This example illustrates generally how every verbal act assumes at minimum a congruency of register for speaker and audience, and how tuning to the wrong channel results in a kind of verbal static. More specifically, it also illustrates how the

Ottoman-era word was quite radically out of place in this particular twentieth-century urban exchange. But we should not lose sight of the fact that this same word, *čardak*, along with myriad other lexical and morphological curiosities, was perfectly appropriate within the register of South Slavic epic (where a more up-to-date or simply unidiomatic term would have been inappropriate). Consider the aorist tense, for example, likewise stigmatized as archaic in standard (conversational or literary) Serbian and Croatian, but absolutely commonplace and expected in the epic. To take another genre from South Slavic, the system of color designations in the women's domain of magical charms or *bajanje* is sufficiently obsolete that not even the skilled practitioners themselves are able to explain certain of its lexical vagaries. Is it then any wonder that both the Homeric register and the registers of South Slavic epic and charm consist not of the relatively smooth surfaces typical of contemporary standard languages, but rather of idioms that reveal great internal heterogeneity both synchronically (in a mélange of dialect varieties) and diachronically (in the collection of historically disparate forms)? One needs to know how to command the particular idiom of expression, which may from one perspective seem composite and uneven but has a functional unity of its own, in order to communicate effectively within a given genre or in a given situation.[12]

It is of course the bard who must achieve that level of fluency in the traditional idiom, but it is also and equally his or her audience, who is always more than a fiction. Without listeners (and later, readers) who can perceive according to the encoded signals of the register, even the most finely crafted work of verbal art will fall on deaf ears. This other bookend of the communicative process, the audience/reader, has been much neglected in studies in oral tradition, primarily because of the misplaced, nearly exclusive focus on orality and a lack of awareness of how focused, specialized, and therefore economical a medium a traditional register is. If we can sense how delicate and yet powerful an instrument such a dedicated variety of language can be, then we can cast off the straightjacket of mechanism versus aesthetics that has plagued the study of bards and their works from many times and places, and begin to understand how traditional oral art can inform even textual compositions.

For one thing, we have long known that traditional registers do not simply disappear with the advent of writing. Face-to-face composition in performance may disappear, giving way to performance of memorized works (unwritten but largely fixed) or even to the pregnant silence of authored texts, but the medieval European vernaculars, for instance, occupy a middle ground, continuing to use the idiom developed in oral tradition. The Old English or Anglo-Saxon canon includes many examples of poems with clear sources in Latin manuscripts or other signs of indebtedness to the written word, and yet they show ongoing allegiance to the traditional register.[13] Likewise with Old French *chansons de geste*, some of which were certainly composed pen in hand but all of which use the medieval French poetic register appropriate to their genre.[14]

What these "post-oral" productions have in common with "true oral" poetry in their respective cultures is a shared register, a common expressive instrument that through its idiosyncratic focus promotes a highly economical kind of signification. As I have argued elsewhere, a noun-epithet formula for a person or god amounts to a shorthand characterization, a traditionally approved way to summon that character to narrative present in all of his or her complexity (*Immanent Art* 17–33). The tell-tale detail—Achilleus' swift feet, Odysseus' wiliness, Athena's bright eyes—is a nominal signifier, a part that stands institutionally for a whole that lies beyond the reach of textualization. To that nominal part the audience/reader brings the experience of other works in the traditional constellation, other experience in this same register; together, operating within a special code that by virtue of being strictly limited in its general applicability is also densely reverberative within its dedicated area, performer/author and audience/reader co-create the work of art. To put the matter proverbially, *tradition is the enabling referent* for the communication.

The other part of this significative proverb holds that *performance is the enabling event*. That is, in the first instance, the fact of performance—with its many linguistic, paralinguistic, and nonlinguistic dimensions—betokens, as Richard Bauman has phrased it (9), "a transformation of the basic referential . . . uses of language. In other words, in artistic performance of this kind, there is something going on in the communicative interchange which says to the auditor, 'interpret what I say in some special sense; do not take it to mean what the words alone, taken literally, would convey'." This keying of performance survives in texts as a set of rhetorical signals, in the form of cues such as special codes, figurative language, parallelism, special formulae, appeal to tradition, and disclaimer of performance (Bauman's examples, 16). The event, whether the actual experience or its rhetorically induced facsimile, empowers the act with an emergent, focused meaning by engaging a context in which the register can do its special significative work.

Whether via experience or through rhetorical signals, then, the performer and audience enter what I call the *performance arena*, an abstraction that names the "place" where they go to communicate in the traditional register. In actual face-to-face interaction, this is a geographically and chronologically defined locus, unique among other actual loci, but its importance stems not from that real-world uniqueness but from its functional coincidence with all other times and places that collectively constitute the tradition. An audience member attending one bard's performance in village A on Wednesday and his sister attending another bard's performance of a similar story in village B on Sunday will effectively have entered the same arena. In the same way, a latter-day reader of a transcribed version of either of the two performances will, according to the limits of his or her experience and of the semiotic transformation from event to text, also be coming to essentially the same place. Even the reader of a text composed pen in hand by a literate author—but a text that still uses the traditional register to some extent—will be trying to gain admission to the performance arena. Literacy or literate composition per se does not necessarily imply segregation in a single camp, nor is mere orality or literacy adequate justification for an exclusivist, parochial criticism. Using the register means engaging tradition as the enabling referent and performance (even if rhetorical) as the enabling event, and these continuities simply supersede the constructed and finally false dichotomy of "oral versus written." Even at the distance of an authored text, the bard's audience is always more than a fiction.

If both parties are able to enter the performance arena, and if both are fluent in the register devoted to the given speech-act, then the verbal transaction will take place with what we may call a heightened *communicative economy.* Instead of having to establish or invent a mythic history for this or that character, for instance, the bard will simply invoke it by using one of the agreed-upon, traditional designations to accomplish the complete, complex characterization at a single, deft stroke. "Swift-footed Achilleus" furnishes one example of this phenomenon; "Little Red Riding Hood" does the same for another, equally more-than-fictional audience. Instead of straining the limits of author-reader interaction to discursively sketch the echoic, multifacteted heroic background for a major combat or a companion's death (if indeed that could ever be done), the bard simply couches the immediate description in the timeless, reverberative language of cognate combats or deaths, language that has many times before placed the momentary and foregrounded in the enriching context of the continuous background. In cases like these, the proper question is not why the bard chose to deploy the hackneyed scene yet again, but how the moment in question is brought to life—without "repetition"—by the institutionalized traditional meaning that naturally accompanies the recurrent scene. Story-patterns, likewise redolent with accumulated traditional signification, also convey value-added meaning for a bard and an audience who speak the same language: anyone familiar with Return Songs from any of their myriad representations in Indo-European traditions[15] knows that Odysseus will finally reach Ithaka, in disguise as a beggar or prisoner, will participate in a flurry of recognition scenes as he tests family and friends, and will eventually (re-)win the wife he left behind when called away to an unexpected war.

Communicative economy, and the artistic dynamic it licenses, stems from the bard's and audience's joint use of the traditional register. They leave behind the general-purpose standard language in favor of a highly focused set of linguistic integers that generations of bards and audiences have endowed with metonymic meaning—the spoken part standing for the unspoken (and unspeakable) whole.[16] In choosing this channel for negotiation of meaning, neither the bard nor his audience is indulging in an antiquarian pursuit, nor, crucially, are they forswearing "creativity" by limiting themselves to a narrowed range of expressive and perceptual possibilities. The language is streamlined so that it can bear a greater, more densely packed significative burden; by deferring responsibility for a broader range of discourse, the traditional register—dedicated in the same fashion that certain computer systems are productively excused from all-purpose operation and dedicated to a single purpose—makes possible a heightened level or rate of exchange, an increased communicative economy.

Immanent Art and *The Presence of the Word*

Because the role of the audience is so crucial to the bard's intelligibility in this highly economical medium (in other words

to maintaining a continuity of reception), I have elsewhere characterized the art of oral tradition—the bard's and the audience's
art—as *immanent*. In defining immanence as "the set of metonymic, associative meanings institutionally delivered and received through a dedicated idiom or register either during or on
the authority of traditional oral performance" (*Singer*, 7), I have
tried to direct attention to what is implied in the very use of
register and entry of the performance arena. Just as the bard of
the African Mwindo epic projects the "whole story" from the
single episode that is the immediate extent of his customary
performance, and just as the Indian *bhopo's* assistant points to
a single frame of the visual representation of the Pabuji epic to
imply the whole,[17] so any given phrase, scene, or tale has an
immanent traditional meaning that is made present to it in the
act of performance (which also includes the act of being a more-
than-fictional audience). This kind of signification persists, with
inevitable modifications, of course, in transcriptions and authored texts: as long as the requisite interpretive competence
remains resident in bard and audience, the circuit is complete
and the verbal transaction remains an immanent art.

   This special mode of communicative negotiation, which emphasizes semantic dimensions that are more than literal and conventionally textual, highlights the fundamentally arbitrary
relation between word and meaning, and compares in its imme-
diacy and situatedness to what Walter Ong conceives of as the
dynamics of the "oral word." Ong reminds us of the basic unwrit-
tenness of words, as against the visual representations we teach
ourselves to understand as primary:

> Reduced by writing to objects in space, words can be compared with
> other objects and seen to be quite different. But reduced by writing
> to objects in space, they are one remove from actuality, less real (al-
> though more permanent) than when they are spoken. . . . That is to
> say, the spoken word does have more power than the written to do
> what the word is meant to do, to communicate. (*Presence* 114, 115)

This distinction is of a piece with his claim that "words are
not signs" (*Orality and Literacy* 75–77), where he distinguishes
between the visual cue and the utterance for which it stands by
chirographic, typographic, or electronic fiat. It also finds a parallel with two of his characteristics of orality, namely that orality
is both "close to the human lifeworld" (42–43) and "empathetic
and participatory rather than objectively distanced" (45–46). In

all cases Ong stresses a certain metaphysical presence as uniquely a quality of the spoken and heard word, entailing the direct and unimpeded involvement of speaker and hearer in an ongoing exchange that demands continual participation and cannot be held at arm's length.

Ongian presence and the concept of immanence briefly elaborated above dovetail in their concern for the immersion of traditional oral discourse in a determinative context. What is more, this context is not optional—since it cannot be deferred or even selected (as one option of many)—but institutionalized, present, immanent to the event of verbal exchange via oral tradition. The situation is clearest in a bard's actual oral performance, where invocation of the context begins with entry of the performance arena and the first few syllables of communication within the dedicated register.[18] Once started down this road, bard and audience make expressive and interpretive decisions from within the summoned context, and latter-day readers seeking to impose their own notions of meaning must therefore wrestle with more than the frequently vast divergences in historical and cultural knowledge: lacking an awareness of implied context, they must continually run the risk of co-creating a work that denies the presence or immanence that was (and should remain as much as possible) a constitutive feature of that work. If Homer or one of his bardic counterparts seems to nod, then, we should consider whether it might in fact be the reader—denied a natural context by the semiotic incongruencies of expressive and interpretive media—who is dozing.

Audience: License and Responsibility

What I want to suggest in closing, in the spirit of an essay that tries to make informed connections among traditional oral performances and written works with roots in oral tradition, is that presence and immanence straightforwardly project an audience that is more than fictional, and an audience that is equally important for the interpretation of transcriptions and even authored texts. In this emphasis I may seem to be departing somewhat from Ong's basic typology of oral, written, printed, and electronic, but I would respond first that his scholarship has always maintained that each stage subsumes what went before

(though not a few scholars have omitted that essential, rationalizing step from their understanding of his revolutionary thinking).
Perhaps more importantly, my focus on immanence as a function
of performance arena, register, and communicative economy is
intimately bound up with his radical notion of the presence of
the word. It is precisely the value-added signification of the
word, empowered through the enabling event of performance and
the enabling referent of tradition, that persists into transcriptions
and texts, and that remains strong, durable, and vital beyond the
reach of textualization—as long as there also remains an audience able to close the loop. Such texts, which may otherwise like
"worlds of wanwood leafmeal lie," harbor a singular, if latent,
significative vigor that the fluent audience, again much more
than a fiction, will recognize and sustain. Later, if or when that
precious context is irretrievably lost, if or when insufficient evidence survives to project presence or immanence to any reasonable degree, this singular vigor will in fact perish. At that point
textual dynamics—always a force in transcribed performances,
and more obviously, of course, in authored texts—supersedes
extratextual concerns, and the expression and perception associated with verbal art begins to proceed under the primary aegis
of another set of rules.

What, then, is the ultimate responsibility of the more-than-
fictional audience, and here we include all bards' audiences—
those attending an actual performance, those dependent on a
transcription of the event, and those who read authored texts
with roots in oral tradition? In short, it is to maintain a continuity
of reception. Without knowledge of the expressive and perceptual register, without the ability to enter the performance arena,
none of these audiences will be able to construe what the bard
is communicating so economically. In special reference to transcriptions and authored texts, this responsibility amounts to using the traditional rhetorical signals—inscriptions of cues for
re-performance, if you will—to foster an artistic illusion that
originates in oral tradition and persists in texts. In so doing we
put the lie to the mirage of mere linearity and sequence uni-
formly projected by the inherent spatialization of texts; we quash
the embedded assumption of instance-to-instance repetition in
favor of a reality punctuated by recurrence, by reverberative moments, by familiar and resonant events that seem to happen "for
the first time now." In such a fecund context no well-told story

is ever stale, no talented performer ever workaday, and no truly fluent audience ever only fictional.

Notes

1. For a similar perspective on the responsibilities of the reader/audience, see the Receptionalist theory expounded by Jauss (e.g., "Literary History") and by Iser (e.g., *Implied Reader* and *Act of Reading*), as extended to the study of traditional oral works by Foley, *Immanent Art*, chap. 2.

2. Sections of the following argument are derived from Foley, *Singer*, esp. chap. 1–2.

3. On the history of the oral–formulaic approach to studies in oral tradition, also known as the Parry–Lord theory, see Lord, *Singer* and *Epic Singers*; Foley, *Oral-Formulaic Research*, with updates in the journal *Oral Tradition* (for bibliography), and *Theory* (for methodology).

4. These figures are chosen not only for their eminent position in the history of English literature, but also because scholars have in fact studied them from the perspective of oral tradition. On Chaucer, Middle English literature, and oral tradition, see especially Parks, Amodio; on Shakespeare, see Trousdale; on Spencer, see Webster.

5. Cf. Nagy 31f. Another dimension of the contemporary cultural ascendancy of writing and things written is tersely described by Ong: "'Preliterate' presents orality—the 'primary modeling system'—as an anachronistic deviant from the 'secondary modeling system' that followed it" (*Orality and Literacy* 13).

6. This approach has affected more that 130 separate language areas to date. See further note 3.

7. Most egregiously, Magoun for Old English poetry. For a history of related developments in this area, see Foley, *Theory*, 65–74; for more recent analysis and scholarship on Old English, see Foley, *Traditional Oral Epic*, chap. 6 and 9.

8. The determinative importance of social context has been increasingly recognized over the past two decades; see esp. Bauman and Briggs; Hymes, *In vain*; Foley, *Singer*, chap. 1.

9. Against the many useful generalizations developed in this field, it is essential to counterpose a full appreciation of the idiosyncratic, identifying differences among forms. I construe these aspects of individuality as "traditional–dependence," "genre–dependence," and "text–dependence" (esp. *Traditional Oral Epic* 1–10).

10. For bibliography on these and other patterns, see Foley, *Oral–Formulaic Research*, with updates in *Oral Tradition*. On these particular examples, see Fenik (battle), Hansen (assembly), and Lord, *Singer*, 186–97 and Foley *Traditional Oral Epic*, chap. 10 (Return).

11. Cf. Halliday, *Language*, 111 (italics mine): "A register can be defined as the configuration of semantic resources that the member of a culture typically associates with a situation type. . . . Since these [semantic] options are realized in the form of grammar and vocabulary, the register is recognizable as a particular selection of words and structures. But *it is defined in terms of meanings*; it is not an aggregate of conventional forms of expression superposed on some

underlying content by 'social factors' of one kind or another. It is the selection of meanings that constitutes the variety to which a text belongs."

12. For examples, see Foley, *Singer*, chap. 4 (Serbian charms), 5 (the Homeric Hymns), 6 (the Old English *Andreas*).

13. E.g., the relationship between the Old English *Andreas* and its source (see Foley, *Traditional Oral Epic* 344–54; *Singer*, chap. 6).

14. See esp. Duggan, *Song of Roland*; "Théorie"; "Mode".

15. On this pattern, which is attested in Serbian and Croatian, Bulgarian, Turkish, Albanian, Russian, and medieval English in addition to ancient Greek, cf. Foley *Traditional Oral Epic*, chap. 10.

16. Spoken versus unspoken must finally be a phenomenological distinction, since what is "present" to a performance or even a phrase must include both what is lexically denoted and what is institutionally implied within the performance arena and through the dedicated traditional register. A corollary to this theorem is that outside the performance arena and register, the same range of immanent meanings is not in force, remaining unavailable to performer or audience.

17. On the Mwindo epic, see Biebuyck; on the Pabuji epic, Smith, 54–70.

18. It is no exaggeration to say that the entire panorama of a South Slavic Return Song (parallel to the *Odyssey* story) is, for the fluent audience, implied in the very first line or two. The prisoner cries out in his misery from a Christian jail (e.g., *"Pocmilijo sužanj nevoljniče, / Iz tamnice od Janjoka bana"*; "The unwilling captive cried out, / From the ban of Janok's prison"; traditional), and immediately not only the impending Devastation but also the eventual Return, Retribution, and (Re-) Wedding are proleptically made present. Far from simply removing all suspense from the rest of the performance, this immanent dimension provides the bard and audience a highly resonant framework within which to forge what will always be a unique as well as a traditional experience.

Works Cited

Amodio, Mark C., ed. *Oral Poetics in Post-Conquest England*. New York: Garland, 1994.

Bauman, Richard. *Verbal Art as Performance*. Prospect Heights: Waveland Press, 1977.

———and Charles L. Briggs. "Poetics and Performance as Critical Perspectives on Language and Social Life." *Anthropology* 19 (1990): 59–88.

Ben-Amos, Dan. "The Seven Strands of Tradition: Varieties in Its Meaning in American Folklore Studies." *Journal of Folklore Research* 21 (1984): 97–131.

Biebuyck, Daniel P., ed. and trans., with Kahombo C. Mateene. *The Mwindo Epic from the Banyanga*. Berkeley: University of California Press, 1969.

Duggan, Joseph J. "Le Mode de composition des chansons de geste: Analyse statistique, jugement esthétique, modèles de transmission." *Olifant* 8, no. 3 (1981): 286–316.

———. *The Song of Roland: Formulaic Style and Poetic Craft*. Berkeley: University of California Press, 1973.

———. "La Théorie de la composition orale des chansons de geste: les faits et les interprétations." *Olifant* 8, iii: 238–55.

Fenik, Bernard C. *Typical Battle Scenes in the Iliad*. Wiesbaden: Steiner, 1968.

Fine, Elizabeth C. *The Folklore Text: From Performance to Print.* Bloomington: Indiana University Press, 1984.

Finnegan, Ruth. *Literacy and Orality: Studies in the Technology of Communication.* London: Blackwell, 1988.

———. *Oral Poetry: Its Nature, Significance and Social Context.* Cambridge: Cambridge University Press, 1977.

Foley, John Miles. "Field Research on Oral Literature and Culture in Serbia." *Pacific Quarterly Moana* 7, ii (1982): 47–59.

———. *Immanent Art: From Structure to Meaning in Traditional Oral Epic.* Bloomington: Indiana University Press, 1991.

———. *Oral-Formulaic Theory and Research: An Introduction and Annotated Bibliography.* New York: Garland, 1982.

———. "Folk Literature." *Scholarly Editing: A Guide to Research.* Ed. David C. Greetham. New York: Modern Language Association, 1995. 600–626.

———. *The Theory of Oral Composition: History and Methodology.* Bloomington: Indiana University Press. Rpt. 1992.

———. *Traditional Oral Epic: The Odyssey, Beowulf, and the Serbo-Croatian Return Song.* Berkeley: University of California Press, 1990. Rpt. 1993.

———. *The Singer of Tales in Performance.* Bloomington: Indiana University Press, 1995.

Halliday, M.A.K. With Angus McIntosh and Peter Strevens. *The Linguistic Sciences and Language Teaching.* London: Longmans, 1964.

———. *Language as Social Semiotic: The Social Interpretation of Language and Meaning.* London: Edward Arnold and Baltimore, MD: University Park Press, 1978.

Hansen, William F. *The Conference Sequence: Patterned Narration and Narrative Inconsistency in the Odyssey.* Berkeley: University of California Press, 1972.

Hymes, Dell. *"In vain I tried to tell you": Essays on Native American Ethnopoetics.* Philadelphia: University of Pennsylvania Press, 1981.

———. "Ways of Speaking." *Explorations in the Ethnography of Speaking.* Ed. Richard Bauman and Joel Sherzer. 2nd ed. Cambridge: Cambridge University Press, 1989. 433–51, 473–74.

Iser, Wolfgang. *The Act of Reading: A Theory of Aesthetic Response.* Baltimore: Johns Hopkins University Press, 1978.

———. *The Implied Reader: Patterns of Communication in Prose Fiction from Bunyan to Beckett.* Baltimore: Johns Hopkins University Press, 1974.

Jauss, Hans Robert. "Literary History as a Challenge to Literary Theory." Trans. Elizabeth Benzinger, from chs. 5–7 of *Literaturgeschichte als Provokation der Literaturwissenschaft. New Directions in Literary History.* Ed. Ralph Cohen. Baltimore: Johns Hopkins University Press, 1974. 11–41.

Lord, Albert Bates. *Epic Singers and Oral Tradition.* Ithaca: Cornell University Press, 1991.

———. *The Singer of Tales.* Cambridge, Mass.: Harvard University Press, 1960.

Magoun, Francis P., Jr. "The Oral-Formulaic Character of Anglo-Saxon Narrative Poetry." *Speculum* 28 (1953): 446–67.

Nagy, Gregory. *Pindar's Homer: The Lyric Possession of an Epic Past.* Baltimore: Johns Hopkins University Press, 1990.

Ong, Walter J. *Orality and Literacy.* New York and London: Methuen, 1982.

————. *The Presence of the Word: Some Prolegomena for Cultural and Religious History.* New Haven: Yale University Press, 1967. Rpt. New York: Simon and Schuster, 1970.

————. "The Writer's Audience Is Always a Fiction." *Publications of the Modern Language Association* 90 (1975): 9–22. Rpt. in his *Interfaces of the Word: Studies in the Evolution of Consciousness and Culture.* Ithaca: Cornell University Press, 1977. 53–81.

Parks, Ward. "The Oral-Formulaic Theory in Middle English Studies." *Oral Tradition* 1 (1986): 636–94.

Smith, John D. *The Epic of Pabuji: A Study, Transcription, and Translation.* Cambridge: Cambridge University Press, 1991.

Trousdale, Marion. "Shakespeare's Oral Text." *Renaissance Drama* 12 (1981): 95–115.

Webster, John. "Oral Form and Written Craft in Spenser's *Faerie Queene.*" *Studies in English Literature* 16 (1976): 75–93.

Section Two
Ongian Readings

Incarnations, Remembrances, and Transformations of the Word

WERNER H. KELBER

> major developments, and very likely even all major develop-
> ments, in culture and consciousness are related, often in un-
> expected intimacy, to the evolution of the word from primary
> orality to its present state. But the relationships are varied and
> complex, with cause and effect often difficult to distinguish.
> —Ong, *Interfaces of the Word*

WORDS ARE FUNDAMENTALLY SPOKEN WORDS, LIVING IN THE EVANES-
cent actuality of sound, and shifts from sound to silence, and
from temporality to spatiality, bring about alienation and complexification of human thought. In capsule form, this is the thesis
which has been central to Walter J. Ong's lifelong probings into
the technologizing processes of communication. Although
strictly speaking a scholar of Renaissance thought and its particular manifestation in French Ramism, Ong's investigations
have taken him from primary orality through rhetoric to chirography and typography all the way to the world of electronic com-
putations. His work blends orality-literacy studies and literary
criticism, psychology and media reflections, philosophy and theology, technology and cosmology, into a rich phenomenology of
culture and consciousness. Deeply grounded in our humanistic
tradition, vigorously interacting with psychoanalysis and the
biological sciences, and profoundly insightful about the implica-

---

This essay is a revised version of the Milman Parry–Albert Lord Lecture
delivered on 11 October 1993, at the University of Missouri, Columbia, under
the title "Language, Memory, and Sense Perception in the Religious and Technological Culture of Antiquity and the Middle Ages," and published in *Oral
Tradition* 10, no. 2 (1995): 409–50. The editors wish to acknowledge the kind
permission of *Oral Tradition* and John Miles Foley to reprint this version of
the Parry–Lord Lecture.

tions of the electronic culture, Ong, the Catholic priest, is one of those rare thinkers whose work inducts us into a genuinely catholic citizenship of the global village.

This essay pays tribute to Walter Ong by developing some implications of his thought across ancient and medieval culture. Its broad and rather sweeping scope is not meant to be taken for another metahistory, for I share postmodernism's anxiety about the futility (and vanity) of global narrative ambitions. History resists assimilation to single research patterns. But in tracing some of Ong's enduring insights, I seek to identify issues of long-standing and persistent urgency resonating across the technological and religious culture of our ancient and medieval past.

I

"Speech is a powerful ruler" (Helen 8: *logos dynastes megas estin*). With these words, the fifth-century Sophist, rhetor, and rhetorician Gorgias invoked the critical issue of language. Ostensibly, the idea of language he has in mind is shaped by the media conditions of his own culture. The *Logos* is perceived here neither as sign nor signification, nor as carrier of meaning nor revealer of truth, but as a potent ruler governing his subjects. The power attributed to the *Logos* relegates it to the world of oral communication and performance. Language is a force, orally processed and operative in relation to hearers. It is a perception which has retained its hold on Western culture bequeathing to it a myriad of linguistic, philosophical, and political problems.

What interested Gorgias most about the functioning of language was its aesthetics of reception: "Of *logoi* some give pain, some pleasure, some cause fear, some create boldness in hearers, and some drug and bewitch the soul by a kind of evil persuasion" (Helen 14). The arousal of both displeasure and pleasure, and of fear and pity, was the primary objective of the spoken *logoi*. Among words, Gorgias singled out the metered language of the poetic tradition which effected fearsome horrors, tearful sympathies, and melancholic desires (Helen 9). He did not entirely dismiss the rational aspects of language. Occasionally he attended to speech as a *techne*, an art of rhetoric. But his main interest lay in the development of a psychology of the emotive powers of oral communication. The efficaciousness of words meshed with the form of the soul, impacting it, molding it, and converting it. It is this affective persuasion of the soul which lay at the heart of Gorgias's theory of language.

The alliance Western culture has forged with the powers of oral speech is an addictive but uneasy one. Gorgias himself introduced the celebrated metaphor of the *pharmakon*. Words affected the soul as the drug does the body (Helen 14). In speech, the processes of healing and poisoning were mysteriously mingled, swaying the psychic condition for better and for worse. Under the powerful spell of speeches, the soul was liable to be cured no less than deceived (*apate*). Pressed for an explanation for this ambiguous operation of language, Gorgias invoked the realm of magic and religion. The spell of words was perceived to be closely allied with magic and witchcraft (de Romilly). Insofar as poetic performances stirred passions and converted souls, they placed themselves above rational probings. Divine both in origin and in their inspirational effect, they created a godlike trance (*enthousiasmos*) among hearers. Speech when thus put into effect by accomplished oral practitioners was a form of divine madness.

When Plato refused to admit the poets into his well-ordered state (Rep. 605b; 607b), he pointed to the emotive and magical impact of their words. He did not mind telling us that theirs was the theater of a woman, whereas men have learned to retain control over their passions (Rep. 605d, e). His chief objection, however, did not rest on the problematic linking of poetic emotions with gender, but on the issue of *mimesis*. The mimetic art practiced by "friend Homer" (Rep. 599d) and his fellow poets corrupted the soul and destroyed its rational part by fashioning phantoms removed from reality. Had Homer been able to truly educate people, he would have "possessed not the art of imitation but real knowledge" (Rep. 600c). Plato himself lacked the temporal distance to appreciate the cultural, linguistic implications of his tirade against the Homeric, poetic tradition. It was Eric Havelock's illuminating work on Plato (1963) which explicated *mimesis* in terms of a millennial experience of oral composing and traditioning. Shaping language in rhythmic, memorable fashion and composing it via the oral processes of imitation, the poets encouraged recitation and learning through repetition. But as far as Plato was concerned, knowledge acquired by imitation and repetition was of little value. His resentment toward the poets could thus well be understood as a revolt of the literate mind against the oral hegemony of Homeric, poetic culture.

Although Plato's philosophy was a major beneficiary of the rationalizing effects of chirography, the philosopher could not bring himself to embrace the new technology as a matter of principle. While resorting to writing himself, he lamented the corrosive effects of the new medium, basing his objections on a thoroughly oral apperception of language. Writing, far from assisting memory, implanted forgetfulness into the human souls (Phaedr. 275a). Written words were antisocial because they segregated themselves from living discourse. Frozen into "majestic silence," they stare at readers, telling them "just the same thing forever" (Phaedr. 275d). Chirographic products were rather like children who had lost their parents, unable to defend themselves and liable to fall into the hands of the wrong people (Phaedr. 275e). Writing, finally, was an unacceptable exteriorization of thought which only gave the appearance of wisdom (Phaedr. 275a). Ideally, understanding was achieved by the "internal scribe" who wrote into the book of our soul (Phaedr. 39a). These were all arguments characteristic of a mind deeply versed in oral culture, distrustful of the impact of writing, and committed to the living, dialogical, and interiorizing powers of speech.

Resentful of the magical powers of speech, in revolt against the poetic mentors of ancient Greece, and distrustful as well toward the new technology of writing, Plato redefined the oral, rhetorical tradition in terms of dialectic. Its objective was to keep words alive in the flow of discourse and to forestall ideological sedimentation. Unfettered by scribal constraints and mimetic routine, dialectic was an oral mode of communication flexible enough to facilitate replacement of anything with something else, should the need arise. But it was a "discourse of reason" (Rep. 532a), far removed from Gorgias's magical comprehension of speech and unimaginable without the rationalizing effects of writing. Dialectical reasoning isolated and defined subject matters, divided and subdivided them, until it reached "the limit of division" (Phaedr. 277b). Proceeding in this analytical fashion, it was designed to lead the soul away from the particulars and toward the contemplation of "the very essence of each thing" (Rep. 532a). One of the boldest features of the Platonic dialectic was its ambition to arrive at the nature of things "apart from all perceptions of sense" (Rep. 532a–b). The quest for knowledge was to be transacted "by thought itself" (Rep. 532a–b), as it were. Language was thereby transformed into a catalyst of cognition, displacing its powers of emotive incitement, and rhetorical persuasion.

Plato's daring project to purify thought by the exclusion of the senses flies in the face of ancient theories of knowledge. For orality and rhetoric, as well as the art of scribality, traditionally engaged the human sensorium and played the sensory register in the interest of retention, emotive incitement, and persuasion. Walter Ong's phenomenology of culture and consciousness has given ample evidence of the oral affinity between sound and thought (1967, 111–75). But knowledge was conceived of by analogy with seeing no less than hearing. Both vision and voice were sense analogues for the intellect. That the human sensorium should be excluded from pursuits of knowledge in the interest of pure thought was largely unthinkable in ancient and medieval culture.

A *locus classicus* for sense perception was memory, the esteemed "treasure-house of eloquence" (Quintilian, Inst. Ora. 11.2.1). Long before the art of memory was assigned a place of honor in rhetoric, its significance was recognized in mythology. According to myth, Mnemosyne, the goddess of memory, bore Zeus nine daughters, the Muses, who personified different modes of poetry, the arts, and sciences. Mnemosyne, mother of the Muses, the myth informs us, was the origin of all our civilized labors and a well-spring of culture. An imaginable female, a corporeal similitude herself, she embodied memory. Her daughters who carried the attributes of wax tablet and pencil, the flute and lyre, the tragic and comic mask, the scroll and a celestial globe, represented a civilization which was constituted by writing and music, tragedy and comedy. But whether they facilitated sound or vision, speech or writing, they always functioned as the daughters of Mnemosyne. Memory was the central civilizing authority.

From Aristotle we have received one of the earliest, strikingly philosophical testimonies to memory. His treatise *On Memory and Recollection* introduced a key feature of memory, namely the theory of images. Responding to external stimulation, memory retained a sense content, a visual representation of the objects. On this principle, all our thoughts and perceptions were deposited in memory by way of images: "we cannot think without images" (450: a: *kai noein ouk estin anou phantasmatos*). Even conceptual thought, Aristotle insisted, interacted with and was mediated by the sensorium (450, a 10). Memory cannot process understanding as a function of pure thought.

Cicero (*De Orat.* 2, ixxxvi, 351–60), the anonymous author *ad Herennium* (3.16.28–24.40), Quintilian (*Inst. Ora.* 11.2), and many others resumed the tradition of memory's *imagines* and *loci*. It was going to be "the stock definition to be forever repeated down the ages" (Yates, 6). The challenge was to create a condition which was favorably disposed to the retention of what was to be remembered. First, one had to invent figures, marks, or portraits which adhered the longest in memory. Since all images required an abode, one must secondly use a large number of mental places clearly defined, in orderly arrangement, and separated at measured intervals. Memory was thus perceived entirely in spatial terms; for example, as a house divided into many rooms, and its principal operating mechanism was the storing of images in localities. The memory tradition challenged both theories of pure thought and verbocentrism. In ancient culture, it was widely understood that both hearing and seeing mediated the processes of recollection and understanding. While the boundaries between aural and visual experience were often blurred, the visual nature of mental representations was widely taken for granted. "Of all the senses, sight is the keenest," Cicero tells us (1942, 357: *acerrimum autem ex omnibus nostris sensibus esse sensus videndi*), postulating the cognitive superiority of vision, a motif which will be replayed by Aquinas, Leonardo, John Locke, and a myriad of others. But when we consider that words such as phantasy (*phantasma*), imagination (*imago*), and rhetoric itself, essential components of the oral, rhetorical tradition, have largely become pejorative terms, we also recognize the changes in consciousness that distance us from our ancient heritage.

Augustine, a practicing rhetor and trained rhetorician himself, singled out the apostle Paul as paragon of Christian oratory: "With what a river of eloquence [his words] flow, even he who snores must notice" (1958, 4.7.12). Indeed, Paul's letters, the earliest canonical literary products, operate in the mode of argumentation intent on producing conviction in audiences (Kinneavy; Wuellner 1977, 1987). If Plato was the dialectician in search of a reasonable alternative to sophistic deception and the *ancien regime* of oral, poetic authority, and Aristotle the analytical rhetorician who made the *ars rhetorica* safe for philosophy, Paul was a practicing Jewish-Christian rhetor ever mindful of his message's reception in the hearts and minds of hearers. Academic and popular convention, however, unmindful of the ancient reputation of Paul's rhetorical skills, has frequently identified him as Christianity's first self-conscious theologian. In this role he is perceived as a thinker who isolated for reflection generic topics such as christology or eschatology, and who conceptualized notions of faith, Spirit, and works. But to perceive him in this classic theological fashion is to deliver him to the time-honored rival of rhetoric, to logic. Standing in the rhetorical tradition, the apostle did not seek truth abstracted from the pragmatics of concrete human interaction. Increasingly we learn to see him as a master in discerning the persuasive potential of given issues and concerns and in constructing appropriate epistolary responses.

A principal technique of apostolic persuasion was to adopt and revise key terms introduced by his addressees. One remembers Socrates' advice given to Meno that in discourse we "must employ terms with which the questioner admits he is familiar" (Meno: 75d). Accordingly, Paul's thought proceeded in a dialectic of adoption and revisioning, a process which kept his language inescapably focused *ad hominem*. Each letter, therefore, involved readers in a different intellectual orbit and in a distinct semantic field. In toto, the Pauline corpus presents itself as a kaleidoscopic experience, confronting us with multiple rhetorical situations. This is a principal reason for the difficulties modern readers encounter in comprehending the apostle's letters. The casuistry of Paul's letters runs counter to theological, logical premises, prompting charges of inconsistency, of intellectual inferiority even. But rhetoric, not logic, is the key to Paul. If logic considers an audience at all, it thinks of a single, universal audience. Paul the rhetor thought and wrote in interaction with multiple audiences. Or, in the words of Carruthers, "rhetoric does not normalize an occasion, it occasionalizes a norm" (181).

True to the ethos of rhetoric, Paul shaped his message to preconceived ends. His repeated pronouncements on the Law, for example, did not originate in a dispassionate analysis of the human condition under the Law, which in turn prompted the solution in Christ. Quite the opposite, it was the experience of redemption in Christ which moved him toward a reconsideration of the role of the Law. In the words of E. P. Sanders, "the solution precedes the problem" as far as Paul's attitude toward the Law was concerned (422). Whereas Platonic dialectic, propelled by a rigorous sifting of ideas, aimed at discovering truth, rhetoric "knows its conclusions in advance, and clings to them" (Ong 1983, 2). Thus while Paul's message adhered to and evolved out of human life situations, his premises and conclusions were known in advance. The principal test of truth was loyalty to

Christ, to the gospel, as well as to him, the apostolic messenger. Partiality, not objectivity was desirable.

Paul the rhetor favored a fundamentally oral disposition toward language (Kelber 1983, 140–83). He deployed the term *gospel* in predominantly auditory contexts and in reference to the oral proclamation. To be effective, the gospel needed to be proclaimed and heard. The idea of responding to his addressees by way of a written gospel narrative appeared to be entirely foreign to his mode of thinking. Hearing, not sight, was accorded pride of place in his economy of the sensorium. It was the supersense which facilitated interiorization of sounded words and faith. Heart was the anthropological metaphor of human interiority and intentionality (Jewett 305–33). It was also the central receptive organ of the Spirit (Gal. 4: 6; 2 Cor. 1:22) and of the proclaimed word (Rom. 10:8). Preached words entered human hearts, engendered faith, and in turn generated confession. Paul's media advise that "faith comes from hearing" (Rom. 10:17) contributed to Christianity's abiding commitment to the tradition-honored, oral/aural sense of words across centuries of increasingly technologized transformations of language. If to Homer we owe the legacy of the "winged words" (*Iliad* 1.201, et al.), from Paul we have received the metaphor of the light-footed word that "runs" (2 Thess. 3:1: *ho logos tou kyriou treche*) across the mediterranean *oikoumene*, carried as it were by the apostolic feet.

As is the case with all categorizations, rhetoric illuminates principal aspects of Pauline language, while simultaneously obscuring features which are outside the rhetorical ethos, or even in tension with it. To assert something is to disregard something else. There is present in Paul's letters a potentially conflictual relation with rhetoric. When in I Corinthians the apostle castigated the "wisdom of the world" (1:20) as a strikingly oral, rhetorical phenomenon, referring to it as the "superiority of speech and wisdom" (2:1: *kath' hyperochen logou e sophias*) or the "seductive (persuasive) words of wisdom" (2:4: *peithoi[s] sophias [logois]*), he sowed the seeds of a persistent Christian ambivalence about the culture of rhetoric. Unwittingly, he anticipated the later Christian distinction between a *sapientia huius saeculi* versus the genuinely desirable *sapientia spiritualis*. What should be noted is that Paul was not unfamiliar with the traditional philosophical anxiety about sophistic vanities and empty eloquence. He would rather stand accused of being "unskilled in speech" (2 Cor. 11:6: *idiotes to logo*) than use the gospel for the advancement of his personal benefit. Still, his own reservation toward the wisdom of words was not based on the philosophical urge to cleanse language of its magical roots in the dialectical search for truth, but rather on the revolutionary kerygma of the cross of Christ which inverted, as he saw it, human values, turning wordly wisdom into foolishness and God's foolishness into genuine wisdom (1 Cor. 1: 18–25).

In the first five centuries of the common era the merits and demerits of rhetoric were subject to debate, and the compatibility of rhetoric with the Christian proclamation remained controversial. As is well known, many of the Latin and Greek fathers were trained in the art of rhetoric, and some were teachers of rhetoric themselves. Tertullian, Cyprian, the three great Cappadocians, John Chrysostom, Jerome, and, above all Augustine, come to mind. They assimilated rhetoric, but rarely by way of unreflective osmosis. Conscious of the linkage between medium and message, rhetorical culture and the *doctrina Christiana* (Christian teaching, not doctrine!), theologians pondered the question whether rhetoric would compromise the gospel. "What," Tertullian asked provocatively, "has Athens to do with Jerusalem, or the Academy with the church?" (7.9: *quid ergo Athenis et Hierosolymis? quid academiae et ecclesiae?*). A matter of great consequence was the promotion of biblical texts to canonical status, creating a mode of privileged authority unknown to Greco-Roman culture. Increasingly, Christian theologians trained as rhetors and rhetoricians had to come to terms with Scripture, be it as source of a new rhetoric or as counterpart to the old rhetoric. In tracing their knowledge and identity to the new authority of the Bible, they discovered a homiletic mode of discourse, long established in Jewish hermeneutics. *Homily*, this Christian type of preaching, legitimated biblical texts as principal inspiration and organizers of the proclamation. The Christian homily was thus a type of rhetoric which was "basically determined by the order of the material in the text, to which may be added material from other texts" (Kennedy 1980, 136). As a consequence, homiletic discourse came to be a rhetoric strongly filtered through the medium of the privileged text.

In spite of the canonization of Scripture which privileged texts and textually based thematic preaching to a high degree, memory was far from being ejected from the Christian tradition. Augustine himself offered a sustained meditation on the mystery of memory. Standing in the rhetorical tradition, he adopted the spatial metaphor of memory, including the deposition of *imag-*

ines at mnemonically advantageous *loci*. He was enraptured with "that vast court" of memory, this "large and boundless chamber," "replete with numberless secrets and inexpressible windings," "the plains and caves and caverns," "innumerable and innumerably full of innumerable kinds of things." Stored in these vast chambers of memory were not the things themselves, but their icons, ready to be recalled to sight in the act of remembering. "Great is the power of memory, excessive great, o my God, a large and boundless chamber; whoever sounded the bottom thereof?" he exclaimed (Conf. 10, 8.15: *magna ista vis est memoriae, magna nimis, deus meus, penetrale amplum et infinitum, quis ad fundum eius pervenit ?*) It is noteworthy that Augustine's conversion to the Bible and prodigious chirographic activity in no way diminished his enthusiasm and need for the memory tradition of ancient rhetoric.

And yet, Augustine struck out on new ground as he probed the deep space of memory. Significantly, his encomium of memory culminated in an exploration of selfhood and knowledge of God. His memory, he mused, facilitated remembrance of what he had done, where and with what feelings. As he lifted the imaged experiences into the full light of his interior vision, he came face to face with his own self. Memory was thus a facilitator of consciousness, and a consciousness interiorly allied with visual powers. At the same time, he felt that memory should also be of assistance in fostering knowledge of God. He had come to know God, and where else could God be found but in memory. But as he traversed the vast spaces of his memory, Augustine also had to admit to himself that he could find neither place nor image of God. There was a sense in which his search for God arrived at the limits of the ancient art of memory. Knowing God without finding him in his interior recesses, Augustine was compelled to reach beyond memory.

He took up the issue of memory once again in *De Trinitate*, a psychological study of the trinity unparalleled in patristics. In book eleven he developed the threefold dynamics of the mind which resemble those of the supreme Trinity. Of the many trinitarian structures of the mind he uncovered, the most important one for our purpose was that of memory, vision, and will. The perception of external impressions, internal visualization, and the concentration of the mind, while representing different properties and faculties, are under the guidance of the will united in trinitarian unity. As far as memory was concerned, Augustine metamorphosed the rhetorical base of mind and memory into the metaphysical realm of trinitarian psychology.

Given the high prestige verbal performance, analysis of speech, and modes of argumentation enjoyed in Greco-Roman civilization, Christianity, itself centrally concerned with proclamation, was compelled, sooner or later, to define its identity vis-à-vis classical rhetoric. No Christian writer in the first five centuries of the common era addressed this issue more thoughtfully than Augustine. In *De Doctrina Christiana*, "one of the most original [books Augustine] ever wrote" (Brown, 264), he sought to negotiate the marriage between the ancient institution of rhetoric and scriptural authority. Eloquence, he stated, could not be rejected out of hand, even though it was intimately associated with rhetoric. What was more, non-artistic discourse would cripple the Christian proclamation. Basically, Augustine agreed with Cicero's insight concerning the interdependence of wisdom and eloquence (Cicero 1949, 1.1.1.; Augustine 1958, 4.1). His plea was not, however, for a Christianization of Ciceronian rhetoric. *De Doctrina Christiana* was meant to be a reflection on the interpretation and teaching of a biblically grounded Christianity. He assumed both the centrality of the Bible and a biblical rhetoric intrinsic to the central book. Admittedly, the rhetoric of the Bible may fall short of the oratorical and ornamental features of pagan rhetoric, but by refraining from a more polished language, the Bible did communicate what it needed to say. There was yet another feature which distinguished biblical language. Whereas absence of sophisticated pomposity was one of the hallmarks of scriptural rhetoric, obscurity and ambiguity of meaning was another. Augustine was in fact at great pains to show how many biblical passages were written in veiled language. The separability of expression from meaning, a commonplace in allegorical theory, was thereby canonized in Christian hermeneutics. The obscurities of biblical writings were themselves "part of a kind of eloquence" (1958, 4.6, 9) which exercised our mental faculties to search for hidden meaning. Consequently, the expositor's primary task was neither the demonstration of rhetorical flourishes, nor an appeal to the emotions, but the raising to consciousness of "that which lay hidden" (1958, 4.11.9).

In the end it would appear that Augustine, never fully persuasive on the matter of a biblical rhetoric, adopted a hermeneutic dictated by scribal sensibilities. What concerned him most was not the efficaciousness of biblical language, but its character of signification. Not content with reflections on the allegorical tensiveness in Scripture, he proceeded to elevate the latter to a linguistic, theological signs theory. Postulating a distinction between sign (signum) and thing (res), Augustine stated that "no one should consider [signs] for what they are but rather for their value as signs which signify something else" (1958, 2.1.1). All words, spoken and written, were perceived to be signs, mere prompters, as it were, signifying the authentic res. In part at least, Augustine's signs theory was born under the pressures of literate sensibilities, for by itself speech knows of no external verification. It clearly problematized the concept of the affective and performative powers of language. When measured against the ethos of rhetorical efficaciousness, signs were obstacles to the presenting powers of the word. Consequently, oral presence was deferred in the interest of a higher goal of unity. Thus, the readers of allegorical and ambiguous scriptural passages should be inspired to contemplate words in their minds, to move from one hint to another, and from discovery to discovery, each one opening up further depths, and to arrive ideally at the love of God and the vision of God.

In the Western tradition, Augustine's fateful distinction between signifier and signified was a major contributor to a linguistically based bipolarity of metaphysical magnitude which manifested itself in such dichotomies as exteriority versus interiority, the letter and the Spirit, the sensible versus the intelligible, the written text and the transcendental Logos, temporality versus eternity, and so forth. In the end, it may be said that Augustine's absorption of rhetoric into scribal culture created a "metarhetoric" (Murphy 287), or perhaps more succinctly, a Christian hermeneutic of communication at the heart of which lay the metaphysical nature of language. In this fashion, it made an indelible impact on medieval concepts of language, buttressing a world of analogies and correspondences.

II

A Christian Codex dated before 1000 C.E. depicts Pope Gregory the Great (540–604 C.E.) as interpreter of Scripture. The miniature carries the title: *Pope Gregory I inspired by the Holy Spirit* (Gumbrecht/Pfeiffer, 726–29). His left hand rests on an open book which is placed on a lectern. Undoubtedly, the book represents the holy Bible. In his right hand Gregory holds another book which is closed. Decorated with a golden cover it likewise appears to be a copy of the Bible. A white dove, representation of the Holy Spirit, sits on the right shoulder of the Pope. The dove's beak is wide open and placed near the ear of the Pope: the Holy Spirit inspires the Pope. Gregory's eyes are directed neither toward the viewer nor toward the books. His is a posture of auditory concentration. He is listening to the words of the dove whispered into his ear. Behind the Pope, separated by a curtain, sits a scribe. In his right hand he holds a stilus, a sharp slate-pencil, and in his left hand a writing tablet. With the stilus he points toward the dove, source of inspiration, and with his writing tablet he gestures toward the Pope, possessor and mediator of Scripture. Presumably, the scribe receives the Pope's dictation transmitted to him through mediation of the Spirit.

This miniature may serve as a central metaphor for both the grand simplicity and the notable complexity of the linguistic and religious culture of the Middle Ages. While the authority of the Bible had been firmly established, its written status raised a host of hermeneutical questions. Although generally understood to be the unified Word of God, the Bible was likewise perceived to be written in veiled language. It was, therefore, in need of interpretation. Encoded in the miniature were differences which called for hermeneutical mediation. The Spirit, source of inspiration and represented by the dove, was a world removed from the Pope, two worlds apart from the bibles, and three stages away from the scribe behind the curtain. Moreover, the open book of revelation was placed side by side with the closed book, and both bibles were separated by the curtain from the scribe who was about to commit interpretation to writing. Thus medieval culture, centered on the Spirit, the Pope, the Bible, and the scribe, has set into motion a process of triple mediation. Assisted by mediation through the Spirit, the Pope opened the closed book of the Bible and mediated his reading to the scribe, who in turn committed the dictation to writing, thus producing yet another text. The very text-centeredness of the Bible eclipsed issues of oral power and performance, moving scribality and interpretation to center stage.

Partially influenced by the growing dominance of the Bible and fostered by monastic and scholastic traditions, an increasing output of manuscripts was generated which lay at the basis of medieval cultural and intellectual life. Still, if one wishes to grasp the Middle Ages from the perspective of communications changes, one must imagine trends of the type of *la longue durée*. The period roughly from the fall of Rome to the invention of

printing saw a general shift from oral performance to chirographic control of writing space. Manuscripts increasingly became important tools of civilized life, and from the eleventh
century onward an ever-growing scribal culture shaped the processes of learning. It bears repeating, however, that this picture of
the textualization of the medieval world is correct only on the
macro-level of history.

Medieval scribality was a craft which required mastery of a
variety of tools and skills. The production of manuscripts was
hard labor, "a seasonal activity like football" (Troll 118), but
rarely of a gratifying intellectual nature. Insofar as scribes were
copyists, they worked in the interest of preservation and transmission of knowledge; when they took dictation, they served as
catalysts of orally dictated compositions. But whether they copied or took dictation, scribes were craftsmen, not intellectuals
eager to think for themselves and to advance knowledge.
Whether medieval scribality constituted a form of monastic discipline or of paid service on behalf of rulers and administrators,
it was always manual labor, indeed drudgery, which did not advance the scribes' *libido sciendi* any more than it encouraged
their urge for self-expression and individuation.

More importantly, the effects of manuscript technology were
not directly translatable into literacy. We do well to keep scribal
textuality separate from literacy. As a craft revolution, scribality
enhanced the availability and status of texts. But the literate revolution (e.g., the formation of a broadly based and informed read-
ership) did not get underway until the sixteenth century under
the impact of print technology. In medieval culture, not only did
literacy remain the privilege of the few, but reading and writing
did not inevitably combine to form a literate mentality. Reading
was widely practiced as an oral activity (Balogh; Saenger). To be
sure, aids to visual apperception increased slowly. Punctuation,
word and chapter divisions, initially introduced in support of
oral reading, facilitated visual encoding of information, and
gradually silent copying and even silent reading. Still, far into
the high Middle Ages "reading was regarded as an active ener-
getic exercise, requiring good health, and not as a passive seden-
tary pastime" (Saenger, 382; cf. 377–82). The recipients of texts
were often listeners who did not necessarily know how to write,
while scribal copyists were frequently unable to comprehend
what they wrote. Reading was linked with dictation and recitation of texts more than with private reflection. What constituted
"literate" intellectualism was thus not necessarily the combined

skills of reading and writing, but to a high degree an audiovisual apperception and remembrance.

Undoubtedly, the high culture of medieval learning, which formulated intricate philosophical, religious, and linguistic options with signal keenness of intellect, was the beneficiary of a growing textuality. Once ideas and experiences were enshrined in writing, they assumed, irrespective of their oral functioning, a status of stability, disposed toward depersonalization, detachable from the oral biosphere, and hence subject to reflection and analysis.

There was, however, an additional feature which uniquely assisted medieval coherence and consciousness: the deployment of the Latin language. Medieval intellectualization owed as much, if not more, to the use of Latin as to scribal productivity. For at least a thousand years, roughly from the sixth to the sixteenth century, the Western Middle Ages were under the governing influence of Latin. *Litterati* were primarily those canonists, diplomats, administrators, and theologians who had mastered Latin— which may or may not have included the ability to read and write (Stock, 26; Troll, 112). Latin became a standard of medieval high culture and the vehicle of theological, philosophical, as well as scientific achievements. Coleman's observation that the assiduous study of grammar in certain monastic circles "was meant to teach a way to reach heaven through *latinity*" (145), could well be extended to the aspirations of many clerical *litterati*: Latin was perceived to be the linguistic medium which aided in the ascent to heaven.

Even though manuscripts eventually came to function as artificial memory or data bases in their own right, medieval scribality and latinity did not displace memory from Western culture. Quite the opposite. For centuries the growing body of texts only intensified and complexified demands made on memory. Not only was there more and more complicated material that had to be processed, but changing cultural circumstances enlisted memory into new services.

The French Cistercian reformer Bernard of Clairvaux, who represented medieval monasticism at its highest development, contributed to the conversion of memory from a rhetorical theory of retention to one of religious reconstruction. Steeped in the monastic experience, he found little meaning in memory as a "treasure-house of eloquence" or a palace filled with precious icons. As he experienced it, memory was a house which stinks intolerably (*De Conv.* 6.8), and "a sewer" (3.4). "The stomach of my memory," he exclaimed, "is crammed with so much muck"

(3.4). He advised his audiences to "close the windows, lock the doors, block up the openings carefully" (6.8) through which so much filth has infiltrated and clogged up memory. While Bernard was careful to state that memory itself should be left intact, he demanded a purification, a "blanching" of its blemishes and discolorations (15.28). In this process, the senses and sensual experiences which left stained marks and filthy traces on memory (3.4) should not be erased altogether, but retrained (5.7) and enlisted in the service of smelling, inhaling, tasting, seeing, and hearing the delights of charity, hope, and spiritual pleasures. Memory thus reconstructed—purged and equipped with a converted sensory base—was able to facilitate the believers' gradual attainment of spiritual purity (Song of Songs, 11.1). Bernard, steeped in monastic discipline, turned memory, rhetoric's treasure-house of knowledge and Augustine's instrument of self-knowledge, into a vehicle of conversion.

Scholasticism, one of the supreme philosophical and theological achievements of the Middle Ages, registered in different ways the cultural revolution marked by scribal productivity and latinity. One hallmark of scholastic culture was the compilation and juxtaposition of biblical, patristic, and philosophical authorities. The project was animated by the fundamental axiom of the compatibility of theology and philosophy. The two disciplines were perceived to be two distinct, but reconcilable sources of revelation. The need for compiling seemingly discordant authorities could in part at least be attributed to the textualization of medieval learned culture. It was forced upon scholastic theologians by the steady growth and growing diversity of Latin texts. The assemblage of discordances, the comparative disposition, the contraposition of authorities, and the desire to seek clarification amidst authorial dissonance were all features traceable to growing intellectual diversity based on a rapid enlargement of the textual database. This is precisely what the scholastic theologian Peter Abelard conceded in the prologue to *Sic et Non Incipit Prologus* 1, a compilation of seemingly contradictory authoritative statements on 150 theological issues. What necessitated his labors, he wrote, was the vastness of verbal materials (*tanta verborum multitudine*) which appeared to be not only in themselves different (*non solum ab invicem diversa*), but truly also contradictory (*verum etiam invicem adversa videantur*).

While driven by the conditions of a textual revolution, the scholastic method of processing thought remained indebted to a form of dialectic. Adopting a pattern of threefold thematization, issues were isolated and discussed by way of explication of objections, argumentation of resolution, and refutation of objections (Grabman 1.28–54). Rather than proceeding along the lines of a sequential, discursive logic, the scholastic art of structuring thought still operated in the tradition of a disputatious dialectic. But the scholastic dialectic differed from the Platonic dialectic which had intended to keep thought alive in the flow of living discourse. The dialectic of St. Thomas' *Summa Theologiae*, for example, was characterized by a nonemotional, stylized quality of thought and a severe asceticism of verbalization. In its passion for rational penetration, the *Summa* constructed argumentation in a highly formalized dialectic. Formal logic and disputational technique fed on each other. It is generally acknowledged that the strategies of scholastic dialectic originated in the medieval system of academic learning (Grabman 1.31–32; Coplestone 2.214–15). Unlike the Platonic dialectic, the scholastic form of disputation was divorced from the oral, ethnic biosphere, and deeply indebted to the Latin manuscript culture. It was in university settings that teachers endeavored to formalize thought processes and convey knowledge by prompting students to raise objections to propositions, by directing the processes of argumentation, and by formulating final resolutions. In this cultural context Thomas helped shape the tradition of the academic dialectic into an instrument of high-powered precision, composing in a Latin that was neither that of the ancients, nor of the Fathers, but of a distinctly scholastic diction.

The question of what memory was and how it collaborated with the mind had to be assimilated to the new intellectual orbit of scholasticism. In substance, Thomas reiterated the ancient rhetorical theory of the mnemonic *imagines* and *loci*, adding the advice that one must cleave with affection to the things to be remembered in order "to keep the shape of images intact" (Summa 2.2, quaest. 49: *conservat integras simulacrorum figuras*). Despite a studied cultivation of memory and its corporeal images, Thomas strove to disengage the issue from its traditional domain of rhetoric and to reassign it to ethics. Memory, originally the mother of the nine muses, had become one of eight components of prudence, the governing queen of all moral values. Since it was the business of prudence to secure knowledge about the future based on past or present experience (quaest. 47), and memory sought to store knowledge about the past (quaest. 48), prudence was dependent on memory. Prudence and memory cooperated in the interest of discerning matters in advance so as to facilitate the right course of action. Although well informed of the ancient theory of memory, Thomas refrained from commending memory as "rhetoric's treasure-house of eloquence." The scribal, textual culture of the thirteenth century may well have been a contributing factor in divesting memory of its strictly rhetorical, mnemonic rationale, promoting it instead as a helpmate of prudence based on considerations of practical reason (quaest. 47: *quod est finis practicae rationis*).

William of Ockham, whose thought is frequently viewed in connection with the nominalism of the fourteenth and fifteenth centuries, remains "to this day the most controversial thinker of medieval intellectual history" (Klein 1556). His model of cognition manifested both the height and incipient demise of scholasticism. Best known for his antirealist position in the controversy over the universals, the Franciscan friar rethought epistemology and helped clear the way for what came to be known as the *via moderna*. In the perspectives we have developed, he epitomized a medieval dominance of logic, sharpened in rapport with a flourishing scribality, as well as a growing reserve toward rhetoric, dialectic, and imagination.

It was a deeply held conviction of medieval realism that language, memory, and sense perception cooperated in the interest of universal knowledge. In fact, divine universals, eternally true realities, were the appropriate objective of the mind's operations. The crux of Ockham's controversial work was to problematize the reality corresponding to universals, be they abstractions in the mind or ideas in God. He did not concede extramental reality to universals. There was, in his view, no reasonable way to prove metaphysical prior presences to which mind and memory could aspire.

Ockham's skepticism concerning philosophical realism moved the particular, the experiential, and the contingent to the center of inquiry. Consequently, his model of language and thought focused with unprecedented force upon the status and quality of distinctiveness, including the particularity of texts. Scripture, indeed all texts, were assumed to be operating according to something akin to an intrinsic linguistic economy, and the operations of the mind, everybody's mind, were such that they could comprehend the internal textual logic. One looks in vain for a special commitment to rhetoric. Language, clearly perceived to be written language, assumed a new status. Gorgias's oral theory of language, which had postulated the affective persuasion of the soul, appeared to be a thing of the distant past, while the Augustinian signs theory, which had postulated the metaphysical nature of language, had fallen under suspicion. As Ockham came to see it, scribal compositions were not meant to arouse emotions any more than to signify universals. Rather, they had an almost autosemantic reality to themselves. Memory, divorced from its rhetorical, metaphysical, and ethical obligations, was assigned the principal role of remembrance of the past. If words still had the attributes of signs, they signified an almost Proustian remembrance of things past.

Ockham's model of mind and language was subtly informed by the technology of scribal communication. From the eleventh century on, manuscripts were increasingly the working material for the cultural elite. That Ockham himself was a privileged and eager beneficiary of scribal culture is well established. "His whole scholarly life until 1330 was spent in the greatest of European universities, his circle the most 'bookish' of the time" (Caruthers 158). The year 1330 marked a watershed in his life. In that year he moved, in compliance with a papal ruling, to a Franciscan convent in Munich where he lived, cut off from all major university libraries, until the end of his life in 1349. Whereas the Munich period saw the publication of distinctly political, ecclesiastical writings, virtually all of his philosophical, theological books were written prior to 1330. How important a role written materials had played in the formulation of his theology is underscored by the bitter complaints he issued from Munich about the unavailability of books (Dialogus).

Let us return to the picture of Gregory the Great which had staged the authorities of the Pope, the Bible, the Spirit, and the scribe in a dramatization of medieval hermeneutics. The most consequential implication of Ockham's theology was a decentering of the Pope in the interest of a sharpened focus upon the Bible, and the application of a *cognitia intuitiva*, an immediate cognitive apprehension of Scripture. The text-centeredness of the Bible, recognizable to a degree already in the miniature of Gregory the Great, had thereby acquired a sense of exclusive authorial objectivity. With a force unknown to previous thinkers, Ockham has moved the textual authority of Scripture and its individual interpreters to center stage, anticipating events which would not come to historical fruition (and explosion) for another two hundred years. The focus upon biblical authority and the attribution of interpretive powers to individual human cognition prepared the way for a potentially conflictual relation between the authorities of Bible and Pope. Indeed, Ockham already asserted two hundred years prior to the reformers that Scripture had precedence over the Pope.

From the viewpoint of hermeneutics it is evident that the *via moderna*, which came to elevate the *sensus literalis* to the exclusion of all other senses and to embrace the principle of *Scriptura sui Interpres* (Scripture is its own interpreter), was unthinkable without Ockham's reversal of Thomistic Aristotelianism whereby universals alone were the proper object of knowledge. If individuals alone have reality, the interpreter of the Bible is thrown back upon the internal logic and economy of scriptural language. The Bible as central grammatological authority is thereby reinforced in ways unheard of before.

III

In paying tribute to the work of Walter Ong, this essay sought to suggest degrees of connectedness between oral and chirographic incarnations of the word and the structuring of thought. Our premise is furthest removed from the notion that language, and different embodiments of it, are comprehensible as neutral carriers of ideological freight. Rather, the proposal is that modes of communication were themselves statements of thought and shapers of cognition. Glancing over the long haul of ancient and medieval history, we made a set of observations concerning shifting roles of language, memory, and sense perception. Speech as divine madness was viewed as the product of a linguistic culture dominated by an orality largely untamed by the powers of chirography. Rhetoric, taking advantage of the technology of writing, made speech conscious of itself (Ricoeur 10) and subservient to civic life. Few experiences enhanced Western text-consciousness more deeply than the canonical centering of the Bible. It helped reshape ancient rhetoric into Jewish and Christian modes of homiletics and engendered an unceasing flow of midrashic texts and commentaries. Memory, the wellspring of all civilized life, was a continuing theme in ancient and medieval culture, which despite the increasing production and availability of books remained in fundamental ways memorial rather than documentary (Carruthers). But the *praxis* of memory changed as different media circumstances exempted it from strictly rhetorical obligations and enlisted it instead into the service of ethical, metaphysical, and historical remembrance. The fundamentally oral/rhetorical conviction of the cognitive value of the sensorium was widely shared by ancient and medieval thinkers. Plato's striving after pure, disembodied thought never became the majority rule. Elsewhere in ancient and medieval thinking, cognition was perceived to be sensory cognition. But a growing manuscript culture and the possibilities it brought for detached thought left its impact on the role of the sensorium as well. Scholasticism's categorization of the *sensibilia* and the *intelligibilia* acknowledged both the foundational role of the former and the superiority of the latter. For the cultural elite, the works of chirography slowly but surely restructured oral, rhetorical consciousness and brought about a transformation of language into the medium of cognition. This process was fostered by the privileging of Latin which developed into a fine-tuned instrument for rational discourse while rapidly forfeiting its marketability in a world of ethnic and vernacular turmoil.

Works Cited

Abelard, Peter. *Sic et Non.* Edited by Blanche B. Boyer and Richard McKeon. Chicago and London: University of Chicago, 1976–77.

Anonym. *Ad Herennium.* Translated by H. Caplan. Loeb Classical Library. Cambridge, MA: Harvard University, 1954.

Aristotle. "On Memory and Recollection." In *Parva Naturalia*, translated by W. H. Hett. Loeb Classical Library. Cambridge, MA: Harvard University, 1936.

Augustine. *S. Aureli Augustini Confessionum.* Edited by Martin Skutella. Stuttgart: Teubner, 1981.

———. The Trinity (*De Trinitate*). Translated by Stephen McKenna. The Fathers of the Church 45. Washington, D.C.: Catholic University Press, 1962.

———. On Christian Doctrine (*De Doctrina Christiana*). Translated by D. W. Robertson, Jr. The Library of Liberal Arts. New York and London: Macmillan, 1958.

Balogh, Josef. "Voces Paginarum." *Philologus* (1926) 82: 84–109, 202–40.

Bernard of Clairvaux. *Saint Bernard on the Song of Songs; Sermons in Cantica canticorum.* Translated and edited by a religious of C. S. M. V. London: A. R. Mowbray/New York: Morehouse-Goreham, 1952.

———. *Sermons on Conversion.* Translated with introduction by Marie-Bernard Said, OSB. Kalamazoo, MI: Cistercian Publications, 1981.

Brown, Peter. *Augustine of Hippo.* Berkeley and Los Angeles: University of California Press, 1969.

Carruthers, Mary. *The Book of Memory. A Study of Memory in Medieval Culture.* Cambridge: Cambridge University Press, 1990.

Cicero, Marcus Tullius. *De Oratore.* Books 1, 2. Translated by E. W. Sutton. Cambridge: Harvard University Press, 1942.

————. De Inventione, De Optimo Genere, Oratorum Topica. Translated by H. M. Hubbell. trans. Loeb Classical Library. Cambridge, MA: Harvard University, 1949.

Coleman, Janet. Ancient and Medieval Memories. Studies in the Reconstruction of the Past. Cambridge: Cambridge University Press, 1992.

Copleston, Frederick, SJ. A History of Philosophy. Garden City, NY: Image Books, 1985.

de Romilly, Jacqueline. Magic and Rhetoric in Ancient Greece. Cambridge, MA and London: Harvard University Press, 1975.

Gorgias of Leontini. "Helen." Reden, Fragmente und Testimonieu. Edited and translated by Thomas Buchheim. Hamburg: Felix Meiner, 1989.

Grabman, Martin. Die Geschichte der Scholastischen Methode. Vol. 1, 1909; Vol. 2, 1911. Berlin: Akademie Verlag, 1956 (reprint). Gumbrecht, Hans Ulrich/K. Ludwig Pfeiffer, eds.

Gumbrecht, Hans Ulrich, and K. Ludwig Pfeiffer, eds. Materialität der Kommunikation. Suhrkamp Taschenbuch 750. Frankfurt/Main: Suhrkamp. Thomas, 1988.

Havelock, Eric A. Preface to Plato. Cambridge, MA: Harvard University, Belknap Press, 1963.

Homer. The Iliad of Homer. Translated by Richmond Lattimore. Chicago and London: University of Chicago Press.

Jewett, Robert. Paul's Anthropological Terms. A Study of Their Use in Conflict Settings. Leiden: E. J. Brill, 1971.

Kelber, Werner H. The Oral and the Written Gospel. The Hermeneutics of Speaking and Writing in the Synoptic Tradition, Mark, Paul, and Q. Philadelphia: Fortress, 1983.

Kennedy, George A. Classical Rhetoric and its Christian and Secular Tradition from Ancient to Modern Times. Chapel Hill: University of North Carolina Press, 1980.

Kinneavy, James L. Greek Rhetorical Origins of Christian Faith. New York and Oxford: Oxford University Press, 1987.

Klein, J. Die Religion in Geschichte und Gegenwart. 3d. ed., IV, s.v. "Ockham, Wilhelm von (ca. 1285–1349)."

Murphy, James J. Rhetoric in the Middle Ages. A History of Rhetorical Theory from Saint Augustine to the Renaissance. Berkeley: University of California Press, 1974.

Ockham, William of. Philosophical Writings. Translated, with introduction and notes by Philotheus Boehner. Indianapolis/Cambridge: Hackett Press. [n.d.]

Ong, Walter J., SJ. The Presence of the Word. Some Prolegomena for Cultural and Religious History. Reprint, New Haven and London: Yale University Press, 1967; Minneapolis: University of Minnesota Press, 1981.

————. "Foreword." In The Present State of Scholarship in Historical and Contemporary Rhetoric. Edited by Winifred Bryan Horner. Columbia and London: University of Missouri Press, 1983.

Plato. "Republic." Translated by Paul Shorey. Collected Dialogues. Edited by Edith Hamilton and Huntington Cairns. Bollinger Series 71. Princeton University Press, 1989.

————. "Phaedrus." Translated by R. Hackforth. Collected Dialogues. Edited by Edith Hamilton and Huntington Cairns. Bollinger Series 71. Princeton University Press, 1989.

Quintilian. *Institutio Oratoria*, vol. 4. Translated by H. E. Butler. London: William Heinemann / New York: G.P. Putnam's, 1922.

Ricoeur, Paul. *The Rule of Metaphor.* Translated by Robert Czerny with Kathleen McLaughlin and John Costello, S.J. Toronto: University of Toronto Press, 1977.

Saenger, Paul. "Silent Reading: Its Impact on Late Medieval Script and Society." *Viator* 13 (1982): 367–414.

Sanders, E. P. *Paul and Palestinian Judaism. A Comparison of Patterns of Religion.* Philadelphia: Fortress, 1977.

Segal, Charles P. "Gorgias and the Psychology of the Logos." *Harvard Studies in Classical Philology* 66 (1962): 99–155.

Stock, Brian. *Listening for the Text. On the Uses of the Past.* Baltimore and London: Johns Hopkins University Press, 1990.

Tertullian. "De Praescriptione Haereticorum." In *Corpus Christianorum*, Series Latina; Tertulliani Opera, Pars I. Turnholti: Typographi Brepols Editores Pontifici, 1954.

Troll, Denise A. "The Illiterate Mode of Written Communication: The Work of the Medieval Scribe." In *Oral and Written Communication: Historical Approaches*, edited by Richard Leo Enos, 96–125. Newbury Park/London/New Delhi: Sage, 1990.

Wuellner, Wilhelm. "Paul's Rhetoric of Argumentation in *Romans:* An Alternative to the Donfried-Karris Debate Over Romans." (1977). In *The Romans Debate*, edited by Karl P. Donfried, 152–174. Minneapolis, MN: Augsburg, 1987.

————. "Where is Rhetorical Criticism Taking Us?" *CBQ* 49: 448–63.

Yates, Frances A. *The Art of Memory.* Chicago: University of Chicago Press, 1966.

"Lewedly To a Lewed Man Speke": Chaucer's Defense of the Vulgar Tongue

JAMES R. ANDREAS

Rousseau NOTES CURIOUSLY THAT "WRITING IS NOTHING BUT THE REP-resentation of speech; it is bizarre that one gives more care to the determining of the image than to the object" (qtd. Derrida 27). Not so for Chaucer, who evinced a populist predilection for the oral, vulgar tongue over written, polite, formally poetic language throughout his literary career and developed a sophisticated theory about the oral source for poetic discourse early on in his dream visions, particularly in *The House of Fame*. While Chaucer may have been considered the "Father of the English Language" by some of his and our own contemporaries, he was more interested in and influenced by the "Mother Tongue," that "gret dyversite / In Englyssh and yn wrytyng of oure tonge" which he celebrates at the end of *Troilus and Criseyde* (5. 1794–95).[1] Chaucer undoubtedly knew that his great and often acknowledged predecessor in the poetic craft, Dante, praised the oral "vernacular" in *De Vulgari Eloquentia* as nobler than the "artificial" language of the Romans which must be learned by the chirographic rules of "grammar."

> What I call "vernacular speech" is that which babies become accustomed to from those around them when they first begin to articulate speech; or, as it could be put more succinctly, I would claim as vernacular speech that which we learn without any rules in imitating our nurse. We can also acquire another speech which is dependent on this one called by the Romans "grammar". . . . Of these two (kinds of speech), then, the vernacular is the nobler; both because it is enjoyed by the whole world, . . . and because it is natural to us, while the other is more an artificial product. (3–4)

Dante considered the oral vernacular superior as a poetic language because it was universal—everyone speaks the native tongue—and because it is natural, whereas grammatically reconstructed speech, presumably in writing, is artificial. All speak. Only the chosen few are taught to read. And speech is a natural medium, instinctive to the human being, as Noam Chomsky has shown, and physiologically produced without mediation of stylus or vellum. The first human interlocutor, according to Dante, was no less than God himself. Moreover, Dante takes great pains to prove that Adam and Eve necessarily spoke in the vernacular, the "mother tongue," the original language of "Petramala," that mythical place which is everybody's "home town."[2]

Anticipating Mikhail Bakhtin, Marshall McLuhan, and Walter Ong, Chaucer often theorized about the priority of the utterance, "however smale," "lewed" and "churlish" over scripted, "gentil" writing. For Bakhtin, speech is primary, while the literary genres derived from it, however complicated in form and content, remain secondary: After all, language enters life through concrete utterances (which manifest language) and life enters language through concrete utterances as well. The utterance is an exceptionally important mode of problems (Bakhtin 1986, 63).[3]

As Charles Owens has demonstrated so insistently, Chaucer may have apprenticed as a "writer," translator, and adapter of "olde" texts that were designed to be *read*, but he quickly developed an interest in and a talent for *speaking* "pleynly" and "ful brode," as the narrator of the *Canterbury Tales* insists he must in the *General Prologue*.[4] Chaucer's works are riddled with explanations about the primacy of speech "experienced" as opposed to written texts that are "authored," which then come to represent the "dictates" of "auctoritee." As "Mother of our Tongue" or at the very least, "the 'Father' of our Mother Tongue," Chaucer took considerable pains in his poetry to justify using the speech of the *vulgus*, the plain folk, and even deliberately *vulgar* language as opposed to the artificial language of *policy*, academe, and the court. In fact, he may well have realized his comic and Christian potential as a poet largely because of this choice. Although writers usually end up as the great *texts* of a civilization, they achieve that distinction by representing the living *voices* of their people.[5]

It is difficult for us to appreciate the power the written word has assumed in our daily lives or the courage it takes for a writer to privilege or even use the "vulgar tongue" in his or her work. Our "signature" alone conveys the power of the written word to command destinies: to "sign" means to write; contracts are "authorized" by chirograph exclusively, by signing a name on paper. Oral and gesticular agreements honored and binding for centuries—handshakes, sharing a meal, smoking a pipe, pledging ourselves to another in marriage—are now rituals no longer bound by legal authority. These rituals and signs are not "authorized" because they are not authored, in other words, put down on paper as words to "sign, seal, and deliver" a bargain. Women recently have been pressured to sign their own children away, authorizing unnatural actions by scribbling their names on a page in a moment of financial panic. Taking music lessons means we learn to *read* music, not necessarily to play and rarely to improvise or *compose*, but merely perform someone else's music by reading a score. Only the vulgar musical forms—blues, jazz, rock, rap—are improvised like everyday speech and are taught by developing listening/mimetic skills with the emphasis always on spontaneous composition, originality, and innovation. Tradition in the oral arts inspires new creation rather than bland performance or blind imitation of cherished texts. Most of us in the United States never learned to speak and comprehend a second language, because it was assumed that languages had to be taught "by the book" through translating and writing, and we were never exposed to other languages aurally or orally.

The social motive for mandating script above utterance is simple and insidious: oral performance, as moral mandarins and modern politicians are learning once again to their chagrin, is not easily controlled, suspended, amended, censored, and shaped for proper popular distribution and consumption. The speaker intrudes and interrupts the smooth flow of prosaic, predictable discourse that can be checked and edited by licensing authorities in script. Script tends by its private nature toward the monologic, speech, to the dialogic, as Bakhtin has so persuasively argued. And while the chirographic mistake can be erased or "rubbed out," the tongue "slips," as Freud says, and he reminds us "there are no accidents."[6]

Speech has a way of erupting radically—or "interrupting," as we say—into the social sphere, doing its social or political damage and evading detection simply because it leaves no trace of itself behind except memory, which is equally intangible. As Walter Ong says, "Sound exists only when it is going out of existence. It is not simply perishable but essentially evanescent . . . There is no way to stop sound and have sound. . . . If I stop the movement of sound (as opposed to moving pictures), I have nothing—only silence" (1982, 32). The sound of the utterance, in other words, leaves little "evidence" (from *video*, "to see") of the disruption it might have caused, and even if it does, it can be withdrawn or erased with an "I'm sorry" or "I was only kidding"—verbal ploys indulged by the many voices that constitute and actually seem to create Chaucer's poetry. Scripted or printed texts, on the other hand, are physical objects that must be funded, published, and licensed before they reach a general public which must, of course, be literate, in other words, privileged with a carefully scripted and controlled education. Moreover, once the text is set down on the page, values can be attached arbitrarily to this or that word, and interpretation of the language can be controlled through learned notation, documentation, and gloss. The scripted language used in such texts must inevitably move toward the abstraction that writing itself demands in the long run, the process of standardization that will sanitize and normalize local speech with its dialectical idiosyncrasies and inevitable vulgarities. The speech of the *vulgus*, the folk, will be rendered "polite" by "policy" and, if need be, by the licensing "police"—that is, the censors who will be in charge of the literary establishment within a hundred years after Chaucer's death.

Recently in *The Social Chaucer*, Paul Strohm has suggested that Chaucer's unique poetic style would be inconceivable without the implied audience which it so conspicuously addresses. "The idea of art without audience would probably have seemed either contradictory or absurd to Chaucer, if in fact he could have entertained it at all. The word 'audience,' as he uses it, remains close to its etymological sense of 'those within hearing,' and his own poems almost always contain references to those who 'hear' or 'harken' or to whom he is 'telling' his 'tale'" (1989, 47). To understand the radical assumption of this position, that Chaucer's greatest works are designed consciously to appeal to a live *audience*, a congregation of listeners, we should pause to appreciate how thoroughly our approach to literature, to "belles lettres," has been conditioned by the primacy of the written over the uttered word. We are taught that Chaucer was a great "writer" rather than a great "speaker" or even "poet." The classes we took in Chaucer for the most part were taught by lecture, that is "readings," from the Latin *lego*. The approach taken to Chaucer throughout most of the modern period has been allegorical or exegetical: when his texts approached the vulgar spectrum of everyday speech, they have been allegorized, in other words *re-scribed*—rewritten to conform to the norms of the *polis*—rather than *de-scribed*, that is unwritten, and reproduced or interpreted orally in the speech that Chaucer always reminds us was mimetically transcribed in the first place. D. W. Robertson, whose exegetical theories held sway over Chaucer criticism for nearly two decades, taught that through allegory "a discipline is thus afforded for the exegete. Those passages which promote charity or condemn cupidity are to be left with their literal significance; but all figurative interpretations must promote the love of God and one's neighbor. If they do not, the interpreter is either deceived or deceiving, and the interpretations are false" (295). It is not difficult to see how such an interpretive approach would target "vulgar" speech for critical emendation and mark it ultimately for the censor's scissors. Even the so-called "speeches" we hear on Chaucer at academic conferences are typically documents that are written, read, and only intermittently spontaneous orally. We are taught from age five on to read privately and silently, as Saint Augustine marveled early in the age of chirography that Ambrose did, "reading like this in silence, for he never read aloud" (1961, 114).[7]

Today a person is considered odd if she reads to herself aloud or, for that matter, if she even talks aloud to herself. Although reading has become a private affair, speaking remains necessarily a public one. However, Chaucer, as an oral poet from the *Parliament of Fowls* through the *Canterbury Tales*, was primarily a social poet, as Paul Strohm has recently reminded us, because oral intercourse is the foundation for social grouping and development:

> A special property of the *Canterbury Tales* is the extent to which its generic and stylistic variety is couched in polyvocality, in its embrace of separate and distinctive voices as a means of asserting social difference. Chaucer's poetry was always polyphonic, permitting the juxtaposition of separate themes and generic structures within the external form of a given work, but it becomes increasingly polyvocalic in its capacity to contain unreconciled voices as we move from the avian disputants of the *Parliament* to the distinctive and ultimately incompatible voices of Troilus and Pandarus and Criseyde to the yet fuller degree of autonomy assigned to the diverse Canterbury speakers. (168)

It may well be that our greatest writers, our novelists and poets, appeal because they speak in the unmediated voice of orality, or at least create the impression and the context that they are voicing their texts. We have only to think of the great comic poets and writers to hear those voices speaking directly to us, voices like those of Homer, Shakespeare, Twain, Hemingway, Joyce, Vonnegut, O'Connor, Welty, and, as Bakhtin has shown, Dostoevsky.

It is their compelling oral appeal that frightens authorities into censoring their texts in order to silence disruptive voices, even to this day, as the censored Shakespeare plays in high school literature texts so graphically demonstrate.[8]

Some of the major cultural critics of the twentieth century including Eric Havelock, Walter Ong, Marshall McLuhan, and Mikhail Bakhtin, conditioned as they were by an age that invented electronic amplification of the human voice, have pioneered the rediscovery that *language*, from the Latin root *lingua*, is first and foremost a *tongue*. Rhetoricians, dealing primarily in oratory, have assumed from time immemorial that oral speech was the primary datum of language and its perfection in discourse, the major objective of rhetoric. Geoffrey of Vinsauf, a thirteenth-century rhetor Chaucer read and quoted, entitled his prose treatise on poetics the *Documentum de modo et arte dictandi et versificandi*—the art of speaking and versifying. Yet, Walter Ong tells us that "writing and print, despite their intrinsic value, have obscured the nature of the word and of thought itself, for they have sequestered the essentially participatory word— fruitfully enough, beyond a doubt—from its natural habit, sound, and assimilated it to a mark on a surface, where a real word cannot exist at all" (1977, 21). Speech, on the other hand, defines our very being and existence as a species. Script is a mere five thousand years old and has been used since its invention almost exclusively, in terms of volume, for bureaucratic purposes. John Fisher reminds us that the Chancery, not Chaucer, was the real *father* of English writing, especially in prose, the form language takes in a chirographicly conditioned culture. Artistically, more often than not, in all recorded poetry, in all the dramatic texts, and in most of the great novels written by the likes of Aristophanes, Petronius, Rabelais, Shakespeare, Cervantes, Fielding, Twain, Joyce, Celine, Salingar, and Vonnegut, dialect and dialogue assume primary importance in the construction, style, and impact of the text. Readers or spectators are treated like auditors, confidantes, participants, coaxed here into alliance, teased there into opposition. Chaucer was our pioneer and perhaps our greatest proponent of the primacy of speech in the literary process. Without the oral cacophony of his busy dreams, his birds, his lovers, and his pilgrims, we might never have had the great dramatic dialogue of Shakespeare or Wordsworth's insistence that poetry should not simply imitate prior poetic texts, but should be shaped by the living language, the language spoken "by men to men": a revolutionary concept whose time seems always past and always future bound, because of what Walter Ong has called the "imperialism," and Elspeth Stuckey, the "violence of literacy."

Chaucer is one of the preeminently oral poets of the English language as received by the modern world. How could he have been anything else, living in the twilight of the chirographic age, just a century before the Guttenberg era was launched by the technology of the printing press? Chaucer, with tongue in cheek no doubt, underscores the inadequacies of the manuscript transmission of texts in his wonderful little poem, "To Adam Scryven," which has the revealing subtitle, "Geffrey unto Adame his owen scryvene." He scolds the scribe who is assigned the meticulous tasks of copying the texts of his most overtly classical efforts, the *Boece* and *Troylus*. The scribe willfully introduces his own "newe" ideas in the text which the poet must rub and scrub off the page to erase:

> But after my makyng thow wryte more trewe!
> So ofte a daye I mot thy werk renewe
> It to corecte and eke to rubbe and scrape;
> And al this is thorough thy neglygence and rape!
> (*Short Poems*, 15, ll. 4–7)

These are strong words, but probably delivered in that spirit of "game and pley" Chaucer so often evokes. The author prefaces his scolding with a warning to the scribe not to pour too long over the pages because his dandruff dirties up the leaves! "Under thy long lokkes thow most have the scalle." Even the cloddish properties of manuscript technology seem to get on Chaucer's nerves here, but he is really teasing his scribe about the natural tendency in the folk transmission of stories to improve on the original—that deepest and most enduring legacy from the oral tradition of "makyng" poetry, the very tendency that most probably produced over a millennia the only perfect poems ever created, the *Iliad* and *Odyssey*.[9]

Walter Ong credits Chaucer and Boccaccio for inventing "frame stories" where "the reader can imagine an oral disputation," and where he or she can "pretend to be one of the listening company—of men and women who tell stories about one another during a pilgrimage" (1982, 103). Chaucer's poetry frequently raises crucial questions about the differences between oral and written texts that are difficult to perceive when one is dominated by one mode or the other. In written or printed texts the author is alienated from her own voice by the medium which transcribes the utterance. Voice is produced by an absolutely natural technology: originating in the diaphragm and lungs and transmitted by larynx, tongue, teeth, and lips to the ear of the listener, the audience. In scripted utterance, the author is distanced geographically and temporally from the reader, and in extreme cases credited with a property that a speaking voice is rarely granted—omniscience. The narrator is elevated to the status of "authority." Chaucer, as he demonstrates in the *Wife of Bath's Tale* and at the end of the *House of Fame* when he announces the arrival of the "man of greet auctoritee" who never shows, routinely eschews or even deconstructs claims to authority and omniscience in the interest of "experience" and *ethos*, that is, maintaining intimate contact with an audience always suspicious of claims to authority. It is also interesting to note that the pilgrims in the *Canterbury Tales* never quite make it to the shrine. There is no return journey, no "final word." The *Canterbury Tales*, a collection of many fragments strung together almost haphazardly, resembles nothing so much as a "great conversation," a polyphonic symphony of disagreement, rejoinder, "requital," and interruption.

Chaucer is reader friendly because, like a speaker, he takes pains to introduce himself informally to his audiences, often by name, as illustrated in the lyric poem to his scribe quoted above, in most of the dream visions, and in the *Canterbury Tales* where he assigns himself two stories, arguably the worst two tales on the pilgrimage. John Ganim has produced a book on the subject of Chaucer's sense of "theatricality," which is a product of the "multivocality" and voiced nature of the *Tales* as text rather than an attempt to "stage" a pilgrimage dramatically in imitation of the processional structure of medieval pageant plays:

> I am suggesting that we consider the formal presentation of the *Canterbury Tales* as akin to a linguistic rather than an architectural gesture. Given the fiction of the *Canterbury Tales* as talk, as recorded speech, I would stress the illusion of multivocality in Chaucer, not only in the fluctuating relationship between teller and tale, but between tale and tale, and between Chaucer and his sources. (Ganim 4–5)

An author/speaker is necessarily present in orally simulated texts, reading, reciting, or even improvising his or her tale. Several manuscripts picture Chaucer reciting what presumably were his own poems to audiences gathered at courts or in gardens. In one interesting illumination from the fifteenth-century manuscript of Thomas Hoccleve's *De Regimine principum,* the poet is depicted in old age pointing to the manuscript to his left as if to suggest that although the author may be dead, his "litel book" lives on in script. The audience is also a physical presence in texts prepared for oral delivery or performance, and that presence is continually acknowledged in Chaucer's texts. Chaucer's dream visions each begin with reference to a book that the author has been reading, a text that, interestingly enough, often puts the author of the text we are reading to sleep. In *Book of the Duchess,* the "fable" is the story of Ceyx and Alcione found in Ovid's *Metamorphoses* and adapted by Machaut in *La Fonteinne Amoureuse.* The first thing Chaucer does is oralize the text by retelling the "tale." The text is then scrambled in a dream which Freud tells us is often conditioned and inspired by oral puns.

Another article on our subject might be a demonstration of how Chaucer goes about reoralizing ancient epic or "letteres olde," as he explains in the opening lines of Parliament of Fowls:

> For out of olde feldes, as men seyth,
> Cometh al this newe corn fro yer to yere,
> And out of olde bokes, in good feyth,
> Cometh al this newe science that men lere.
>
> (ll. 22–25)

In his *Letters and Social Aims,* Emerson tells us that "Language is a city to the building of which every human being brought a stone." Emerson might well have had Chaucer's House of Fame in mind here, for our poet early on in the dream visions depicted language as a building: a huge, drafty place where every word ever uttered represents a brick in the floating edifice of language, a building Chaucer himself takes us along to visit on the back of his garrulous eagle who gives him a lesson in the physics and poetics of sound. The image is perfect: speech is a hall where sounds congregate and reverberate, seem to disappear, and then resurface, assuming in the process the eternal status that Augustine assigns to memory in the *Confessions.* We know buildings have long been designed with such properties in mind, including our own capitol, where secret acoustics were early on put to nefarious political use—our first "bugging." More importantly, in all the dream visions, especially the *House of Fame,* Chaucer is articulating a physiological and a poetic theory of language as primarily sound rather than authored text—sound, however "lowde or pryvee, foule or faire," that rises to the House of Fame and is duly registered and recorded for all of eternity there. In short, oral speech, which is received "by experience" as the Eagle remarks, is just as "sound" a source for insight as the written texts of "auctoritee." This, according to the Eagle, is vindication for "speaking lewedly to a lewed man" to "shewe hym swyche skiles / That he may shake hem be the biles." It also shows that vulgar as well as polite speech rises; words are themselves *good* in the Neoplatonic, vertically privileged scheme of things. Sound is heaven-bound, if not legally binding. The letter on the page is dead; the word on the lips, living. The immaterial properties of speech sounding and resounding, the same properties that keep "one's word" from being legally binding, are the very properties which give it spiritual and Christian value, not to mention comic potential, because living speech, as Freud tells us, is "slippery" and open to ironic word play and undercutting through pun and parody. Taking a person "on his word"—his oral word—is an act of faith and trust, if not a legally binding contract.

I want to go through the pertinent passages in the *House of Fame* line by line to demonstrate how carefully, albeit comically, Chaucer privileges the vulgar tongue through the eagle on whose back he rises, like sound itself, to the heavens. Most of the text in book 2 is dialogue between the eagle, who acts as the author's tutor, and Geffrey who will wake from the dream to compose the text itself. The eagle begins with a lecture on the nature of speech as sound, the first lesson for an aspiring author who might easily be lulled into supposing that the great scripted texts of a culture are primary and authoritative:

> "Thou wost wel this, that spech is soun.
> Or elles no man myght hyt here;
> Now herke what y wol the lere.
> "Soun ys noght but eyr ybroken,
> And every spech that ys yspoken,
> Lowde or pryvee, foule or faire,
> In his substaunce ys but aire. . . ."

> (ll. 762–68)

First of all, it is fascinating that a bird is providing the oral catechism for the budding poet here. Do symphonies start as bird calls? We should remember Chaucer's love of birds in other contexts: his transcription of the noisy parliament of fowls, a meeting where birds *parley*, that is *talk*, and, of course, his two beast fables, the *Nuns' Priest's Tale* and the *Manciple's Tale*, which are both "for the birds too" and debate the notion of the right use of utterance, whether in singing or speaking. Chaucer encourages us to remember our affinity with birds through speech. Birds are the only species we teach to speak our languages—particularly the vulgar tongue—and they teach us theirs as well, for we have contests all over the world to see who among us can best whistle and cry like the birds. And like the birds, our utterances are typically squabbles over territory and sex.

> "Now hennesforth y wol the teche
> How every speche, or noyse, or soun,
> Thurgh hys multiplicacioun,
> Thogh hyt were piped of a mous,
> Mote nede come to Fames Hous.
> I preve hyt thus—take hede no—
> Be experience: for yf that thow
> Throwe on water now a stoon,
> Wel wost thou hyt wol make anoon
> A litel roundell as a sercle . . ."

(ll. 783–91)

The eagle's subject here is the favorite topic of medieval rhetoricians, those who study *speech* or *oratory*: that is, how speech is *amplified* and conveyed. As Ong says, amplification is the chief verbal device in an oral culture. The eagle's proof is "experience." He is teaching "litel Geffrey" a medieval theory about sound which still rings true: sound is a wave, and like a wave, it travels outward in ever larger circles and is never fully dissipated in terms of the energy it carries. For Chaucer, sound, however small, vulgar, or seemingly insignificant, reaches a kind of comic and cosmic equivalent of Plato's Realm of Ideals or Wordsworth's mansion of Beauteous Forms, although I think Chaucer is perfectly serious here.

For Chaucer "Fame" does not mean celebrity conveyed through inscription by the powers that be, although that meaning obtained by the fourteenth century. Fame, from the Latin *fama*, means "rumor," or better yet, "gossip"—that staple of oral, folk, or vulgar communication. Writers as communicators are fascinated with gossip; think of all of Shakespeare's characters who romp off stage after the comedies to a "gossip's feast." Myth, in a sense, can be described as "meta-gossip." The myths of the western world to this very day, myths that circulate in our gossip columns, on our talk shows, and in magazines like *People*, are

as scandal-ridden as the *Metamorphoses*, and they can get their
writers in the same deep trouble Ovid suffered at the hands of
Augustus. In the passage quoted just above we learn that sound
operates vertically like authority, but its power, like gossip,
comes from the ground up, just as words and farts do in the
Miller's and Summoner's fabliaux:

> "Everych ayre in other stereth
> More and more, and speche up bereth,
> Or voys, or noyse, or word, or soun,
> Ay through multiplicacioun,
> Til hyt be atte Hous of Fame.
> Take yt in ernest or in game . . ."
>
> (ll. 817–22)

"A man may say full sooth in game and pley," Harry Bailley tells
us, and the eagle speaks truly here. Whether we like it or not,
and whether the utterance is profound or trivial, as pure sound,
one utterance is as good as the next and therefore as worthy of
imitation by the writer as the great texts that precede his or
her own. The eagle proceeds to compare human utterances with
smoke, fire, and the sound of musical instruments. In the hierarchy of elements, uttered words rise, printed words, fall. It's all
a matter of "grace and gravity," as Simone Weil reminds us in
the twentieth-century:

> "Now have I tolde, yf ye have in mynde,
> How speche or soun of pure kynde
> Enclyned ys uypward to meve—. . .
> Of every speche, of every soun,
> Be hyt eyther foule or faire
> Hath hys kynde place in ayre . . ."
>
> (ll. 823–25, 832–34)

Again, content is not the issue: words themselves rise neutrally
and are not to be judged here below. What sentiments for an
aspiring writer, especially a writer with comic or Christian aspirations! All words are fair game for the artist. Nothing verbal is
alien to the oral poet, nothing high or low, sacred or obscene. It
may well be that the very notion of obscenity is a function of
chirographic cultures. We know that licensing is the method by
which the written language literally "dictates" to its oral parent.
Words cannot be recorded as obscene until some concept of a
"standard" language emerges which is surely a product of the

chirographic frame of mind. "Standard English" is the imitative
language dictating its own technology to the parent oral tongue.
Vulgarisms, barbarisms, and obscenities in an oral culture are
simply products of colorful usage. Most words designated as
"obscene" in dictionaries today are words considered not "fit to
print" and were so designated until well into the twentieth
century by the infamous dashes D. H. Lawrence excoriated. No
such dashes exist in the manuscripts that record these terms
from the Middle Ages. Actually, vulgarisms are residues of the
dominance of the hated oral tongue. "Fuck," "shit," and "cunt"
are the vulgar terms that trace back to Germanic roots in our
language. "Intercourse," "feces," and "pudendum," the so-called
"polite" terms for bodily parts and functions, are derivations
from alien languages that are mastered through or even transcribed by chirographic methods and hence are "fit to print."
"Pudendum" is my personal favorite of these polite terms. In
standard English it is the privileged word, although its root in
Latin means "that which shames." The eagle makes it plain, like
"plain speech itself," that words are to be duly recorded and
registered in script from the oral tongue without regard to hurt
feelings, sensitive egos, delicate sensibilities, or standards of polite discourse. The conclusion the garrulous eagle draws is, as
the kids say, "radical":

> "Than ys this the conclusyoun,
> That every speche of every man,
> As y the telle first began,
> Moveth up on high to pace
> Kyndely to Fames place.
> "Tell me this now feythfully,
> Have y not preved thus symply,
> Withouten any subtilite
> Of speche, or gret prolixite
> Of termes of philosophie
> Of figures of poetrie,
> Or colours of rethorike?"

(ll. 848–59)

As Bakhtin remarks, "ears are antiofficial" (1986, 141). Every
person's speech rises to Fama's palace as the physics and physiology of sound prove. None of the procedures of chirographic
culture—logic, flowers of rhetoric, sophistic subtilty—is needed
to experience or utilize the power of speech. All little Geffrey
can utter in response to this demonstration, like Adeodatus in

Augustine's *De magistro*, is "Yis." The inescapable, but oft forgotten conclusion of the lesson is:

> "Aha," quod he, "lo, so I can
> Lewedly to a lewed man
> Speke, and shewe hym swyche skiles
> That he may shake hem be the biles
> So palpably they shulden be."

(ll. 865–76)

Raw speech provides, as poets from Chaucer through Wordsworth to Frost have been affirming for centuries, the *data* of the poet, the speech that Wordsworth claimed was spoken—by man to men—unrefined, unamended, unpolished, not the carefully crafted rhetoric and the poetic refinement of the schools as they were modified by what Ong calls chirographic culture and technology. As Bakhtin insists, "speech genres" are "primary"; literary genres are "secondary."

> It is especially important here to draw attention to the very significant difference between primary (simple) and secondary (complex) speech genres. . . . Secondary (complex) speech genres—novels, dramas, all kinds of scientific research, major genres of commentary, and so forth—arise in more complex and comparatively highly developed and organized cultural communication (primarily written) that is artistic, scientific, sociopolitical, and so on. During the process of their formulation, they absorb and digest various primary (simple) genres that have taken form in unmediated speech communion. These primary genres are altered and assume a special character when they enter into complex ones. *They lose their immediate relation to actual reality and to the real utterances of others* (italics mine). (1986, 61–62)

Utterance, the primary datum for literature, is transformed in chirographical and typographical transmission which necessarily alienates it from the living, growing "real" world of language, that is orality.

In the absence of "bird bills" on human beings, Chaucer leaves little room for doubt about how he thinks words should shake us. It is fascinating that Mephistopheles gives much the same advice to Faust in Goethe's great poem:

> "But you will never reach the people's hearts,
> Unless you speak to them straight from your own.
> Diction! That's rubbish, fit for puppet plays.

My good Magister, force is what we need!
Don't be a cymbal-tinkling ass!
Won't friendship, love, and brotherhood
Express themselves without a rhetoric class?
And when you've something real to say,
Do you have to hunt for words all day?"

(Quoted Mann 10)

Speech changes, of course, although the authorities appoint grammarians and lexicographers to monitor and impede the process of oral drift and development. Nevertheless, the life-blood of speech, like love, is change, or so says the narrator in Chaucer's *Troilus and Criseyde:*

Ye knowe ek that in forme of speche is chaunge.
Withinne a thousand yer, and wordes tho
That hadden prys now wonder nyce and straunge
Us thenketh hem, and yet they spake hem so,
And sped as wel in love as men now do.
Eke for to wynnen love in sondry ages,
In sondry londes, sondry ben usages.

(2.22–28)

Speech is "sondry," variable in its usage, and from that diversity distinction and excellence arise. The function of the artist is not to freeze the process of utterance in script or print, but to record the change and exchange of words as they emerge, evanesce, and evaporate.

One incontrovertible fact emerges about the Canterbury pilgrims in Chaucer's greatest poem, the *Canterbury Tales,* which is perhaps the greatest narrative poem in English or any other vernacular language: they were "diverse folks" because "diversely they spoke." Chaucer restates his defense of the vulgar tongue as powerfully as it can be articulated at the outset of the pilgrimage, and I will quote it nearly in full here:

But first I pray you, of youre curteisye,
That ye n'arrette it nat my vileynye
Thogh that I speke hir wordes properly.
For this ye knowen al so wel as I,
Whoso shal tell a tale after a man,
He moot reherce as ny as evere he kan
Evrich a word, if it be in his charge,
Al speke he never so rudeliche and large,
Or ellis he moot telle his tale untrewe.

Or feyne thyng, or fynde wordes newe.
He may nat spare, althogh he were his brother;
He moot as wel seye o word as another.
Crist spak hymself ful brode in hooly writ,
And wel ye woot no vileyneye is it.
Eek Plato seith, whoso kan hym rede,
The wordes moote be cosyn to the dede.

(l. 725–42)

These are *provocative* words; they "call forth" a voiced response
as the poem *in toto* always has, and as the individual "tales"
themselves provoke among their tellers. Courtesy is associated
conventionally with scripted, standard speech, "villainy," with
the vulgar tongue. "Vileynye" is the problematic word here. It is
interesting to note that the term "vileynye," like "vulgar" from
the same root which gave us "folk," have both become pejorative
and even deprecating words: "vileynye," from the French "vil-
lein," meaning villager or rustic, has come to mean "criminal"
in modern English. Chaucer as narrator, however, will speak "vil-
lainously" in the *Canterbury Tales*. He will relate one word just
as readily as the next, because all have been uttered, however
"rudeliche and large." And if he does not, he lies. One word is
as good as another, vulgar or polite, as we have been taught in
the *House of Fame*.

The authorities who vindicate this practice of "rehearsing"
and reporting real words about real actions are none other than
Plato and Christ, the two architects of medieval Neoplatonism
and Christianity. As Arrian says with reference to the discourses
of Epictetus which he recorded, the great teachers do not write,
they speak their truths directly:

> These discourses are such as one person would naturally deliver
> from his own thoughts, extempore, to another; not such as he would
> prepare to be read by numbers afterwards. . . . When he (Epictetus)
> uttered them, he aimed at nothing more than to excite his hearers to
> virtue. . . . when Epictetus himself pronounced them, his audience
> could not help being affected in the very manner he intended they
> should. More evidence of the fact that the great teachers never wanted
> their thoughts, their sayings, their teachings fixed in print, made
> public to be quoted out of context or expurgated or distorted or "held
> accountable." (1)

Both Christ and Socrates spoke directly to their disciples. Many,
including the Gnostics, feel that the "scriptures" their lives and

dialogues inspired have distorted their teaching. To be sure, the "word in the beginning" was oral, not scripted. Words, like sticks and stones, may hurt brothers, but they must be repeated because they guide the race in its choices, dreams, and prayers.

I want to conclude with some quotations by modern *authorities* about keeping language open and accessible to the folk who create and recreate it everyday. Kierkegaard identifies the silencing of voices, what we call "shutting up"—the first words many of us remember being taught at home, school, and church—with "unfreedom" and the demonic.

> The demoniacal is shut-up-ness unfreely revealed. . . . Freedom is precisely the expansive. It is in opposition to this we would employ the word "shut-up," in an eminent sense for "unfreedom." . . . The demoniacal does not shut itself up with something, but shuts itself up; and in this lies the mystery of existence, the fact that unfreedom makes a prisoner precisely of itself. Freedom is constantly communicating (it will do no harm to take into account even the religious significance of this word); unfreedom becomes more and more shut-up and wants no communication. (59)

Humor, liberty, and even religious understanding can only be experienced through the living communication of open speech. Spinoza understood the Hebrew word for prophet was *nabi*, which means speaker or interpreter (36). Chaucer in turn invented a form of communicative discourse and of dialogical exchange that no other poet in English has ever been able to imitate, largely because of its religious drive and dimension that may be traced to its oral roots.

Alice Walker reiterates for us the ultimate consequences of shutting up and alienating a culture from its mother tongue in *Living by the Word*. "It is language more than anything else that reveals and validates one's existence, and if the language we actually speak is denied us, then it is inevitable that the form we are permitted to assume historically will be one of caricature, reflecting someone else's literary or social fantasy" (58). Chaucer's language is free, "unruly," open, "heteroglossic," polyphonic, polyvocalic, and occasionally even "polyglossic," to use Bakhtin's suggestive terminology. The new vocabulary and syntax that Chaucer introduced into English has been shown by Thomas Ross and others to have been derived as much from his observation of slang, jargon, obscenity, "sklaundre" and colloquial idiom as from Latinate neologism and grammatical prescript or from the official courtly language of the long dominant dictates of the scripted Latin and Norman culture of his own time. The nearly incomprehensible dose of "in-language" exchanged between the Pardoner and the Host in the *Canterbury Tales* or the professional jargon of the Man of Law or Merchant, or the scatology of the Summoner, Reeve, or Miller, or the "damnation" of the Alchemist because he refuses to speak openly to his fellow pilgrims, all illustrate Chaucer's decisive privileging of *talk* in his tales. "The Father of English" then is not so much interested in the declaratory language of doctrine and edification delivered in the monologic style of *auctoritas*, or what Bakhtin calls the "official culture," as he is in the "interface" of dialogue within the living matrix of linguistic experience that is speech: the "vulgar," mother tongue.

Notes

1. All quotations are taken from the edition of Chaucer's poetry edited by John Hurt Fisher.

2. "Since human commerce is carried on in so many and such different languages that people in many instances cannot make themselves understood to others, with or without words, we must hunt down that language which a man would use had he neither mother nor nursing, had he gone through neither schoolboy stage nor adolescence. In this, as well as in many other cases, Petramala is the most important city and the 'home town' of the greater part of the children of Adam" (Dante 8).

3. The theory of Bakhtin, whose major works are listed below, is shot through with sentiments such as these because the primacy of the uttered word in linguistic and literary phenomena is his essential premise.

4. For discussion of Chaucer's abiding interest in oral folklore, see also Carl Lindahl who writes: "By the middle of the 1380's, Chaucer seems to have been ready for an even more dramatic change, ready to embrace forms and styles more closely suited to his expressive needs and personality. These techniques had been developed orally to fill much the same needs that Chaucer felt. Therefore, he turned to folktale and folk rhetoric at the end of his career" (171).

5. Standard studies on Chaucer and oral poetics which have influenced my thinking include the work of Bronson, Chaytor, Crosby, Finnegan, Havelock, Huot, Koff, Olson, and Zumthor.

6. "Although the ordinary material of speech of our mother-tongue seems to be guarded against forgetting, its application, however, more often succumbs to another disturbance which is familiar to us as 'slips of the tongue'" (Freud 69).

7. Augustine speculates that Ambrose may have read "to himself" to avoid conversation and save his voice for sermons, but goes on to explain that private reading is the truly spiritual means of nourishing the soul.

8. On the relationship of literary censorship to the power structure, see Susan Jansen. On the subject of censorship of Shakespeare in secondary textbooks, see articles by Andreas. As an example of a censored Shakespearean text used extensively in secondary schools today, see *Adventures in Reading*.

9. Few of the shorter, so-called "lyric" poems of Chaucer have generated the kind of controversy "Adam Scriveyn" has, with scholars raising questions about its authorship, topical allusions, and figurative interpretations. In his edition of Chaucer's poetry, F. N. Robinson corroborates my suggestion that the poems "reveals some of the anxieties which beset an author before the invention of printing" (521), and John Hurt Fisher agrees in his commentary, characterizing the poem as an "exasperated expostulation" of an author to his copyist about textual accuracy (671). A generation of scholars, inspired by John Manley (see Peck's bibliography, p. 101), however, eagerly tried to identify the real "Adam," stretching credibility to the point of suggesting that "Scriveyn" might perhaps have been a surname. R. E. Kaske has enriched this investigation, offering "that [Chaucer] . . . actually had a scribe named Adam and is capitalizing on the happy correspondence between his name and that of *clericus Adam*." He sees the typological source for the name in a popular twelfth-century poem found in a number of continental manuscripts entitled *Clericus Adam*. "In any case, this evidently popular picture of a *clericus* Adam writing about the sin of the first Adam makes one wonder whether Chaucer may not be playfully introducing a similar position in his warning to *Adam Scriveyn*." Chaucer might be saying, "Look here, *clericus Adam*, you little bungler, don't you disfigure *my* handiwork the way your namesake disfigured that of God!" (115–16).

Seth Lehrer has recently advanced the most controversial reading of the poem, suggesting in the process that it might even have been written by John Shirley, one of the staunchest of Chaucer's imitators and successors: "It is to John Shirley that we owe attributions of a half dozen of Chaucer's shorter poems and to Shirley that we owe the information on the circumstances of these and many others" (119). Shirley, in a sense, recast the manuscripts and poetic career of his master as an "act of canonization," placing "Chaucer's poetry in the biographical contexts of production" (120). "Shirley presents himself as this laboring Adam to Chaucer's near-divine authority, a someone who had transcribed the whole of the *Boece* and who had, throughout his life, copied the bits and pieces of the *Troilus* as they struck his fancy" (121). What is pertinent to my argument here is that Shirley, although he is the *textual* successor and editor of Chaucer, feels free in what Ong calls a "manuscript age" to amend, complete, and even compose texts which he can thus attribute to his master, much like an oral poet would improvise on the formulas and themes of his great poetic predecessors. "For John Shirley, then, the canonicity of *Adam Scriveyn* lies in its participation in a system of transmission—indeed, the preoccupations of the poem are the very systems of transmission that confer a canonicity on authorized production" (143).

John Stowe was the first editor to print "Adam Scriveyn," appropriately, on the very last page of his edition of Chaucer's works published in 1561.

Works Cited

Adventures in Reading. Orlando: Harcourt, 1985.

Alighieri, Dante. *De Vulgari Eloquentia. Literary Criticism of Dante Alighieri.* Translated by Robert S. Haller. Lincoln: University of Nebraska Press, 1973.

Andreas, James R. "Neutering Romeo and Juliet." In *Ideological Approaches to Shakespeare: The Practice of Theory.* Edited by Robert Merrix and Nicholas Ranson, 227–42. Lewiston, NY: Mellon, 1992.

———. "Silencing the Vulgar and Voicing the Other Shakespeare." *Nebraska English Journal* 35 (1990): 74–88.

Augustine. *Confessions.* Translated by R. S. Pine-Coffin. New York: Penguin-Viking, 1961.

Bakhtin, Mikhail. *Art and Answerability: Early Philosophical Essays by Mikhail Bakhtin,* Edited and translated by Michael Holquist. Austin: University of Texas Press, 1990.

———. *The Dialogic Imagination: Four Essays.* Translated by Caryl Emerson and Michael Holquist. Austin: University of Texas Press, 1981.

———. *Problems of Dostoevsky Poetics.* Translated by R. W. Rostel. Ann Arbor: Ardis, 1973.

———. *Rabelais and His World.* Translated by Helene Iswolsky. Cambridge: Massachusetts Institute of Technology Press, 1968.

———. *Speech Genres and Other Late Essays.* Translated by Vern W. McGee, edited by Caryl Emerson and Michael Holquist. Austin: University of Texas Press, 1986.

Bronson, Bertrand H. "Chaucer's Art in Relation to His Audience." In *Five Studies in Literature,* 413–32. Berkeley: University of California Press, 1940.

Chaucer, Geoffrey. *The Complete Poetry and Prose of Geoffrey Chaucer.* Edited by John H. Fisher. New York: Holt, 1989.

———. *The Works of Geoffrey Chaucer.* Edited by F. N. Robinson: Cambridge, MA: Houghton Mifflin, 1957.

Chaytor, H. J. *From Script to Print.* Reprint, London: Sidgwick and Jackson, 1945; 1966.

Crosby, Ruth. "Chaucer and the Custom of Oral Delivery." *Speculum* 13 (1938): 413–32.

———. "Oral Delivery in the Middle Ages." *Speculum* 11 (1936): 88–110.

Derrida, Jacques. Quoting Rousseau's *Fragment inedit d'un essai sur les langues.* In *Of Grammatology,* translated by Gayartri Spivak. Baltimore: Johns Hopkins University, 1974.

Epictetus. Preface from "Arrian to Lucius Gellius" to Epictetus' *The Moral Discourses.* Translated by Elizabeth Carter. London: Everyman's, 1910.

Finnegan, Ruth. *Oral Poetry: Its Nature, Significance, and Social Context.* Cambridge: Cambridge University, 1977.

Fisher, John Hurt. *An Anthology of Chancery English.* Knoxville: University of Tennessee Press, 1984.

Freud, Sigmund. "Mistakes in Speech." *Psychopathology of Everyday Life.* In *The Basic Writings of Sigmund Freud,* translated by A. A. Brill. New York: Random, 1938.

Ganim, John. *Chaucerian Theatricality.* Princeton, NJ: Princeton University, 1990.

Geoffrey of Vinsauf. *Documentum de modo et arte dictandi et versificandi.* In *Les arts poétiques du XIIe et XIIIe siècles: Recherches et documents sur la technique litteraire du moyen age,* edited by Edmond Faral. Reprint, Paris: Champion, 1924; 1962.

Havelock, Eric A. *The Literate Revolution in Greece and Its Cultural Consequences*. Princeton: Princeton University, 1982.

Huot, Sylvia. *From Song to Book: The Poetics of Writing in the Old French Lyric and Lyrical Narrative Poetry*. Ithaca, NY: Cornell University, 1987.

Jansen, Susan. *Censorship, The Knot That Binds Power and Knowledge*. New York and Oxford: Oxford University, 1988.

Kaske, R. E. "*Clericus Adam* and Chaucer's *Adam Scriveyn*." In *Chaucerian Problems and Perspectives: Essays Presented to Paul E. Beichner*. Edited by Edward Vasta and Zacharias P. Thundy, 114–18. Notre Dame: University of Notre Dame Press, 1979.

Kierkegaard, Soren. *The Laughter Is On My Side*. Edited by Roger Poole and Henrik Strangerup. Princeton, NJ: Princeton University, 1989.

Koff, Michael. *Chaucer and the Art of Storytelling*. Berkeley: University of California Press, 1988.

Lehrer, Seth. "The Complaints of Adam Scriveyn: John Shirley and the Canonicity of Chaucer's Short Poems." In *Chaucer and His Readers: Imagining the Author in Late-Medieval England*, 117–46. Princeton, NJ: Princeton University Press, 1993.

Lindahl, Carl. *Earnest Games: Folkloric Patterns in the Canterbury Tales*. Bloomington: University of Indiana Press, 1987.

Mann, Thomas. *Essays*. Translated by H. T. Lowe-Porter. New York: Vintage, 1957.

Olson, David R. "From Utterance to Text: The Bias of Language in Speech and Writing." *Harvard Educational Review*. 47 (1977): 257–81.

Ong, Walter. "Transformations of the Word and Alienation." In *Interfaces of the Word*. Ithaca and London: Cornell University Press, 1977.

———. *Orality and Literacy: The Technologizing of the Word*. London and New York: Metheun, 1982.

———. *Rhetoric, Romance, and Technology*. Ithaca and London: Cornell University Press, 1971.

Owen, Charles. *Pilgrimage and Story-Telling in the Canterbury Tales: The Dialectic of "Ernest" and "Game."* Norman: University of Oklahoma Press, 1977.

Parr, Roger, translator. *Documentum de modo et arte dictandi et versificandi*. Milwaukee: Marquette University Press, 1968.

Peck, Russell A. *Adam Scriveyn*. In *Chaucer's Lyrics and Anelida and Arcite: An Annotated Bibliography: 1900 to 1980*, 101–02. Toronto: University of Toronto Press, 1983.

Robertson, D. W. *A Preface to Chaucer*. Princeton, NJ: Princeton University Press, 1957.

Ross, Thomas W. *Chaucer's Bawdy*. New York: Dutton, 1972.

Spinoza, Baruch. *The Philosophy of Spinoza*. Edited by Joseph Ratner. New York: Modern Library, 1936.

Strohm, Paul. *Social Chaucer*. Cambridge, MA: Harvard University Press, 1989.

Stuckey, Elspeth. *The Violence of Literacy*. New York: Heinemann/Boynton Cook, 1991.

Walker, Alice. *Living by the Word*. New York: Harcourt, 1988.

Zumthor, Paul. *Oral Poetry: An Introduction*. Translated by Kathryn Murphy. Minneapolis: The University of Minnesota Press, 1990.

What the King Saw, What the Poet Wrote: Shakespeare Plays before King James

ALVIN KERNAN

OVER THE YEARS WALTER ONG HAS LED THE WAY IN THE STUDY OF what he sums up briefly in his magisterial book, *Orality and Literacy The Technologizing of the Word* (1982), as "the dynamics of the orality-literacy shift." Along with Innis, McLuhan, and Havelock, Ong defined this field of study in theoretical terms and wrote many chapters of its history, particularly in the Renaissance. The following is offered as a case history of the complex interaction of orality and literacy during the Renaissance when literacy was replacing orality as the privileged mode of knowledge.

When James the Sixth of Scotland became the king of England in the spring of 1603, the playing company in which Shakespeare was the resident playwright and a major shareholder was, almost immediately, made the royal troupe, the King's Men. Shakespeare thereby became the king's official playwright, and from the Christmas celebrations at Hampton Court in 1603, his new plays and many of his old still in repertory were performed before the king and his court on a variety of occasions. Shakespeare continued to work in the public theater, the Globe, downtown, but his Stuart drama—*Othello, Lear, Macbeth,* and *The Tempest,* among others—was written with the knowledge that the plays would be eventually performed at court before the royal patron.

History has left no record of what James thought of the Shakespeare plays designed to his interests, though he did once call for a second performance of the old play *The Merchant of Venice.* But we do have a number of extremely interesting descriptions of James in the court theater, as well as Shakespeare's descriptions of how those "command performances" at the palace were experienced from the players' side of the stage. Putting the two together approximates what happened when Shakespeare and his fellows performed at Whitehall.

155

Theater at the court took place in one of the great halls of the palace, which was arranged for performance in the manner the Venetian, Orazio Busino, zooms in on at a performance at Whitehall:

> At about the 6th hour of the night [10 o'clock] the king appeared with his court, having passed through the apartments where the ambassadors were in waiting. . . . On entering the house, the cornets and trumpets to the number of fifteen or twenty began to play very well a sort of recitative, and then after his Majesty had seated himself under the canopy alone, the queen not being present on account of a slight indisposition, he caused the ambassadors to sit below him on two stools, while the great officers of the crown and courts of law sat upon benches. The Lord Chamberlain then had the way cleared and in the middle of the theatre there appeared a fine and spacious area carpeted all over with green cloth. In an instant a large curtain dropped, painted to represent a tent of gold cloth with a broad fringe; the background was of canvas painted blue, powdered all over with golden stars. (*Calendar of State Papers Venetian*, 15, 1617–19, p. 112)

James went faithfully to the court plays, especially when his own players performed, and made his views of them known, but he was not exactly stagestruck. He "liked or disliked as he saw cause" Dudley Carleton said, "but it seems he takes no extraordinary pleasure in [plays]. The queen and prince [Henry] were more the players' friends" (15 January 1604).

A man who disliked crowds, and after several attempts on his life feared them too, the king was never very relaxed or comfortable on the occasions when plays were performed in overheated halls ablaze with candles and crammed with people. Plays at court usually came at the end of protracted and wearying feasting and dealings with the king's courtiers and entertaining foreign ambassadors. Much wine and heavy food had been consumed, and the hall was crowded and hot from the heat of bodies and the candles that furnished light. Under these pressures James often became touchy and sometimes did not conceal his annoyance with some of the dull, pretentious stuff he had to watch. At a performance of a Latin play, *Ajax Flagellifer*, in Christ Church Hall, Oxford, on the evening of 28 August 1605, "The King was very weary before he came thither, but much more wearied by it, and spoke many words of dislike" (Nichols, 1.550). Things got even worse the next night after another day of elaborate ceremonies:

> That night, after supper, about nine, began their Comedy called *Vertumnus*, very well and learnedly penned by Dr. Gwynn. It was

acted much better than either of the other [plays the king had seen] and chiefly by St. John's men, yet the King was so over-wearied at St. Marie's, that after a while he distasted it, and fell asleep; when he awaked, he would have bin gone, saying, "I marvel what they think me to be," with such other like speeches shewing his dislike thereof, yet he did tarry till they had ended it, which was after one of the clock. The Queen was not there that night. (Nichols, 1.552)

On the occasion of a masque produced by Francis Bacon and performed by the gentlemen of two of the Inns of Court celebrating the Princess Elizabeth's marriage in 1613, the king became so exhausted and testy that the performance had to be postponed. The hall was stifling, as usual, and Chamberlain wrote Alice Carleton that "the King was so wearied and sleepie with sitting up almost two whole nights before, that he had no edge to it." Bacon was understandably devastated by the king's refusal to see his masque, and entreated "his Majestie, that by this disgrace he wold not as it were bury them quicke." But, Chamberlain goes on, "I heare the King shold aunswer, that then they must burie him quicke for he could last no longer, but withall gave them very goode wordes and appointed them to come again on Saterday" (18 February 1613).

As the king grew older and more impatient with court ceremonies, the outbursts at theater in the great hall got louder and more testy. One of the spectators at a masque, a Venetian as observant as Iago, describes the atmosphere, the explosion, and then a wonderful anecdote about how a courtier genius handled the situation:

> we were so crowded and ill at ease that had it not been for our curiosity we must certainly have given in or expired. . . . [the dancers] performed every sort of ballet and dance of every country whatsoever such as passamezzi, corants, carianes. . . . Last of all they danced the Spanish dance, one at a time, each with his lady, and being well nigh tired they began to lag, whereupon the king, who is naturally choleric, got impatient and shouted aloud. "Why don't they dance? What did they make me come here for? Devil take you all, dance." Upon this, the Marquis of Buckingham, his Majesty's favourite, immediately sprang forward, cutting a score of lofty and very minute capers, with so much grace and agility that he not only appeased the ire of his angry lord, but rendered himself the admiration and delight of everybody. (*Calendar of State Papers Venetian*, 15, 1617–19, p. 111)

Things could get much worse at the theater when James was present, and did at the drunken theatricals on the occasion of the visit of the royal brother-in-law, Christian of Denmark, at Theobalds in the summer of 1607. Cecil, the king's chief secretary, had arranged for a "representation" of the Queen of Sheba coming to Solomon, designed to gratify the king's image of himself as the judicious Solomon. Sheba began by offering the kings jellies, creams, and other rich foods, but spilled them in the lap of the Danish king. When he, covered with the mess, rose to dance with her, he was so tipsy that he fell and had to be carried off to bed. Faith, Hope, and Charity were now to appear but were already totally smashed, and after mangling their speeches, they reeled about and spewed before collapsing in a stupor. Victory approached in armor with a sword but got so confused she had to be led away to sleep on the steps of the chamber. Next,

> did Peace make entry, and strive to get foremoste to the King; but I grieve to tell how great wrath she did discover unto those of her attendants; and, much contrary to her semblance, most rudely made war with her olive branch, and laid on the pates of those who did oppose her coming. (Harrington, 1.351)

Obviously no one at court paid close attention to plays when they were performed there—there were too many other things going on—and indeed the king was seated at royal performances in a way that made hearing and seeing the play far less important than his visibility to the remainder of the audience. In an argument between court officials and college dignitaries at Christ's Church, Oxford, in 1604 about the placement of the "state," the canopy covering the royal chairs and the platform on which they were fixed, the college people producing the play wanted the state located at the point in the hall where the king would be at the focal point of the perspective scenery and where he could best see and hear the play. The court officials, who prevailed, however, insisted that the state be placed where the king could hear or see the play only with difficulty but where he could clearly be seen by the remainder of the audience, who would be watching him rather than the play (Chambers, 1.228).

The king, not the play, was the thing at court performances, but at times when the play really interested him as on a visit to Cambridge in March of 1615, the king did pay attention to the play. The university wined and dined the court with no expense spared and amused it with a series of plays, plus a number of "acts and disputations" in Divinity, Law, and Physic. Chamberlain was in the party and described the festivities to Carleton in a letter from London of 16 March that gives a good picture of university theatricals staged for royal visits:

> The Kinge and Prince lay at Trinitie College where the playes were represented, and the hall so well ordered for roome that above 2000 persons were conveniently placed. . . . The second night was a comedie [George Ruggle's *Ignoramus*] of Clare Hall with the helpe of two or three goode actors from other houses, wherein David Drommond in a hobby-horse, and Brakin, the recorder of the towne under the name of Ignoramus a common lawier bare great parts: the thing was full of mirth and varietie, with many excellent actors . . . but more than halfe marred with extreme length. (Letter #225)

Chamberlain obviously enjoyed the shows and was favored with a place near enough the king that he "had the hap to be for the most time within hearing, and often at his heales." From this position where he could see and hear the king, like Horatio at *The Murder of Gonzago*, Chamberlain could tell that he was "exceedingly pleased many times both at the playes and the disputations" and with the Latin play in the manner of Plautus, *Ignoramus*, that was the hit of the visit. The play was a long, five-hours traffic of the stage, an incredibly complicated romance, but inserted into it was a satire on "common" lawyers, those who argued for the supremacy of the common law over the king's prerogative and the authority of ecclesiastical courts. *Ignoramus* ("we know of no such crime") was at that time the legal term used by grand juries to indicate that they could find no grounds for an indictment, and in the play "the principal character was a pompous, silly old Inns-of-Court lawyer named Ignoramus—intended, actually, as caricature of the Cambridge town recorder, Brackyn, with whom the university had long been at odds. But the moment Ignoramus appeared, the audience saw him as Lord Coke to the life" (Bowen, 358). Sir Edward Coke, lord chief justice of the King's Bench, was the great defender of the English common law against the king's prerogative. He was engaged in a bitter struggle with his monarch at that time, and James roared with laughter, clapped frequently, and called out "Plaudite" as Ignoramus-Coke, spouting pig latin and legalese, strutted the stage, attacked bishops and laymen, and courted a young girl with bawdy macaronic verses, "Et *dabo* FEE SIMPLE, *si monstras* love's pretty dimple."

James couldn't stop laughing at the play, and according to Cambridge witnesses tried to have it brought to London. When that proved impossible, he visited the university two months later after a hunting trip, purposely, Chamberlain implies, to see *Ignoramus* again (letter #229). At any rate, the play was put on for him a second time. According to James Tabor, registrary of the University, "About 8 of the clock the play began and ended about one: his majesty was much delighted with the play, and laughed exceedingly; and oftentimes with his hands and by words applauded it" (Mullinger, 2.544). Coke, who was a graduate of Trinity, was not amused, and made a quarrel of it, attacking scholars from the bench, but wincing from that time on whenever the term "Ignoramus" was heard in Westminster Hall. Chamberlain reported that the play had "so netled the Lawiers that they are almost out of all patience, and the Lord Chief Justice [Coke] both openly at the Kings Bench and divers other places hath galled and glaunced at schollers with much bitternes" (letter #229). Chamberlain thought, however, that "yt was a scandal taken rather than geven."

On another theatrical occasion when the king was himself the object of a stage satire, he was not so amused. The French ambassador, M. de la Broderie, wrote on 8 April 1608 to his friend the Marquis de Sillery, that the boy players, the Children of Blackfriars, had in March of that year satirized James's Scottish followers and showed his majesty a mighty hunter, drunk for a month, cursing heaven over the way a hawk flew and beating one of his gentlemen for injuring a hound. The king was so enraged that he swore that the players would have to beg their bread in the future and ordered all London theaters closed on 29 March with the threat of permanent closure (Chambers, 2.53; 3.257).

Matters could get even more serious when the king was present and what was staged for him caught his attention. Girolamo Lando, the Venetian ambassador, would almost seem to have had *Hamlet* in mind in his description of a performance of a play, close but not exactly like Fulke Greville's *Mustapha*, in January 1620, at the court. He thought the story worth recounting to their sereneties back in Venice "owing to the mystery it involves":

The Comedians of the prince, [Charles] in the presence of the king his father, played a drama the other day in which a king with his two sons has one of them put to death, simply upon suspicion that he wished to deprive him of his crown, and the other son actually did deprive him of it afterwards. This moved the king in an extraordinary manner, both inwardly and outwardly. (*Calendar of State Papers Venetian*, 16.111)

Lando then went on to make the surprising statement that "In this country however the comedians have absolute liberty to say whatever they wish against any one soever, so the only demonstration [remonstration?] against them will be the words spoken by the king." It would be fascinating to know at what point in the play King James thought that Prince Charles, Hamlet fashion, had used his players to suggest that his father had murdered his elder brother, Prince Henry, as was rumored at the time, and to alarm him with the possibility that Charles might himself prove more dangerous to his throne in the end.

James Stuart was not an unlearned man, quite the contrary. His education at the hands of the humanist scholar George Buchanan had been thorough, extensive, and bookish. Known to some in later years as "the wisest fool in Christendom," he was a considerable linguist, a competent poet, and a writer who actually published books on poetics, politics, witchcraft, and tobacco. He was, that is to say, a Gutenberg man whose consciousness had been formed in large part by print, and yet as the above examples make clear, he still acted in the theater in ways characteristic of public oral situations. With a book in his hand, the Bible by way of conspicuous example, he was a very close reader and a scrupulous interpreter of difficult meanings. But his behavior in the theater demonstrates perfectly the nature of public oral reception. His attention flagged easily, he grew tired and bored, he came to be seen rather than to see and listen, he understood what was going on only in the crudest way, and his full attention was captured only when events on stage bore directly on his own interests.

None of this would surprise any director or actor, long enured to the absence of close attention or sophisticated interpretation in the theater. But the king's playwright, for all his theatrical skills as an actor and long success on the boards as a playwright, was also a man of the written word who was changing the theater by making his oral-visual medium carry the subtle and complex meanings of the printed page. Ong notes that the drama "from antiquity had been controlled by writing. Euripides' tragedies were texts composed in writing and then memorized verbatim to be presented orally" (133). But the written text, with the exception of a few playwrights with a dense literary style like Aeschylus, remained until Shakespeare's time little more than a simple

outline for performance, not a great deal more complicated than
the plots that the *commedia 'dell 'arte* players tacked to the wing
of the stage.

Puttenham in his *Arte of English Poesie* speaks with scorn of
the rude language of the people "in any uplandish village or
corner of a Realme, where is no resort but of poore rusticall or
uncivill people" (150). From such a place did the Shakespeares
come, and to judge by their use of marks for signatures, both the
father and grandfather were illiterate. The better-born mother
may have been able to read, probably could, though female education in even the best families often did not extend to reading
and writing. But the son amassed an astounding, even a miraculous, writing vocabulary. As recorded in the *Harvard Concor-
dance*, the Shakespearean oeuvre, a total of 884,647 words,
(680,755 in verse, 203,892 in prose) uses 29,066 different words.
A use vocabulary of twenty-nine thousand words, along with the
elegant intricacies of phrasing and complex grammatical turns
characteristic of Shakespeare, are the marks of a *writer* rather
than of a *speaker*, and, despite the fact that only half his plays,
though all his poems, were published in his lifetime, ought to
end conclusively the often-heard argument that he is primarily
an oral poet.

The richness of this "great feast of language," to use Shakespeare's own phrase from his language play, *Love's Labour's Lost*,
can only be appreciated in comparison with other great poets.
Of the founding poets of the Renaissance, Dante has 101,499
occurrences in his *Commedia*, 13,770 of which are received
words used more than once (lemmata), while 1,052 words appear
only once (hapax legomena), among which are a number of coin-
ages. Petrarch in the *Canzoniere* has 57,635 occurrences, with a
vocabulary composed of 3,284 words used more than once and
1,207 used only once. Shakespeare's contemporary, the playwright and poet Christopher Marlowe, himself, like his heroes,
a "mighty man of words," used a total of 148,337 words, with a
total vocabulary of 11,448, and, startlingly, hapax legomena of
5,074. Marlowe, of course, wrote far fewer works than Shakespeare, but a comparison made possible by the new computer-
ized Marlowe and Shakespeare concordances shows that had
Shakespeare written the same number of words as Marlowe, he
would, based on the frequency with which different words appeared in his own work, have shown a total vocabulary of 12,744
in contrast to Marlowe's actual 11,448, making him a mightier

man of words than the "dead shepherd" remembered in *As You Like It* for his "saw of might."

If we would like to know what the king and his courtiers thought of the Shakespeare plays performed before them, it would be still more fascinating to know what Shakespeare, half in the theater, half in the study, expected from his audience when his plays were taken up to court. The evidence is indirect, but the playwright has left us a number of dramatic comments on playing in the palace, all of which show disappointment with the conduct and the interpretive skills of audiences in oral performance.

There are internal plays in *The Taming of the Shrew* and *Love's Labour's Lost*, but the full Shakespearean scheme of playing in an aristocratic setting does not appear until *A Midsummer Night's Dream* where a stage-audience made up of the Duke of Athens, Theseus, and his bride, the Amazon queen Hippolyta, sit, along with two other just-married couples, at a wedding celebration in the palace watching a company of artisans turned players. These amateurs, hoping to please the duke and gain a pension of six pence a day for life, put on the "tedious brief scene" and the "very tragical mirth" of *Pyramus and Thisbe*. The play is as bad as can be, "not one word apt, one player fitted," but Theseus having been present at many an awkward public performance given by the common people in his honor has learned the importance of what he calls "noble respect," the necessity of giving "thanks for nothing," and taking "what poor duty cannot do. . . . in might, not merit" (5.1.91). Noble respect substitutes the imagination of the aristocratic audience for the deficiencies of the players, recognizing that "the best in this kind are but shadows; and the worst are no worse, if imagination amend them" (5.1.211).

But despite Theseus's generous intentions, he and the other members of the court audience are more than a little deficient in the needed imagination at the performance. They chatter away, exchange witticisms about the ineptitude of the amateur players, and preen their own sense of social and intellectual superiority. For the Athenian courtiers plays are only a source of amusement, not to be taken very seriously, a way of passing the time until they go to bed and beget heirs for their noble houses. They see nothing in the play, though it has much to say to them, for all its foolishness, about the deficiencies of the imagination from which all of them, not only the players, suffer.

It is in *Hamlet*, however, that Shakespeare offers his most extended comments on the gap between the play as written and the audience at court. The 1601 play was not written specifically for James, though it was performed for him in 1603 on the occasion of his first Christmas in England, but its commentary on the inadequacy of the court audience to the meaning of the play, fitted the Stuart court as well as the Tudor. The players in *Hamlet* are, like the King's Men, a professional troupe, from the city of Wittenberg, not London, cut down to six players in order to travel. The Wittenberg troupe arrives at Elsinore, even as the King's Men came to Hampton Court, to perform before the king and queen and the Danish court with a repertory that includes a very literary play on Dido and Aeneas and another on a sensational murder in Vienna, *The Murder of Gonzago*. The players are servants and are so treated by the king's principal secretary, Polonius. When he is commanded by Hamlet to see them "well bestow'd" and "well us'd," he remarks testily that he "will use them according to their desert," implying that their status is not very high.

The heir apparent, Prince Hamlet, has visited the company's theater in the city many times, getting to know the actors and their repertory, even getting many lines from their plays by heart. He greets them warmly: "You are welcome, masters, welcome all. I am glad to see thee well. Welcome good friends" (2.2.4–21). He jokes familiarly with the boy playing female parts about his voice breaking, and twits one of the younger players about his new beard, "Oh old friend! why, thy face is valanc'd since I saw thee last; com'st thou to beard me in Denmark?" (2.2.422). Hamlet is a theater buff, like one of the young lords or lawyers from the Inns of Court who sat on the stage in the London public theaters, or in the gallery boxes above the stage, and commented learnedly and wittily on the action. Like them, too, he professes the latest neoclassical aesthetic standards and looks down on the popular theater's crudity, its ranting tragedians, melodramatic acting styles—parts "to tear a cat in"—bombastic blank verse, "inexplicable dumb shows," vulgar clowns, and the crude audience of groundlings who stand in the pit.

Despite the familiarity of the prince, the actors know their place. Hamlet jokes with them, but not they with him. They are deferential and quietly agreeable to the courtiers, though Hamlet has to warn the leading player not to mock Polonius behind his back. The players say little, but listen attentively—though they change nothing—when the prince lectures them about his sophisticated views of art, more suitable to the printed text than to the theater—"suit the action to the word, the word to the action . . . o'erstep not the modesty of nature" (3.2.17)—and of play construction—"well digested in the scenes, set down with as much modesty as cunning" (2.2.439). They humor him, and when he recites some lines from a speech in the Dido and Aeneas play that he has particularly liked, the players tactfully applaud his delivery. And when Hamlet asks for a performance the next evening—"We'll ha't tomorrow night"—of *The Murder of Gonzago,* they are ready to perform and can easily manage—"Ay, my lord"—the dozen or sixteen lines which Hamlet "would set down and insert in't."

The players, however deferential to the prince, are still popular entertainers, but with high-culture literary pretensions. Their Dido play is "caviary to the general," and the other item in their repertory, *The Murder of Gonzago,* may contain such primitive theatrical devices as a vice, morality-play structure, and dumbshow, but at its center are a number of long and sonorous speeches, usually cut in performance, which obviously originated in an author's pen. The plays that the actors bring to Wittenberg are, like Shakespeare's own plays, odd mixtures of sensational stage fare and highly wrought verse more suitable for the printed page than for the rough-and-ready world of public performance.

In the end the players do "tell all," for *The Murder of Gonzago* holds the mirror up to the hidden crime, the murder of the old king by his brother, the present king, that is poisoning the Danish state. The Elsinore play fulfills the moral requirements of humanist theater, to please and to instruct, but the audience does not respond, as the theorists predicted, like

> guilty creatures sitting at a play [who]
> Have by the very cunning of the scene
> Been strook so to the soul, that presently
> They have proclaim'd ther malefactions.
>
> (2.3.589)

Claudius sees his murder staged, his conscience is pinched—"O, my offense is rank"—and he retreats to the chapel to pray. But there he quickly finds that he really cannot bear to give up his ill-gotten gains, either Queen Gertrude or Denmark—"My words fly up, my thoughts remain below" (3.4.97). Far from repenting his crime, he decides to commit another murder by sending Hamlet, now too dangerous to keep in Denmark, to England for execution.

The other members of the courtly audience, though the play speaks directly to their realities as well, are even less perceptive than Claudius. Ophelia knows so little of theater or anything else that she cannot puzzle out the obvious meaning of the dumbshow. Gertrude, who may or may not have known about the murder of her first husband by her second, fails to see, or ignores, the mirror of her own unfaithfulness held up to her by the player queen, "the lady doth protest too much, methinks." Even Hamlet, the theater expert, misses the point. He makes vulgar and loud remarks to other members of the audience, baits the actors, and criticizes the play while it is going forward. He interprets the play as if its only purpose were the political one of catching "the conscience of the king." In this it succeeds in the short but not the long run, and only through the most rudimentary part of the play, the dumbshow. Hamlet the sophisticated critic misses entirely the point of the long and formal exchange between the player king and queen that constitutes the major portion of The Murder of Gonzago. This scene shows "the very age and body of the time his form and pressure" in a long exchange in which the queen assures the king that she will never wed again if he should die, and he tells her in sonorous, lofty, very literary tones that though people intend what they swear, human passions change and human purposes weaken. Life goes on, and as it does, it carries people to places they never intended or expected:

> Our wills and fates do so contrary run
> That our devices still are overthrown,
> Our thoughts are ours, their ends none of our own.
>
> (3.2.211)

Closely read and interpreted in the intense Gutenberg fashion, the internal play tells of the helplessness of the human will in the undertow of fate. Everyone in Denmark, most especially Hamlet, is in the end pulled down by a fate that runs contrary to their wills, and Hamlet eventually comes to and phrases an understanding of this process when after his escape from the plot on his life and his direct encounter with death in the graveyard where Ophelia is being buried, he ceases struggling to shape destiny and accepts that "the readiness is all," since "If it be [now], 'tis not to come; if it be not to come it will be now; if it be not now, yet it [will] come" (5.2.220). This is very close to the meaning of the written text in the Murder of Gonzago, but Hamlet, like the rest of the audience, could not hear it in an oral performance in a highly charged public setting.

On the night of performance before the assembled court at Elsinore, the Wittenberg players, despite strains and interruptions, do their work like the professionals they are until the play is broken off by the rising of the agitated king and his call for lights. We hear no more of them and may assume that, like the King's Men so many times, they packed their costumes in their hampers and went off to play elsewhere. Their play had told all, but it was understood by no one and changed nothing.

Shakespeare claims in *Hamlet* a useful purpose for his new-style theatrical art, designed for both page and stage, and assigns it a place of dignity, however minor and subservient to other offices, in the life of the court. *Hamlet* is the Renaissance play, set in all the symbolic places of the palace on which the kingdom centered. Opening on the battlements, where the guard encounters and tries to question a ghost from beyond, the action moves on to the king's presence chamber where affairs of state are dealt with, through various private chambers and public areas, on to the great hall, set up for theatrical performance, and thence to the *prie-dieu* in the royal chapel, to the queen's bedroom, and on out of the palace at last to a field where a great army passes on the way to battle, to the burial ground, and back into the palace to the presence chamber, where the rest becomes silence. In these settings, the vital activities of the Renaissance court are carried out. The mounting of the guard, the dispatch of ambassadors, disposal of children, council, funeral, duel, warfare, marriage, coronation, and, among these other primary social rituals, theater.

Yet even as Shakespeare raises theater to the level of the other major institutions of the state, he recognizes that his extraordinary art mixing the energy of oral performance with the subtlety of the written word is not fully understood even by aristocratic intellectuals like Hamlet, and is altogether a blank to the other self-centered courtiers who watch it. The play may be the thing, but it seldom, if ever, catches the conscience of a king who was often "very weary before he came [to the theater] but much more wearied by it, and spoke many words of dislike."

Note

Material in this article later was used in *Shakespeare the King's Playwright, Theater in the Stuart Court, 1603–1613*, Yale University Press, 1995. Thanks are due the Yale Press for permission to use this material.

Works Cited

Bowen, Catherine Drinker. *The Lion and the Throne, The Life and Times of Sir Edward Coke (1552–1634)*. Boston, 1956.

Calendar of State Papers and Manuscripts Relating to English Affairs, Existing in the Archives and Collections of Venice and in other Libraries of North Italy. 35 volumes. Edited by Horatio Brown, et al. London Historical Manuscripts Commission, 1864.

Carleton, Sir Dudley. *Dudley Carleton to John Chamberlain, (1603–1624), Jacobean Letters*. Edited by Maurice Lee, Jr. New Brunswick, N.J., 1972.

Chamberlain, John. *The Letters of John Chamberlain*. 2 vols. Edited by N. E. McClure. Philadelphia, 1939.

Chambers, Sir Edmund K. *The Elizabethan Stage*. 4 vols. Oxford, 1923.

Harrington, Sir John. *Nugae Antiquae*. 2 vols. Edited by Thomas Park. London, 1804.

Mullinger, James Bass. *The University of Cambridge*. Cambridge, 1873.

Nichols, John, ed. *The Progresses, Processions, and Magnificent Festivities of King James the First*. 4 vols. London, 1828.

Ong, Walter J. *Orality and Literacy, the Technologizing of the Word*. (1982) London: Metheun, 1983.

Puttenham, George. *The Arte of English Poesie*. In Smith, G. Gregory. *Elizabethan Critical Essays*, 2 vols. Oxford, 1904, vol. 2.

Shakespeare, William. *The Riverside Shakespeare*. Edited by G. Blakemore Evans. Boston, 1972.

The Beautiful and the Merely Pleasing: Love, Art, and "The Jinnee in the Well Wrought Urn"

Patrick Colm Hogan

From his earliest writings, and well before the current fashions of Bahktin and Lacan, Father Walter Ong emphasized and elaborated the dialogic nature of speech. Each utterance—spoken, written, taped, encoded on a disk—is essentially intersubjective. Each word is dialogue, perhaps arrested for a time on an unread page, but always beginning with human subjectivity and always aiming toward it. Whether examining literature, religion, or broader issues of history and culture, Ong's work has repeatedly led us back to this: to be human is to be isolated, a consciousness alone seeking communion, but at the same time to be human is to be in dialogue—temporarily failed or temporarily successful—with what is other to this consciousness. To be human, then, is to speak, and to love. For speech is what allows dialogue and, when the aims are not merely practical, love is what sustains it; conversely, communion is the aim of non-pragmatic communication, and communication in some form is the necessary ground for communion.

One of Ong's most illuminating, influential, and beautiful comments on literature—his 1954 essay, "The Jinnee in the Well Wrought Urn"—places the work of literature firmly in this context. He stresses "the sense of communication which rides through the contemplation of a work of art" (18) and conjectures that "the impulse to produce a work of fine art simply cannot arise except within a framework of personal give-and-take, a you-me situation" (20), even if that situation is merely a goal, an idea in the mind of an isolated writer. Because of this, we confuse works of art with people, ultimately with the men and women who create them: "In proportion as the work of art is capable of being taken in full seriousness, it moves further and further along an asymptote to the curve of personality"; as a result, "each work of art is not only an object but a kind of surrogate for a person" (24). "We consider here the case not of passing attention, serious and protracted and repeated. Contemplation of this sort," Ong tells us, "involves love" (20).

In making these observations, Ong's aim is to explain the persistence of personalism—the subjugation of the work of art to the personality of its creator, the substitution of biography for critical interpretation. Personalism is, and will remain persistent, Ong argues, for "in the last analysis, as a matter of full, serious, protracted contemplation and love, it is unbearable for a man or woman to be faced with anything less than a person" (25). However, I should like to consider Ong's insights in another context. Reinterpreted in light of Sanskrit aesthetics, this link between love and art provides, I shall argue, a solution to a central problem in aesthetic theory: the demarcation of the aesthetic from the merely pleasing. This difference has been stressed by many aestheticians, most famously Immanuel Kant (see sections 2 and 3 of *The Critique of Judgement*), and such followers of Kant as Samuel Taylor Coleridge (see "Essay Third" in *On the Principles of Genial Criticism*). Perhaps it was most succinctly formulated by Norman Holland when he asked: "How does the aesthetic pleasure of a poem differ from the simple sensuous pleasure of a well-mixed martini?" (202). Put very simply, and somewhat inaccurately, it is my view that the aesthetic is distinguished from the merely pleasing insofar as it is akin to love. More exactly, aesthetic feeling is not the *emotion* or, as Sanskrit aestheticians would say, the *bhava* of love; rather it is what these aestheticians would refer to as the *sentiment* or *rasa* of love, a sentiment which is, of course, closely related to the emotion, but not identical.

Sanskrit aesthetic theory focuses on the feelings of the spectator or reader. Though neglected by western aestheticians and literary critics, it is, in my view, one of the most valuable theories available for understanding the subtleties of literary response. At its basis is the notion that, in reading a literary work (or, more commonly, seeing a play), the spectator does not experience the emotions depicted in the work—love, fear, sorrow, etc.—but rather experiences something closely associated with them: sentiments such as the erotic, terrible, and pathetic. The distinction is difficult to articulate, but experientially clear. When watching a play about love, we do not actually love the hero or heroine, or the actors playing these roles. But, if the play is successful we do have a sort of intimation of love. When watching a play about terror, we do not actually fear the villain. But we do have an intimation of fear. That intimation is rasa or sentiment.

Though Bharata-muni, Abhinavagupta, and others do not develop the point in this way, the concept of a sentiment may perhaps be defined best in terms of central and peripheral properties of emotions. In our internal lexicon—the "dictionary" each of us has as a part of our mental make-up—we organize concepts into hierarchies such that the more definitionally crucial elements come first, followed by a series of secondary or tertiary beliefs, associations, and so on. (For a nontechnical introduction to the internal lexicon, see Aitchinson.) For example, we may believe that bachelors are slovenly at home or carefree about their personal lives. But clearly these are lower-level beliefs, the highest, "definitional" level being occupied by the idea that bachelors are unmarried men. The same structure holds for emotions. And here, as elsewhere, the hierarchy of beliefs about the emotions parallels a hierarchy of properties of the emotions. Love, anger, fear, and so on, all have properties which we consider definitive, along with a series of associated or less central properties. The central properties of an emotion are typically those which relate it to a real or putatively real person, situation, and so on. The peripheral properties concern the tone of feeling, various ancillary concerns and behaviors, and so on.

The relation between emotions and sentiments is similar to that between terms used literally and terms used metaphorically. Metaphors are, in part, terms used in such a way as to activate certain secondary meanings while blocking central meanings. If I refer to a tall person as a giraffe, I am isolating a single secondary property (height), while blocking the more centrally definitive properties (e.g., non-human animal). Sentiment or rasa may be understood as the production in a person of certain secondary properties of an emotion without at least some of the central properties.

In the case of art, the blocked central properties are frequently those which relate the emotion to a real object. However, this is not to say that sentiment has no object. Rather, it is to say that the object of a given sentiment is in some way inappropriate. Typically, it is inappropriate in being unreal, fiction. The recognition that the object is unreal, so to speak, severs the sentiment from the central properties of the emotion. To take a very simple example, the object of fear is a threatening situation. Fear centrally involves a number of properties, including behaviors such as flight. The object of the corresponding sentiment is fictional, and (unself-consciously) recognized as such by, say, audience members. (If it is not recognized as fictional, disaster will result in the theater.) Thus, when encountering an appropriate fictional situation, audience members may experience an increased heart rate, a rush of adrenalin, and other elements of fright, but they will not believe that they are in danger—in other words, they will discount the reality of the object—and, therefore, they will not flee.

All the sentiments isolated by Sanskrit writers—the erotic, terrible, pathetic, comic, furious, and so on—take objects within the fictional world of the literary work or are otherwise evoked by elements within the work. However, in addition to the sentiment that we experience through a work, we may have another sentiment which takes the work itself as object. It is my contention that when the sentiment of love takes a thing—whether a poem, a sonata, a mountain range, or a human face—as its object, then we have aesthetic experience. Thus the difference between aesthetic enjoyment and mere pleasure is that *aesthetic feeling is the sentiment of love;* mere pleasure is not.

Note that, unlike the other cases in which sentiments operate, the object here is perfectly real. Poems, sonatas, and human bodies are not themselves fictional. However, they are inappropriate objects of love—which takes us back to one of Ong's central points: love is aimed at subjects. Even a human body is not a subject, and it is our awareness of this that makes our aesthetic experience of a tragedy, or a face, or a river, into an experience of sentiment rather than emotion. On the other hand, as Ong indicates, this sentiment is always unstable, always inclined to seek an appropriate object, and thus to become full love—love of the tragedian, love of the person with the beautiful face—rather than remaining the truncated love of aesthetic sentiment.

There is a long tradition linking beauty with love. In the *Symposium*, Plato saw the feeling of love and the feeling of beauty as closely related. Both Burke and Kant saw them as causally linked (see, for example, Kant 108; sec. 10 of Burke). More recently, Mary Mothersill has written that, while "[n]ot everything is possible; for example, getting married and living happily ever after with a novel is not"; nonetheless, "falling in love" seems "literal and non-hyperbolic in its application to aesthetic response. . . . The question is," she concludes, "worth further study" (274). However, here and elsewhere (see, for example, Brown 26 and Sircello 5), aestheticians have recognized the similarity without being able to develop and understand it, primarily

because they failed to recognize the difference between sentiment and emotion, and to note that aesthetic feeling falls under
the former category, love under the latter.

What then is love? Or, more exactly, what is romantic love—
for aesthetic feeling is akin to the feeling of a lover, more than,
say, a parent or a child or a friend (though elements of these
enter, just as they do in romantic love itself). Perhaps the most
central properties of romantic love are: 1) a feeling of pleasure
associated with the object—or, more exactly, a feeling of that
particular form of pleasure defined by love; 2) a consequent desire for the welfare of the object; and 3) a desire for the reciprocation of both the preceding feeling and the preceding desire. The
desire for reciprocity is crucial, and, to some extent, one's feelings of love are contingent upon a sense of reciprocity. Clearly,
this is the feature of love most thoroughly suppressed in the
sentiment of aesthetic feeling. There can be no question of a
poem, a chorale, even a body reciprocating our love—and this is
why personalism is so enduring: we love the poem, but hate the
aloneness of such love.

Concern for the welfare of the object is, in contrast, carried
over from love into aesthetic feeling; we do not want a play to
be lost (or become unavailable), and landscape to be ruined by
construction, a body to lose its form. However, this feature is not
of great interest to the Kantian dilemma, for this concern applies
also to objects which we find merely pleasing: we do not want
gum to lose its taste. There is not even a difference in degree
here. Sex, for example, may very well be merely pleasing, but
most people would respond quite strongly to a threat of lost sex,
perhaps more strongly than to the threat of a lost novel.

Oddly, Kant recognizes the importance of this concern with
respect to the pleasing, but claimed that it was absent in genuine
judgments of beauty. As Kant put it, "when the question is if a
thing is beautiful, we do not want to know whether anything
depends or can depend on the existence of the thing" (38). Of
course, what Kant had in mind is that, for example, in making
an aesthetic judgment about a play, the producer should not be
considering whether or not he or she will profit from the performance. But by the same token, in judging whether or not one
finds the food at a business dinner pleasing, one should not be
considering whether or not the guests will sign a new contract
with one's firm. Kant's demarcation criterion, then, seems entirely irrelevant.

The specific feeling of "love-pleasure" is perhaps the most crucial feature of aesthetic feeling—for this is what we feel when we find a poem or a skyline or a dance beautiful. But in some ways it is the least informative, the feature least theoretically valuable to identify, for it is the least articulable. Presumably, we all know that the feeling of pleasure in being around one's beloved is different from the feeling of pleasure in escaping danger, in seeing one's enemies skewered, or in hearing a good joke. However, I at least find myself incapable of describing that feeling, except in these indirect terms. The same inarticulateness prevents me from describing the experience of aesthetic feeling. Thus, I can only indicate the two and note, but not present, their similarity.

On the other hand, this similarity is associated with a range of other concerns and behaviors, which are descriptively isolable, and which effectively characterize aesthetic feeling. Perhaps the most obvious is the complete absorption of the lover in the beloved. In love, the beloved becomes the center of pleasurable attentions, the rest of the world diminishing to insignificance. As Sartre put it, the beloved is not "seen on the ground of the world as a 'this' among other 'thises,' but the world [is] revealed in terms of [him or her]" (481). In connection with this, the lover conceives of the beloved as unique, irreplicable. This sense of uniqueness involves a careful and caring attention to the beloved—what Leila Tov-Ruach calls "formative attentive regard" (468)—particularly an affection for those details which render him or her unique. Considering the beloved to be unique is, in this way, not a purely abstract commitment; it involves a very palpable dwelling on his or her words, thoughts, and actions. Indeed, often something minute, seemingly insignificant— a turn of phrase, a typical gesture—crystallizes the lover's delight by becoming exemplary of the beloved's uniqueness.

This affectionate absorption is not only to be found in aesthetic experience; it is, according to such writers as Abhinavagupta, its necessary condition. In order to experience *rasa*, we must remove ourselves from the ordinary pragmatic attitude toward the world and adopt, rather, what Amaladass calls the "*dhvani* attitude" (117), an attitude of receptiveness to the *dhvani* or suggestiveness of the work. Suggestiveness is the ability of a work to communicate noncentral meanings and semantic associations and its related ability to evoke the noncentral feelings and associations of *rasa*. Clearly, this potential in a work is actualized only by a reader, viewer, and so on; it is part of a dialogue, as Ong would put it. Moreover, it is actualized only when the reader or viewer is "savoring" the work, dwelling on its details. As Abhinavagupta put it, "Aesthetical experience takes place, as everyone can notice, by virtue, as it were, of the squeezing out of the poetical word. Persons aesthetically sensitive, indeed, read and taste many times over the same poem. In contradiction to practical means of perception, that, their task being accomplished, are no more of any use and must then be abandoned, a poem, indeed, does not lose its value after it has been comprehended" (xxxii).

Moreover, this savoring focuses on the uniqueness of the object. Though it is commonplace to assert that a concern for novelty in art is purely western, in fact all cultures prize unique variation within certain bounds. One culture, historical period, class, or individual may prefer more variation or less; what one group counts as uniqueness, another may count as mere repetition or wild extravagance. But all value uniqueness in some way. Our attention to a poem, for example, involves a careful lingering over everything that sets it apart. Aesthetic experience is a dwelling on each word, the sound, the phrasing, the idea, the implication, or on line or color, on movement or gesture, depending on the art—but in all cases, precisely the sort of detail the lover dwells on in the beloved.

Indeed, in responding to beauty, we also tend to focus on specific details which we take to be particular markers of uniqueness, a curve, a shadow, an image or metaphor or striking phrase, some unique "twist" as Kuntaka called it. Let me illustrate with a personal example—all examples of this are, of course, necessarily personal—a photograph by Ralph Gibson. On the right, in the foreground, we see a guitar, and a man's right hand moving in a slight blur across the strings. Behind the man is a crib, and behind the crib an open door. A child's left hand reaches, barely visible, above the edge of the crib. When I see this photograph, I focus immediately on the child's hand. It is not that the hand in and of itself is beautiful. But without it, the photograph would be banal. With it, the photograph is beautiful. For another viewer, this same detail might make the photograph sentimental; another might find it of no interest either way. I do not mean to indicate that we will all have the same preferences. But we will all lavish our aesthetic attentions on details of this sort.

Perhaps the point will be clearer with a literary example, which we can see and vary. When I read Sappho's lines on seeing Brochea, "A thin fire / runs over my flesh," I dwell upon the thinness of the fire. For me, that detail is delightful, and there is an enormous aesthetic difference between the line as it stands and "A fire / runs over my flesh." Again, not everyone will choose this detail, or even find this line particularly beautiful. But everyone will find some things particularly beautiful and will link that beauty to exemplary details of some sort. In the same way, a lover might focus on a typical phrase, a slight turn of the lip, a gesture, but always some special marks, intimations of difference not delightful in themselves, but details of the beloved, thus a source of delight without which the beloved would be diminished. The same details might provoke indifference or even repulsion in another.

This last point brings us to the issue of evaluation. We tend to think of both love and beauty as good, and the merely pleasing as bad or indifferent. In illustrating the distinction between the aesthetic and the pleasing by reference to a poem and a martini, Holland reenforces this valuative hierarchy, as I did in citing sculpture and chewing gum. However, this is not in and of itself a hierarchized distinction. Someone may find a bombing raid aesthetic and a piece of fruit merely pleasing. Moreover, as this indicates, aesthetic feeling is not in and of itself less conformist or more self-reflective than mere pleasure. Here again, beauty is akin to love—and, we might add, mere pleasure is akin to the (non-amorous) enjoyment of another person. Though we tend to conceive of love as morally good and enjoyment of persons as morally neutral, someone may love Hitler, which is not, I imagine, ethically preferable to enjoying the company of Mother Theresa. Moreover, despite the lover's focus on the uniqueness of the beloved, love, too, is not particularly nonconformist or self-reflective. Indeed, as Soble points out, "love explains why the lover treats the beloved as unique, rather than uniqueness explaining love" (49). Horkeimer and Adorno make precisely the same point about the culture industry, tacitly referring to aesthetic feeling: "Not only are the hit songs, stars, and soap operas cyclically recurrent and rigidly invariable types, but the specific content of the entertainment itself is derived from them and only appears to change" (125).

On the other hand, there is one way in which love and aesthetic feeling are linked with moral goodness, unlike mere pleasure and enjoyment of a person. Specifically, we tend to conceive of the capacity to love and the capacity to experience beauty as admirable character traits (on love, see Brown 124ff; on beauty, see Kant 108). We do not, in contrast, see an ability to experience pleasure as in any way linked with goodness of character. In the case of beauty, this valorization is less pronounced in the west than in less puritanical traditions, though it is to be found in the commonplace that literature humanizes by training our feelings to sympathy. In the Indian tradition, however, the connection is stronger and more obvious. The man or woman who can truly experience beauty is the *sahrdaya*, the one "with heart," the one who can empathize, who can truly bring about the dialogue which is essential to art. While Anandavardhana and Abhinavagupta do not explicitly connect this aesthetic capacity with a capacity for love, the similarities are clear in their writings and elsewhere. (Though, of course, none of this implies that aesthetic sensitivity actually does incline one to increased human sympathy; indeed, this appears to be false, as, for example, George Steiner has argued [see Steiner 61–62]. The point is that we conceive of them in parallel as excellences of character.)

A further property shared by love and aesthetic feeling is closely related to this. Through love and through beauty, we seek unity (I take this to be obvious for love; on beauty, see Milner 131–32). Literary art is not, as for example Robert Scholes implies (26), an analogue of orgasmic sex. That is the merely pleasing—not unity, but forgetting of the self and thus an occlusion of separation. Both love and art aim at a mingling of what cannot help but be separate worlds, isolated souls which really are unbreachably alone, "persons who, in their deep interiors where no other creature can enter, are cut off clean from the rest of the world," as Ong puts it (24–25). This mingling is only symbolized, and necessarily never achieved, by sexual congress. It is this feeling of unity that Abhinavagupta noted when he stressed that the final state of aesthetic experience should be peace, *santi*, and is analogous to union with God in enlightenment (see Gnoli, quoting Abhinavagupta, xxxviii–xlv). Similarly, when Margaret Atwood wrote at the end of a love poem, "I would like to be the air / that inhabits you for a moment / only. I would like to be that unnoticed / & that necessary" (77), she could not have failed to intend a link between her breath speaking this poem and the breath of her beloved reading this poem. Eight centuries earlier, Li Ch'ing Chao expressed this connection more directly when she wrote of a sleepless night after the death of her husband: "I try / To write a poem in which / My tears will flow together / With your tears" (96).

Because they strive for unity, both love and aesthetic feeling can accommodate pain. We can love a person who hurts us or whose suffering hurts us, or find beauty in a work of art that makes us weep. There are limits to this, of course. But the merely pleasing cannot accommodate pain at all. Except in cases of perversion, where the pain is itself a form of pleasure, we are pleased only by what is pleasing. The merely pleasing is not part of something greater—pleasure is consumed in itself. As Kant put it: "everything that pleases is pleasant because it pleases" (40). In contrast, Kant tells us, there is an entire realm of aesthetic feeling, the "sublime," in which "a pleasure . . . is only possible through the medium of a pain" (99). Both love and aesthetic feeling can incorporate displeasure as part of a striving for unity, a unity (temporarily) resulting in peace, in *santi*.

Given this, it is not surprising that love and aesthetic feeling may be causally connected as well. It is a commonplace that love can make us see the ugly as beautiful; the phrase "he or she has a face that only a mother could love" means that only the complete love of a mother could make one think of that face as beautiful—"love" being used here to refer to aesthetic feeling. Conversely, beauty is all too often the source of love. Each leads to the other.

This last point returns us to the issue raised by "The Jinnee in the Well Wrought Urn." Ong points out that our "plenary attention" to or savoring of the work of art inspires love, and thus turns our focus to the author, away from the text. He goes on to say that this is inevitable, and thus that personalism will persist. But why is this the case? Because art, once again, is dialogue. And dialogue brings a concern for reciprocity. And reciprocity is precisely the element which differentiates love from aesthetic feeling. The fact that human interaction is inevitably dialogue necessarily pushes aesthetic feeling toward a desire for reciprocity, thus toward love, thus toward personalism.

I have been seeking here to develop one of Ong's many insights in order to work out some of its implication for issues and conundrums which he himself did not address. Having done this, I should like to conclude by recurring to personalism myself. Over many decades, Father Ong has been an inspiring humanist in both theory and practice. He has not only analyzed and advocated dialogue, but he has engaged in it continually. Certainly, the preceding reflections are an attempt to continue a dialogue begun, brilliantly, by Ong; one of many he has begun in print, with erudition, insight, and wisdom over many years. But I am not referring only to the suspended dialogues of print. As generations of student have learned, Ong's teaching is an ongoing dialogue. Not in the common and false sense that he believes "everyone is entitled to his/her own opinion." Rather, in the sense that Ong sought to have students engage with him in rigorous thought and analysis. When I characterized dialectical pedagogy in *The Politics of Interpretation*, I drew on writing of Lacan in order to place the characterization within a psychoanalytic framework, but my primary model for the teaching itself was Father Ong.

The preceding essay, like everything else human, is then part of dialogue, and tainted by personalism. It is in part a gesture of reciprocation, not only to the dialogue of "The Jinnee in the Well Wrought Urn," but to the much larger dialogue of Ong's teaching, of which his essay is merely a small, crystallized part.

Works Cited

Abhinavagupta. *The Aesthetic Experience According to Abhinavagupta*. Edited and translated by Raniero Gnoli. 2d ed. Varanasi: The Chowkhamba Sanskrit Series Office, 1968.

Aitchison, Jean. *Words in the Mind: An Introduction to the Mental Lexicon*. Oxford: Basil Blackwell, 1987.

Amaladass, Anand., S.J. *Philosophical Implications of Dhvani: Experience of Symbol Language in Indian Aesthetics*. Vienna: Publication of the De Nobili Research Library, 1984.

Anandavardhana. *The Dhvanyaloka of Anandavardhana with the Locana of Abhinavagupta*. Translated by Daniel Ingalls, Jeffery Masson, and M. V. Patwardhan; edited by Daniel Ingalls. Cambridge: Harvard University Press, 1990.

Atwood, Margaret. "Variation on the Word *Sleep*." In *Selected Poems II: Poems Selected and New 1976–1986*. Boston: Houghton Mifflin, 1987.

Bharata-Muni. *The Natyasastra*. Vol. 1. 2d ed. Translated by Manomohan Ghosh. Calcutta: Granthalaya, 1967.

Brown, Robert. *Analyzing Love*. Cambridge: Cambridge University Press, 1987.

Burke, Edmund. *A Philosophical Inquiry into the Origin of Our Ideas of the Sublime and the Beautiful*. Edited by J. T. Boulton. New York: Columbia University Press, 1958.

Gnoli, Raniero. "Introduction." In Abhinavagupta, *The Aesthetic Experience According to Abhinavagupta*. Edited and translated by Raníero Gnoli. 2d ed. Varanasi: The Chowkhamba Sanskrit Series Office, 1968.

Hogan, Patrick Colm. *The Politics of Interpretation: Ideology, Professionalism, and the Study of Literature*. New York: Oxford University Press, 1990.

Holland, Norman. *The Dynamics of Literary Response*. New York: Norton, 1975.

Horkheimer, Max and Adorno, Theodor. *Dialectic of Enlightenment*. Translated by John Cumming. New York: Continuum, 1986.

Kant, Immanuel. *Critique of Judgement*. Translated by J. H. Bernard. New York: Hafner, 1951.

Kuntaka. *The Vakrokt-Jivita of Kuntaka.* Edited and translated by K. Krishna-moorthy. Dharwad: Krishnatak University, 1977.

Li Ching Chao. "Alone in the Night." In *One Hundred Poems for the Chinese,* translated and edited by Kenneth Rexroth. New York: New Directions, 1971.

Milner, Marion. *On Not Being Able to Paint.* New York: International University Press, 1957.

Ong, Walter J., S.J. "The Jinnee in the Well Wrought Urn." In *The Barbarian Within and Other Fugitive Essays and Studies.* New York: Macmillan, 1972.

Sartre, Jean-Paul. *Being and Nothingness.* Translated by Hazel Barnes. New York: Washington Square, 1966.

Scholes, Robert. *Fabulation and Metafiction.* Urbana: University of Illinois, 1979.

Sircello, Guy. *Love and Beauty.* Princeton: Princeton University Press, 1990.

Soble, Alan. *The Structure of Love.* New Haven: Yale University Press, 1990.

Steiner, George. *Language and Silence: Essays on Language, Literature, and the Inhuman.* New York: Atheneum, 1967.

Tov-Ruach, L. "Jealousy, Attention and Loss." In *Explaining Emotions,* edited by A. O. Rorty. Berkeley: University of California Press, 1980.

Breaking the Ice: Some Highlights of the History of *Humor* and *Sense of Humor*

Sr. Anne Denise Brennan, SC

In the making and meaning of words: a companion to the dic-*tionary*, George Henry Valins states that no group of words shows a more "interesting" change in meaning than "those terms adopted into the modern language from the vocabulary of medieval medicine" of which *humor* is the most important (71). Despite Valins's claim, it is difficult to find a systematic and detailed account of the change. Thus, this essay focuses on the eighteenth and nineteenth centuries as dictated by evidence of change in the use of *humor* and the appearance of *sense of humor* during this period, as indicated by comparative studies of various dictionaries and the citations under *humor* in the *OED*. Two works invaluable in accounting for these developments are Edward N. Hooker's "Humor in the Age of Pope" and Ian Watt's *The Rise of the Novel*. Walter Ong's studies of orality, literacy, and the development of consciousness underlie the entire presentation (1967a, 228 and 1982, 153).

Humor is not a simple term nor a simple concept. If, as Groom affirms, words are never used twice in exactly the same way (126), one can anticipate some problems in trying to pin down the meaning of any word. Despite humor's protean qualities (see Empson 252) and Paul Jennings's admonition that *humor* should not be defined (120), as well as Addison's declaration in the *Spectator* of 10 April 1711, that one might more easily say "what is not humor than what is" (Bond 146), it seems, however, that some understanding of the word and of the concept of humor can be managed. Cazamian extends hope when he notes that *humor* is frequently abused, but these unreliable meanings surround a sure center (146). In the essay "Humor et amour" in *Essais en deux langues*, Cazamian suggests how to come to this understanding: rely on usage more than on articulated theories.

In order to understand fully the changes in the usage of *humor* and to appreciate the significance of them, it is important to have some grasp of humor's roots. This, it seems, necessitates knowledge of three things: humoral pathology, humoral doctrine, and Ben Jonson's humoral theory, especially as these are understood in the seventeenth century, which is the background for the changes noted in the eighteenth century. To delineate these theories in detail is neither necessary nor appropriate. Walter Clyde Curry's *Chaucer and the Medieval Sciences* and Charles Read Baskervill's *English Elements in Johnson's Early Comedies* are both excellent sources. Donna Hurley, in her thesis "The Medical World of *Tristram Shandy*," provides insightful information of the humoral doctrine as the outgrowth of humoral pathology. Her account, using Bamborough's *The Little World of Man* (e.g., 22–23, 59), demonstrates the detailed and complicated nature of humoral pathology and the humoral doctrine, something frequently overlooked in discussions of this topic.

Affectations of humors, however, raise a question about the meaning of *humor*, especially related to Jonson's humoral theory. It seems appropriate here simply to remark upon the compatibility of these theories not only with the medical and psychological ideas of the seventeenth century, but also with the philosophical writings held in esteem at the time. For example, the humoral doctrine resonates with Plato's remarks on love in the *Symposium* and with Aristotle's theory of the mean and the extreme.

In its full cosmic scope, the humoral doctrine perceives the person in relation to the four elements and the consequent conditions of hot, cold, dry, and wet. The cosmic dimension and the inherent concern with balance and imbalance (e.g., Curry 10, 205) are the bases of the kinship with Plato and Aristotle.

In the *Symposium*, Plato has Eryximachos say:

> For the healing art, to put it shortly, is knowledge of the body's love for filling and emptying, and one who distinguishes the beautiful and ugly love in these things is the most complete physician; and one who makes them change, so that they get one love instead of the other, and, where there is no love when there ought to be, one who knows how to put it in, and to take out love that is in, he would be a good practitioner. You see, one must be able to make friends of the greatest enemies in the body. Now the greatest enemies are the most opposite, hot and cold, bitter and sweet, dry and wet, and so forth: our ancestor Asclepios, as our poets here say, and I believe, composed our art because he knew how to implement love and concord in these. (*Great Dialogues* 83)

In *The Nichomachean Ethics*, Aristotle states: "the equal is a mean between excess and deficiency. By 'the mean,' in the case of the thing itself, I mean that which lies at equal intervals from the extremes, and this mean is just one thing and is the same for everyone, but when related to us, it neither exceeds nor falls short (of what is proper to each of us), and this is neither just one thing nor the same for everyone" (B.5 1106a 27). Bamborough, in discussing the cosmological dimensions of the humoral doctrine, states clearly that a wise person can achieve control and affect the various planetary and lunar influences, thereby gaining the "Golden Mean," particularly by observing the rule: *Nosce te ipsum* (81).

Continuing in the *Nichomachean Ethics* Aristotle asserts: "Virtue, then is a kind of moderation, at least by having the mean as its aim" (B.5 1106b 28). In the same work, he suggests how to achieve the mean by leaning "sometimes in the direction of excess and sometimes in the direction of deficiency, for by doing so we shall most easily attain the mean and goodness" (B 1109b 34). One can only do this by knowing oneself. Failure to follow this dictum results in going to extremes. Baskervill equates Jonson's humors in *Cynthia's Revels* with Aristotle's extreme (28). Plato's name for this condition is "the ridiculous" as is evident in the dialogue between Socrates and Protarchus in "The Statesman Philebus" (333). Here Plato's reference to "the ridiculous" as a "vice" complements Aristotle's association of the mean, the achievement of balance, with virtue. Interestingly, Coleridge calls the devil the "extreme of all humor" (279). All of this is echoed in the humoral doctrine. There are *peccant* or *sinning* humors which *Stedman's Medical Dictionary* defines as "deranged fluids in the body" regarded as "the direct cause of various illnesses." Bamborough calls any deviation from normal "an illness" in some measure (61).

To the sophisticated twentieth-century reader, the humoral doctrine may seem somewhat naive, but, in the light of seventeenth-century medical, psychological, and philosophical knowledge, the Galenic doctrine is quite plausible (Jefferson 151). The *1773 London Catalogue of Books in All Languages Arts and Sciences . . . Printed in Great Britain since . . . 1700* lists twenty-two entries seemingly related to humoral pathology, including works on the motions of blood (126), bleeding (124), and bath waters (124–26, 130). It is also no wonder that as late as 1760, one finds in the *Index Medicus* the English translation of Quesnay's 1743 discourse to the Royal Academy of Surgery at Paris, the title of which includes: *concerning the vices of humors in which the doctrine of suppuration and various medical and*

chirugical subjects are considered, and experiments recom-
mended, to assist observation in the discovery of the nature,
causes and cure of diseases. Both of these listings indicate the
persistence of at least three important concepts associated with
humor: balance/imbalance; virtue/vice; the extreme and the ridiculous. In a sense they are reducible to fluidity/rigidity.

Against this background one must view the humoral theory
associated with Ben Jonson. Charles Read Baskervill's work includes a masterful chapter, "A Study of Humors" ([34]–75)
which details the theory. Baskervill neatly summarizes Jonson's
use of *humor* as expressing a trait of the inner man, but then
symbolizing it by "outward peculiarities and fashions that in
their turn naturally have the name humor applied to them" (36).
The fact that Jonson does not make equal use of these meanings
of *humor* (Snuggs 119) and the gradual disintegration of a world
view embracing the humoral pathology and humoral doctrine
underlying Jonson's usage of *humor* (Lauter 193), account, in
part, for the reservation of *humor* for the predominant characteristic rooted in nature, for affectation, or for a mere whim or ca-
price. Jensen reminds the reader that during the seventeenth
century the character himself or herself is often called "the humor" (5).

One thing seems clear. Throughout the century and into the
first half of the eighteenth, *humor* is integrally linked with Jonson's humoral theory and the ongoing interpretations of it. The
use of humor in the latter seventeenth century, however, seems
to follow the pattern of simple caricature, focusing on extremes
rather than the mean, on vice or oddity rather than on virtue or
the norm and concomitantly on the ridiculous. The change in
the *Zeitgeist* in the seventeenth century from the more organic,
cosmic, sin-conscious world of the Elizabethans to a courtly life
dedicated to the "ceremony of living" in which affectation becomes an end in itself (Baskervill 20), encourages the use of
humor for these ideas.

Dryden and Shadwell provide good examples of the continu-
ance of this trend. Jensen summarizes Dryden's use of *humor:* it
tends to mean "temperament" in the early and late years of Dryden's career [1631–1700]; most frequently it means "extravagance" or "whim"; it is also used synonymously with
"character" and even to signify a literary genre (61).

Although Dryden appreciates the naturalness of temperament
or humor as a distinguishing factor among individuals, he nonetheless defines *humor* as a "ridiculous extravagance of conversa-

tion" (116, 114). While Dryden stresses "eccentricity," Shadwell echoes Jonson's doctrine from *Every Man in His Humor* (1 576), but presents it in stronger terms in the epilogue to *The Humorists: A Comedy* written in 1671 (241; Jensen 61). Where Jonson simply says the "peculiar quality / doth so possess and draw," leaving, it seem, some possibility for change, Shadwell introduces "with violence," and seems to insist there can be no flexibility, for the will is bent to "**one** side **still**" and this is so in "**all** changes" (241; Jensen 61, emphasis added). For Shadwell, as for Dryden, then, an extreme condition is signified by *humor*, and a strong sense of rigidity is implied.

Shadwell is also very strong in associating humor with what pleases the audience, and that seems to be a recognition of commonality. In the preface to *The Humorist* he says: "For if a man should bring such humor upon the stage (if there be such a humor in the world) as only belongs to one or two persons, it would not be understood by the audience, but would be thought (for the singularity of it) wholly unnatural, and would be no jest to them neither" (186). Shadwell is not alone in this way of thinking. Schlegel suggests that in this period a shift occurs from "English National Comedy" to that of the town of London, with many writers producing "prescriptive fame pieces" (482–83). John Dennis's "A Large Account of the Taste in Poetry, and the Causes of the Degeneracy of It" gives some insight into the change in audiences and their demands from the time of Charles II until the turn of the century (231–37). Dennis claims that the audience in the reign of Charles II, an era "of Poetry and Pleasure" (233), had the leisure "to watch the turns and counter turns of . . . [h]umors, and to trace the windings of them up to their very springs" (235); whereas the later decades, which he calls "a reign of Politics and Business" (233), attract audiences too absorbed in these affairs to be attentive to "the just and harmonious symmetry [sic] of a beautiful design" (237).

Audiences coming primarily to "unbend" (Dennis 237), like many modern television viewers, are satisfied, indeed demand, typicality in the plots and characters presented for their entertainment. The rather large number of banal and stereotypic television situation comedies currently broadcast weekly proves this point. It is easy for writers to slip into simply supplying for demand, although they may claim to be creating in a particular genre, mode, or school. Imitators of Jonson's humor theory fall victim to this. Kerr accuses even the great Beaumont, Fletcher, and Shirley of being influenced by the public; she does, however, distinguish between these and later writers who purport to follow Jonson "more loosely," but who actually do so "less wisely" (121), spawning a spate of repetitive types (122). Dennis attributes this reduction to the accommodation of writers to the humors of the town, meaning the presence in society not of "originals," but mere "coxcombs" affecting certain political and social stances (235).

In commenting on the preponderance of types existing into the mid-eighteenth century, Schlegel suggests the reason is the inability of many lesser writers to seize the "hidden and involuntary emotions" of characters and the resulting contentment with showing surfaces (480, 482). Kerr suggests that part of the reason for the numerous type characters is an inherent danger in Jonson's humor theory (124). Lauter pinpoints this when he remarks that Jonson himself must have been aware of the compulsive, mechanical nature of humor-bound characters (112). It has been observed above, however, that Jonson's language is much milder than is Shadwell's.

It seems obvious that the changes in the *Zeitgeist* and an over-simplified understanding of the humoral doctrine underlying the humoral theory account for the number of types. Louise Turner Forest, in "A Caveat for Critics against Invoking Elizabethan Psychology" warns against seeing the predominant humor as deterministic (663). One of the results of a deterministic interpretation is the equation of *humor* with "mechanical people" (114). Hazlitt speaks of Jonson's characters as being "like machines" (40). Jensen, referring to Watson's work on Dryden, equates "Comedy of Humors" and "Mechanical Comedy" (5). Empson calls "a humor" a "mechanical toy" (85).

It is evident from this somewhat involved presentation that the use of *humor* in the seventeenth century and continuing into the first part of the eighteenth is very much connected with one's theory of characterization. Lauter remarks on the "loose" and "inconstant" use of the word *humor* during this period (193). We may conclude, however, that the term is used to denote several key concepts: temperament, still heavily rooted in physiology; an exaggerated state or eccentricity of character; an affectation; a whim; the character in whom any of these is found.

If the temper of an age is reflected in the objects of laughter in that age (see Gregory 87), it is accordingly reflected in the use of *humor*. The last years of the seventeenth century and the whole of the eighteenth century witness changes that are paralleled in the changes in the use of *humor* and which pave the way for the rise of *sense of humor*. Hooker's article, "Humor in the Age of Pope," presents these changes to mid-century. According to Hooker, the significant fact about *humor* in the early eighteenth century is not that it begins to enjoy its modern meaning (361), but that changes in its use indicate a new understanding of the relation of the individual to society (376). We know that seventeenth-century use often equates *humor* with character. Hook summarizes this usage into two principal ones: a person exhibiting a "singularity with deep emotional roots" or a person "whose fancies, like merry children scramble rowdily throughout the corridor of the soul's mansion where reason ought to prevail" (363; see also McKillop 103). Congreve, writing in 1695, analyzes the works of Jonson and identifies three types of character, reserving *humor* for one type only—those who, like Morose of the *Silent Woman*, exhibit "natural humor" (70).

By 1744, however, *humor* has come into its own, as evidenced by the title of Morris's *An Essay Fixing the True Standards of Wit, Humor, Raillery, Satire and Ridicule*. While not influential in the subsequent history of *humor*, Morris's essay is the most representative of theories and usage of the mid-eighteenth century (Tave 139; Clifford, 5). The two most significant points for the study of the change in *humor* are the separation in the use of *humorist* and *humor* and Morris's actual use of *humor*, which differs from his definitions and descriptions.

Morris's definition relates him to the humoral doctrine with the emphasis on "nature without any embellishment" (23), the oddities and foibles being found in the "temper or conduct of a person in real life" (12, xxv, 13). Unlike Congreve, however, Morris does admit to the inclusion of affected and temporary foibles under *humor* (23), thus carrying on the original theory of Jonsonian humor as presented by Snuggs. For the purposes of this essay, however, Morris's use of *humor* is of greater value than his definitions.

In the introduction to his essay, Morris presents an idea not formulated earlier by the writers already considered in this history. For Morris humor "is **derived from** the foibles, and whimsical oddities of persons in real life" (xxi, emphasis added). Morris's use of *humor* in this instance does not signify a "disposition" nor a "stimulus" eliciting a reaction, such as ridicule, but is itself the "response" (see Chapman and Foot, 1976, 3 for use of words; application to Morris's essay is that of this author). Morris also insists in his introduction that "mirth is not so properly the parent of humor, as the offspring." If mirth is derived from humor, which, for Morris, means the foibles and oddities of people, and if "humor" meaning "response" is derived from the same source, then *mirth* and *humor* are equatable (see xxi).

Reflecting the growing appreciation for individual differences and the concomitant change in the attitude of society toward persons "faithful to their individuating humors," humor as stimulus then elicits mirth rather than ridicule as a response, except in the cases of affectation (see Lauter 192). The word *humor* itself becomes synonymous with mirth and is used to refer to any situation, circumstance, or action eliciting a mirthful response. By extension it also signifies a genre characterized by benevolent presentation of the foibles of people perceived to be following their individual personal passions.

The emphasis on individuality brings a rejection of "types" in favor of "originals." Watt notes that the word *original* changes in the mid-eighteenth century from "existing from the first" to "underived, independent, first-hand" (14). These "originals," "humorists," "characters of humor" or "characters with humors" are much more "human" than the more mechanical and generic "humors of the times" or "humors of the town." Hazlitt, writing of this period in 1819, comments that during the reign of George II (1727–1760), "people become represented in books as well as in Parliament" (121). "Humor" becomes "human" and "humane." Ainger intuits this in pointing out the "jingle" between *humor* and *humane* and in stating that it is characters with "the human touch" that "delight" (236; see also 234 and "Laughter" 400). Kimmins is correct in claiming that the "humanization of laughter" grows along with "higher ideals in national life" (126). Some reflections on the changes in the *Zeitgeist* during the eighteenth century not only provide the background explanations for the change in *humor* from medicine to mirth, but serve as a base for understanding the phenomenon of the rise of *sense of humor* in the early Victorian age.

In speaking of literary patterns, Frederika Blanker suggests that they are records of social evolution analogous to the way Chladni figures in physics serve as graphs of the vibrations producing them (318–19). What is true of the work of art is true also of language (see Groom 185). "The difficulty," as Groom notes, "is to discover what features of a complex civilization bear more directly on the life of words" (185). Regarding the change in *humor*, the features more directly involved are those connected with the change in the relation of the individual to society, and the growing **acceptance** of rather than **ridicule** of those

who are, to use Morris's word, "characters" (see Hooker 369 and
Q. D. Leavis 124). From Hooker's account, it is clear that the
question of ridicule is being discussed at the time in both the
secular and the religious arenas and appreciation of the individual per se is found in both the religious and secular spheres.
Mudrick credits the rising industrialism of the eighteenth century and the dissipation of the "sacramental view of life" with
encouraging interest in the individual (212). Hooker posits that
"Puritanism and mercantilism [are] freeing the individual from
the old social responsibilities, and fixing divine approval upon
individual capitalism and the spread of Protestantism, especially
in its Calvinist or Puritan forms" (60). Williams reports the
change in *individual* from *indivisible* to *singular person* in connection with Adam Smith's *Wealth of Nations* 1776 (134–35).
As the source of the change, Watt recognizes the Reformation
and the rise of national states both threatening the "homogeneity
of Medieval Christendom" (61). That the roots of individualism
lie in the Renaissance is also suggested by Baskervill who sees
it reflected in the change from Chaucer's analysis of people by
class and trade to Jonson's emphasis on temperament with Aris-
totelian and Platonic interest in qualities in individuals (39–40).
This change from emphasis on the group to that of the individual
is reflected in the art and architecture of the Renaissance and
post-Renaissance worlds. Huizinga mentions that framed pictures replace murals; dwellings rather than churches and palaces
become the focus of architectural endeavors; drawing rooms and
bedrooms are of greater concern than galleries; chamber music
becomes popular, and eventually wigs frame faces as frames do
works of art (201, 184). The Acts of Enclosure of 1688, whereby
common land is permitted to be apportioned to private use
(Burke 144), also demonstrates the all-pervading nature of this
change.

By 1690, Temple equates humor with both particularity and
variety of life, claiming that the abundance of humor in English
is due to the remarkable variety of English life, especially the
climate and "ease" of government (198–99; Spingarn 73). The
residual humoral pathology is evident here. In 1695, Congreve
still—but barely—nods in this direction, stressing instead "freedom, privilege and liberty" (75; Spingarn 739) reflected even in
the landscaping of the gardens (see Malins vii, 24, ix).

Students of English history are well aware of the events in the
latter seventeenth century and first half of the eighteenth century
that demonstrate the rise of this liberalizing democratic spirit

to which both Temple and Congreve refer. With the spirit of democracy and the value of the commoner particularly achieved with the work of Sir Robert Walpole and William Pitt (see Thackeray, 1968, 325) comes the toleration and respect for the individual that bear upon the change in the use of humor.

Paralleling these events in the secular sphere are those in the religious realm. Ian Watt writing in his chapter "Robinson Crusoe, Individualism and the Novel" provides a comprehensive discussion of Protestantism's role in developing both religious and economic individualism (60–90). Of note for the purposes of the present study of humor, is the general tenor of Protestantism, especially of Evangelicals and Wesleyans; namely, the importance placed on each person's taking the primary responsibility for individual spiritual direction rather than relying on rules of a church as mediator between the self and God (Watt 74). This belief leads not only to "consciousness of the self as a spiritual entity," but also to a "democratization of the moral and social outlook" (Watt 74). Both Scholes and Kellogg (176) and Watt (74) point out that the roots of this subjective emphasis lie in primitive Christianity, but Watts also clearly asserts Calvin's role in re-establishing and systematizing it during the sixteenth century (75). Most popularly associated with the emphasis on the individual is private interpretation of the Bible (Burke 136). "Literacy" acquired in the home would need a vernacular text, the publication of the Authorized or King James Version in 1611, making just such a text available (Ong, 1971, 113–41, esp. 119–20).

Walter Ong situates the "sola scriptura" of Protestantism in the tides of the "sea of change" in attitude toward the word in the post-Gutenberg world (1967a, 262–86, esp. 272, 164). This is caused, essentially, by the change from "hearing dominance" to "sight dominance" (Ong, 1982, 117–138). The technology of print—writing itself is also a technology (1982, 81–2)—produces an analytic world vision, with its "quality of 'alienation,'" that allows for analytic confrontation (Burke 212). In the wake of the greater proliferation of printed matter, one finds the rise of empiricism and Newtonian revolution. Indeed, Ong calls print the "harbinger" of the latter (1954, 226). As print brings about the "reification of the word" (Ong, 1971, 162; 1967a, 229), the Newtonian emphasis on sight and surface leads to objectification of the universe and also of persons (1967a, 227–28). The earlier Baconian emphasis on the inductive method grows out of this same source (Watt 62). Referring to the works of Bacon, Hobbes, and Locke, Watt brings out the empiricist espousal of the cause of individualism: Bacon's method is used to ascertain information about individuals; Hobbes demonstrates in his writings a regard for the "fundamentally egocentric constitution of the individual"; and Locke insists on the indefeasibility of individual rights versus those of family, Church, and state (62). With these developments comes the loss of influence of the authority of the ancients and of faith with which Huizinga characterizes the seventeenth century (156; see also Ong 1954, 226).

The shift from orality to literacy, especially the rise of print seems, then, to underline the changes in attitude toward the individual and society, so evident in the sphere of science, the realm of religion, the rise of the democratic spirit. Kenneth Burke notes in this regard the passage of the Statute of Frauds (1677) marking the move from the simple "status" agreement to the "contract," that is, from "unwritten form" to "written legality" (144). Thus all the major reasons given for the change in the appreciation of the individual in relation to society which, as shown earlier, affect the concept and use of humor, can be allied to the underlying shift from "hearing dominance" to "sight dominance" accompanying the proliferation of print.

Before leaving this discussion of the shift from orality to literacy in the post-Gutenberg era, which sets the stage for the rise of *sense of humor*, it is important to suggest the connection between this occurrence and what can be said about "originals," "humorists," "characters of humor," and "characters with humor" on the one hand, and "comic humors" on the other. The former are "natural" as opposed to types, and although influenced to greater or lesser degrees by a predominant passion or humor, they are not determined by it; rather, they act in accord with the truth of their beings. "Comic humors" tend to be more mechanical, stereotypical, often affected, without depth and seemingly presenting less possibility of flexibility than the others. That the interest in "originals," "humorists," "characters of humor," or "characters with humor" should surface in the late seventeenth century seems also to reflect the shift from the more oral-aural world to one of sight and print. In the "private words" generated by reading and writing, "the feeling for the 'round' human character is born," such a character being also "deeply interiorized in motivation" and "powered mysteriously, but consistently from within" (Ong 1982, 153). The rise of Romanticism with which the psychological presentation of character is associated in contradiction to the rhetorical mode dominant until that time (Scholes and Kellogg 193) is also important. Here, again, one is forced to return to the underlying shift in consciousness caused by writing, but especially in print. Thomas J. Farrell's discussion of Ong's theories in relation to Eric Neumann's presentation of Jungian stages and to Jean Houston's delineation of psycho-historical stages provides further insight into the issues presented here.

In *Rhetoric, Romance and Technology*, Ong reports that the Age of Romanticism with its concern for "originality" is the result of increasing human control of nature made possible by writing and even more by print as a means of storage and retrieval of knowledge (264, 20; see also 1967, 155). Indeed, Romanticism and technology are "mirror images," he states (1971, 264). While these movements are usually associated with the latter eighteenth century, the shift in consciousness allowing them to flower begins to sprout at the time of the Enlightenment (1967, 129). Congreve's work in the 1690s reflects this rising concern with the individual, and his essay itself presents a quite analytic assessment of the concept of humor. One might also note that Morris's essay indicates that literacy is a part of the world in 1744, for he says, "I call such a person in the **book** of **mankind**, a **"character"** (12; emphasis added).

One final consideration remains: the distancing that results from print also leads to a deeper awareness of one's own interiority. In experiencing the object outside, Ong reminds the reader, one comes to experience oneself (1967a, 228). In the analytic world of print, one can expect the rise of a Descartes. The "Cartesian shift to the point of view of the perceiving individual ego" and the concomitant possibility of defining both inner and outer worlds (Watts 295), brings a greater awareness that people are quite complex, and to treat them as objects can prove, as Ong notes, "embarrassing"; persons exhibit consciousness and are thus "unaccountable intrusions" in the universe, "foreign to objective reality, which is voiceless and normally passive" (1967a, 228).

Hooker makes a similar point in discussing the reasons for the repudiation of ridicule in the early eighteenth century. By 1700, England, he points out, is influenced by Pascal, La Bruyère, and La Rochefoucauld, who stress the fact that humans are "bundles of oddly assorted passions, dimly lighted by reason" (370). This "new look" at the individual brings the realization that the human condition is one in which all share (Mayoux 4), and ridicule yields to mirth. By the mid-eighteenth century the stage is set for the appearance of *sense of humor*, for is not that the term suggested in Mayoux's description: "Ce retour sur soi, c'est le premier mouvement de l'humour; seulement il s'y joint un sentiment, très existentialiste, que l'on est *sujet* pour soi et *objet* pour les autres: le geste de l'humour devient alors partie du rituel d'une sociabilité modeste, familière, entre soi, laissant de côté les catégories de l'absolu" (4).

Although the stage is set and despite Max Eastman's rather cavalier claim that the phrase *sense of humor* is an "expression" in the eighteenth century (168), there seems to be no evidence of such usage. Even in the nineteenth century when the phrase is found, for example, in *Vanity Fair* and *The Egoist*, it is not used frequently. While the words *humor* and *good humor* abound in these novels, *sense of humor* occurs only four times in the former (Thackeray 1962, 30.344; 31.363; 35.324, and 37.451) and *sense of humor* and *sense of the humorous* once each in the latter (Meredith, 377–78, 379). One does not find it at all in such eighteenth-century classics as *Tom Jones* and *Tristram Shandy* nor in such nineteenth-century favorites as *Great Expectations*, *Jane Eyre*, and *Middlemarch*. Since the phrase does occur in Thackeray's work of 1847–48 and Meredith's of 1879, one is led to ask what factors account for its appearance in the mid-Victorian age.

The late eighteenth century and early nineteenth century witness an increase in literacy. Ford Maddox Ford, for example, connects ladies of leisure with the reading of novels (40; see also Cross 118); Beattie mentions the role of printing (441) and Huizinga the "exhuberance of printed matter" (156); Leavis reports the doubling of daily sales of papers from 1753 to 1775 (130); and Stephens notes the beginning of serious study of Old English literature at this time (185; see also 210–11). This phenomenon is reflected even in the discussion on humor. Hazlitt, in his lecture, "On Wit and Humor," refers to humor "as it is shown in books" and seems to see humor as a genre, "an imitation of the natural or acquired absurdities of mankind, or of the ludicrous in accident, situation and character" (15).

Like Morris, who also uses *humor* to signify genre, Hazlitt makes a statement obviously grounded literally. In comparison to Morris's, which focuses on real life and relates that to books, Hazlitt's is completely in the world of books with application to real life left to the reader. Hazlitt also notes that the conversation of his day is "not personal, but critical and analytical" (153), a fact that reflects how deeply internalized print has become in the less than one hundred years between the two essayists.

The relationship between the increase of literacy and the rise of *sense of humor* is based not on the availability of humor in published form—Wells records an influx of this in the late sixteenth century (277)—nor is it based, as Jennings warns, on "being equipped with a conventional book-culture" (121). It is based on the shift, detailed by Ong, from the immersion in an aural-oral world to the experience of the analytic distancing of a sight-space universe born from the technology of writing and confirmed by the advent of the printing press (see 1982, esp. chap. 3 and 4). Ian Watt, in *The Rise of the Novel*, presents a comprehensive account of the state of literacy in the eighteenth century (35–39; see also 42, 43–44, 52–53, 290), and information on literacy in the eighteenth century can be found in many places as seen already. What is important here, however, is that increased literacy provides the concomitant development of interiority which facilitates the "treatment of self as object" (Ong 1981, 159) and allows for the type of analysis of the concepts of humor/ good humor seen in Johnson's *Rambler* (nos. 72 and 141) and Goldsmith's "Enquiry into the Present State of Learning in Europe." As literacy increases in England into the nineteenth century, especially due to the influence of the Benthamites and the *Westminster Review* begun in 1824 (Bowyer and Brooks 5), and as *sense* and *humor* change, the stage is set for the appearance of *sense of humor* as found, for example, in *Vanity Fair*. The works of Jane Austen to whom Phelps attributes both the "good-natured laughter" and "common sense" that refresh English literature after the "long reign—or shall we say rain?" of such "lachrymose literature" as Mackenzie's with his "Man of Feeling" (89, 97, 77; see also Wimsatt and Brooks 297) provides the literary analogue to these points. Also, that same distancing, provided by literacy and the interiorization of print, provides the ability to perceive for herself and then to make the reader "sensible", that is, "aware" (Phillips 39) of the "absurdity of unreasonableness which [Austen] wishes to expose" (Gore 1968, 114).

Austen's usage is of key importance in tracing the rise of the actual term *sense of humor*. Austen carries on Dryden's usage, namely, the association of "common sense" with "judgement" (Jensen 107), this usage being found, as such, in her personal correspondence (Phillips 38; Austen 1952 no. 140, 470). The association of "common sense" and English humor and the specific claim of Phelps that sense of humor is a cure for sentiment reflect the theory of laughter espoused by Gregory and McDougall. They explain laughter as an antidote to "sympathetic pain" to which people are exposed because of the "high sensitivity" of their "primitive sympathetic tendencies" (Gregory 18; see also McDougall 303). While Gregory questions the claim of the anonymous author of "Laughter" that "sense of humor" implies "balanced common sense" (86), his presentation suggests that the two go hand in hand.

E. B. White, quoting from a parody diary of Franklin P. Adams, 28 April 1926, also indicates the belief that the sense of humor acts as antithesis to emotion (see Empson 261). All this again suggests a certain distancing, the ability to discriminate as Goldsmith describes, which, as has already been demonstrated, flourishes with the growth of literacy. Phelps's connection of Jane Austen with this function of sense of humor again situates *sense of humor* in a rather literate age, the first half of the nineteenth century.

In order to have *sense of humor*, however, two additional changes in the use of *sense* are necessary. The first is the use of *sense* to mean perception. Lewis details four possible steps in this development: "experience," "awareness," "consciousness," and finally "an unspecified awareness"; the last of these especially connects with *sense of humor* (142). The second change is the actual formulation of the phrase *sense of*. Lewis also provides a good background image for dealing with the changes in words. He reminds the student that developments do not follow the pattern of an "insect undergoing metamorphosis," but rather "grow like a tree throwing out its branches" (8). So it is with *sense*. While the association of *sense* with "common sense" and "judgement" blooms, so also does the connection between *sense* and "perception" as "unspecified awareness." Lewis points to its use in this way as early as 1612 in Bacon's "Of Praise" (*Essays* 213) and its use in the same way by Wordsworth in "Tintern Abbey" (*Poetical Works* 164), which he writes in 1798 (142). Phillips notes Jane Austen's similar usage—"Jane Fairfax's **sense** of right"—in *Emma* 1816 (38; Austen 446, emphasis added).

The *OED* lists sense as "capacity for perception and appreciation of (beauty, humor, some quality, etc.)" as the ninth of eleven possible usages under the general category of "Faculty of Perception or Sensation." The examples are concerned with perception rather than sensation and have as their object or perception such abstractions as "beautie," "arts and sciences," "the picturesque," and, finally, "humor" in Payn's 1855 *Talk of the Town* (see Payn 222). Of the eight examples, five use *sense of*: one in 1604, one in 1704, and the other three in the second half of the nineteenth century. It seems that *sense of* becomes more commonly used after the turn of the nineteenth century. It is, as quoted above, the form used by Wordsworth in "Tintern Abbey." Empson in his chapter-long discussion of *sense* used in Wordsworth's "Prelude" points out that of the forty-seven times the word occurs in the 1805 edition, its most frequent use is as *sense of* (293). Thus, the early nineteenth century sees the rise of the linguistic form *sense of* as a generalized expression to which the word *humor* can be affixed.

In the early nineteenth century, then, several factors are present in the *Zeitgeist* which combine to foster the rise of *sense of humor.* *Humor* has come to mean *mirth; sense* has come to mean *perception;* the linguistic formulation *sense of* is in use; Victorian society, due to increasing literacy, becomes more and more adept at reflective and reflexive activity. This latter quality is of prime importance for, as Duncan points out in *Language and Literature in Society,* "great laughter is reflexive" (54), especially laughter at oneself. The internalization of writing, especially print, allows the distancing and self-perception necessary to have a sense of one's own humors and those of others, and to recognize the ridiculous in them and in oneself with enough detachment to laugh. Also the change in consciousness occasioned by the shift from the oral/aural world to the visual one, that is, the development of the analytic approach to the concept of sense of humor, creates, in turn, the need to name it.

Despite Carlson's claim that defining *humor* etymologically is "unrewarding" (41), it is a rather enlightening occupation which Thomas repeatedly demonstrates throughout his popular contemporary work, *Late Night Thoughts on Listening to Mahler's Ninth Symphony.* Thomas presents an etymological study about the root *dhghem,* meaning *humus,* from which come *earth* and *humility* (14; see also *Dictionary of English Word Roots* 63). The modern understanding of humor, especially the place of the person in the universe, suggests that *humor* comes from *dhghem.* Indeed, it has been shown that the eighteenth century seems to make this same connection. While the association of *humor* with *humus,* as in helping to keep one's feet on the ground, or the linking of *humor* with *human* and *humane,* are all conceptually admissible, to connect *humor* and *dhghem* is etymologically inaccurate. The editors of the *Comprehensive Etymological Dictionary of the English Language* point out that even the spelling of *humor* with an *h* is due to "folk etymology" (750). Leacock, in his brief etymological discussion of *humor,* rightly focuses on the meaning of *wetness* (8–9), so obvious in its use in humoral pathology, and continuing to underlie both the humoral doctrine and Jonson's humoral theory. The connection of *humor* with wetness and flow fades during the latter seventeenth century when the emphasis is on rigidity, the extreme and the ridiculous, picking up on the diseased humors of the humoral pathology, rather than continuing the fluidity of the etymological root. These more mechanical or "comic humors" tend to dominate the scene, and a comparison of Shadwell's diction with Jonson's demonstrates such a change in emphasis. With the changes leading into the eighteenth century, a humanizing of humor occurs and encouragement to "go with the flow" revives the etymological meaning of *humor*. *Sense of humor*, too, continues in this stream, since the implication of achieving and/or maintaining balance at the mean in relation to the extremes demands flexibility or fluidity in dealing with life. One does not usually associate sense of humor with people who are stiff or rigid or even rather formal unless, perhaps, they exhibit a sense of humor described as *dry*. In discussing O'Connell's "The Sense of Humor: Actualizer of Persons and Theories" in the light of Furlong's "The Flow Experience of Fun in Fun" (35–39, 80), Chapman and Foot underscore this connection between humor, especially sense of humor, and fluidity: "The art of humor—total and flexible concern with both poles of paradox [the mean in relation to the two extremes]—provides the person with the rewarding experience of 'flow,' the total awareness and heightened involvement with activity basic to fun" (1977, 147; see also Collins 3).

Notice, too, that many writers speak of humor in terms of fluidity. L'Estrange, in saying that comedy is "meandering" in a "swifter and shallower current," (258), and George Eliot, in saying that humor "flows along" (81), do so literally; Coleridge, in speaking about humor and "growth from within" (277), does so figuratively. In the light of all this, Eastman is correct in claiming that the essence of humor is "flexibility instead of fixation" and "its food is not unity, but variety" (25; see also Cazamian 114, 132). Such flexibility is the source of humor's healing power as Hershkowitz describes it as "a way of presenting ambiguities which are acceptable, even sought for, and which may serve to make [a] patient tolerate" what is as everyone experiences "not always an 'either-or' world" (139).

Now that the ice has been broken about the highlights of the history of *humor* and *sense of humor*, a final point pertaining to that history is most appropriate. In the presentation of the etymology of *humor* from the Indo-European **wegw*, meaning *wet*, the compilers of *The American Heritage Dictionary of the English Language* cite the Old Norse form *vok* from **vakvo*, meaning a *crack in the ice* coming from *wet spot*. This image seems to provide an excellent summary of the history of *humor* and *sense of humor* and of their functions in life, by focusing on the underlying concept of fluidity/flexibility often unconsciously revealed in the popular contemporary phrase *breaking the ice.*

Works Cited

Ainger, Alfred. "True and False Humour in Literature." In *Lectures and Essays.* vol. 2. 222–54. London: Macmillan, 1905.

American Heritage Dictionary of the English Language. New College Edition, Boston: Houghton-Mifflin, 1981.

Aristotle. *The Nichomachean Ethics.* Translated by Hippocrates G. Apostle. Synthese Historical Library 13. Dordrecht, Holland: Reidel, 1975.

Austen, Jane. *Emma.* Vol. 4 of *The Novels of Jane Austen.* 3d ed. 5 vols. 1933. Reprint, London: Oxford, 1966.

——. *Jane Austen's Letters to Her Sister Cassandra and Others.* Edited by R. W. Chapman. 2d ed. 1932. Reprint, London: Oxford University Press, 1952.

Bacon, Francis. *Bacon's Essays and Colours of Good and Evil with Notes and Glossarial Index.* Edited by Walter Wright. 1862. Reprint, Freeport, N.Y.: Books for Libraries, 1972.

Bamborough, J. B. *The Little World of Man.* London: Longman's, 1952.

Baskervill, Charles Read. *English Elements in Jonson's Early Comedy.* Austin: University of Texas Press, 1911.

Beattie, James. "On Laughter and Ludicrous Composition." In *Essays on Poetry and Music As They Affect the Mind; On Laughter and Ludicrous Composition; On the Usefulness of Classical Learning.* 3d ed., corr. London, 1779.

Blankner, Frederika. "Literacy Pattern As a Graph of Social Evolution: An Inquiry into a New Field." *Twentieth Century English.* Edited by William S. Knickerbocker. New York: Philosophical Library, 1946.

Bond, Donald F., ed. *The Spectator.* 5 vols. Oxford: Clarendon, 1965.

Bowyer, John Wilson and John Lee Brooks, eds. *The Victorian Age: Prose, Poetry and Drama.* NY: Crofts, 1944.

Brophy, Brigid. "A Remorseless Realist." Reprinted in *Jane Austen: Sense and Sensibility, Pride and Prejudice and Mansfield Park: A Casebook,* Edited by B. C. Southam. London: Macmillan, 1976.

Burke, Kenneth. *Attitudes toward History.* 2d ed. rev. Los Altos, CA: Hermes, 1959.

Carlson, Richard S. *The Benign Humorists.* USA: Archon-Shoestring, 1975.

Cazamian, Louis. *Essais en deux langues.* Paris: Didier, 1938.

Chapman, Anthony J. and Hugh C. Foot, eds. *Humor and Laughter: Theory, Research and Applications.* London: Wiley, 1976.

————. *It's a Funny Thing, Humor.* London: Pergamon, 1977.

Clifford, James L., ed. *Eighteenth Century Literature: Modern Essays in Criticism.* New York: Oxford University Press, 1959.

Coleridge, Samuel Taylor. "On the Distinction of the Witty, the Droll, the Odd, and the Humorous; the Nature and Constituents of Humor:–Rabelais–Swift–Sterne." In *The Complete Works of Samuel Taylor Coleridge,* edited by Shedd. vol. 4. 275–85. New York, 1986.

Collins, R. G. "In Search of Humor in Literature." *Thalia* 1, no. 1 (1978): 3–8.

Comprehensive Etymological Dictionary of the English Language. Vol. 1. Edited by Dr. Ernest Klein. Amsterdam: Elsevier, 1966.

Congreve, William. "An Essay Concerning Humour in Comedy: To Mr. Dennis." In *An Essay Fixing the True Standards of Wit, Humor, Raillery, Satire and Ridicule,* Corbyn Morris, 66–75.

Cross, Wilbur L. *The Development of the English Novel.* New York: Macmillan, 1923.

Curry, Walter Clyde. *Chaucer and the Medieval Sciences.* 1926. Reprint, New York: New York University Press, 1942.

Dennis, John. "A Large Account of the Taste in Poetry, and the Causes of Degeneracy of It." In *Theories of Comedy,* edited by Paul Lauter, 215–38.

Dictionary of English Word Roots: English-Roots [and] Roots-English. Edited by Robert W. L. Smith. 1966. Reprint, Totowa, NJ: Littlefield, 1977.

Dryden, [John]. "An Essay of Dramatic Poesy." In *Eighteenth Century Poetry and Prose,* edited by Louis J. Bredvold, Alan D. McKillop, and Lois Whitney. New York: Ronald, 1952.

Duncan, Hugh Dalziel. *Languages and Literature in Society: A Sociological Essay on Theory and Method in the Interpretation of Linguistic Symbol with a Bibliographical Guide to the Sociology of Literature.* Chicago: University of Chicago Press, 1953.

Eastman, Max. *The Sense of Humor.* New York: Scribner's, 1921.

Eliot, George. "German Wit: Heinrich Heine." *Westminster Review* (1856). Reprint in *Essays and Leaves from a Note-Book.* Edinburgh, 1884.

Empson, William. *The Structure of Complex Words.* Norfolk, CT: New Directions, 1951.

Farrell, Thomas J. "Secondary Orality and Consciousness Today." In *Media, Consciousness and Culture: Explorations of Walter Ong's Thoughts,* edited by Bruce E. Gronbeck, Thomas J. Farrell, and Paul A. Soukup, 194–209. Newbury Park, CA: Sage, 1991.

Fielding, Henry. *Joseph Andrews.* Edited by Martin C. Battestin. Middletown, CT: Wesleyan University Press, 1967.

Ford, Ford Maddox. *The English Novel: From the Earliest Days to the Death of Joseph Conrad.* Philadelphia: Lippincott, 1929.

Forest, Louise C. Turner. "A Caveat for Critics against Invoking Elizabethan Psychology." *PMLA* 61, no. 3 (September 1946): 651–72.

Forster, E[dward] M[organ]. *Aspects of the Novel and Related Writings.* Edited by Oliver Stallybrass. Abinger ed. 12. London: Arnold, 1974.

Furlong, William Barry. "The Flow Experience: The Fun in Fun." *Psychology Today.* 10, no. 1 (1976): 35–38, 80.

Goldsmith, Oliver. "An Enquiry into the Present State of Polite Learning in Europe." In *Collected Works of Oliver Goldsmith*, edited by Arthur Friedman, vol. 1. 243–41. Oxford: Clarendon, 1966.

Gore, Catherine. Review of *Women As They Are*. *Edinburgh Review* 53 (July 1830): 448–51. Reprint in *Jane Austen: The Critical Heritage*, edited by B. C. Southam, 113–14. London: Routledge; New York: Barnes, 1968.

Gregory, J. C. *The Nature of Laughter*. London: Kegan Paul, 1924.

Groom, Bernard. *A Short History of English Words*. 1934. Reprint, New York: St. Martin's, 1966.

Hazlitt, William. *Lectures on the English Comic Writers and Lectures on the Age of Elizabeth*. Vol. 6 of *Complete Works of William Hazlitt in Twenty-One Volumes*, edited by. P. R. Howe. Centenary Edition. London: Dent, 1931.

Hershkowitz, Aaron. "The Essential Ambiguity of, and in, Humor." In Chapman and Foot, *It's a Funny Thing, Humor*, 139–42.

Hooker, Edward N. "Humor in the Age of Pope." *Huntington Library Quarterly*, 2, no. 4 (1948): 361–85.

Huizinga, J[ohan]. *Homo Ludens: A Study of the Play Element in Culture*. Beacon Paperback ed. 1955. Reprint, Boston: Beacon, 1970.

Hurley, Donna W. "The Medical World of *Tristram Shandy*." Thesis. Columbia University, 1963.

Index Medicus. Washington, DC: Government Printing Office, 1879–1985.

Jefferson, D. W. "*Tristram Shandy* and the Tradition of Learned Wit." In *Essays in Criticism* 1 (1951): 255ff. Reprint in *Laurence Sterne: A Collection of Critical Essays*, edited by John Traugott, 148–67. Englewood Cliffs, N.J.: Prentice, 1967.

Jennings, Paul. "Humor: The Modern Religion?" In *Essays by Divers Hands*. London: Royal Society of Literature of the United Kingdom 40 (1979): 117–31.

Jensen, H. James. *A Glossary of John Dryden's Critical Terms*. Minneapolis: University of Minnesota Press, 1969.

Johnson, Samuel. *The Rambler: A Periodical Paper, Published in 1750, 1751, 1752*. London, 1826.

Jonson, Ben. *Every Man in His Humor. Complete Plays*. Anglicized ed., edited by Ernest Rhys. 2 vols., 1910. Reprint, London: Dent; New York: Dutton, 1940, 1:559–624.

Kerr, Mina. *The Influence of Ben Johnson on English Comedy 1598-1642*. New York: Appleton, 1912.

Kimmins, C. W. *The Springs of Laughter*. London: Methuen, 1928.

"Laughter." *Edinburgh Review* 215, no. 440 (1912): 383–404.

Lauter, Paul, ed. *Theories of Comedy*. Garden City: Doubleday, 1964.

Leacock, Stephen. *Humor and Humanity: An Introduction to the Study of Humor*. New York: Holt, 1938.

Leavis, Q[ueenie] D[orothy]. *Fiction and the Reading Public*. Norwood Editions. 1932. Reprint, London: Chatto, 1977.

L'Estrange, Rev. A[lfred] G[uy Kingan]. *The History of English Humor*. 1878. Reprint, New York: Franklin, 1970.

Lewis, C[live]. S[taples]. *Studies in Words*. Cambridge: University Press, 1960.

London Catalogue of Books in All Languages, Arts and Sciences That Have Been Printed in Great Britain Since This Year 1700. London, 1773.

McDougall, Williams. "A New Theory of Laughter." *Psyche* (Cambridge), ns 2, no. 4 (1922): 292–303.

McKillop, Alan Dugald. *The Early Masters of English Fiction.* Lawrence: University of Kansas Press, 1956.

Malins, Edward. *English Landscaping and Literature.* London: Oxford, 1966.

Mayoux, Jean-Jacques. *L'Humour et l'absurde: Attitudes anglosaxannes: attitudes francaises.* Oxford: Clarendon, 1973.

Meredith, George. *The Egoist.* Edited by George Woodcock. 1968. Reprint, Middlesex: Penguin, 1979.

Morris, Corbyn. *An Essay Fixing the True Standards of Wit, Humor, Raillery, Satire and Ridicule.* 1744. Reprint, New York: AMS, 1972.

Murdick, Marvin. "Character and Event in Fiction." *Yale Review* 50, no. 2 (1960): 202–18.

OED. 1933 ed. Reprint, Oxford: Clarendon Press, 1961.

Ong, Walter J. *The Barbarian Within: And Other Fugitive Essays and Studies.* New York: Macmillan, 1954.

———. *Fighting for Life: Contest, Sexuality and Consciousness.* Ithaca: Cornell University Press, 1981.

———. *In the Human Grain: Further Explorations of Contemporary Culture.* New York: Macmillan, London: Collier-Macmillan, 1967.

———. *Orality and Literacy: The Technologizing of the Word.* New Accents ser., edited by Terrence Hawkes. London: Methuen, 1982.

———. *The Presence of the Word: Some Prolegomena for Cultural and Religious History.* New Haven, Yale University Press, 1967a.

———. *Rhetoric, Romance and Technology: Studies in the Interaction of Expression and Culture.* Ithaca: Cornell University Press, 1971.

Payn, James. *The Talk of the Town.* Vol. 1. London, 1855.

Phelps, William Lyon. *The Advance of the English Novel.* New York: Dodd, 1919.

Phillipps, K. C. *Jane Austen's English.* London: Deutsch, 1970.

Plato. *Great Dialogues of Plato.* Edited by Eric H. Warmingon and Phillip G. Rouse, translated by W. H. D. Rouse. New York: NAL, 1956.

———. "The Statesman. Philebus." Translated by Harold N. Fowler. Vol. 8 of *Plato in Twelve Volumes,* edited by G. P. Goold, 199–399. Loeb Classical Library. Cambridge, MA: Harvard University Press; London: Heinemann, 1975.

Rhys, Ernest, ed. *Complete Plays.* By Ben Jonson. vol. 1, 1910. Reprint, London: Dent; New York: Dutton, 1940.

Schlegel, Augustus Wilhelm von. From *Lectures on Dramatic Art and Literature.* Translated by John Black. 1808. Reprint in Lauter, *Theory of Comedy,* 324–349.

Scholes, Robert and Robert Kellogg. *The Nature of Narrative.* New York: Oxford, 1966.

Shadwell, Thomas. *The Humorists; A Comedy. Complete Works.* Edited by Montague Summers. vol. 1. London: Fortune, 1927. 176–55.

Snuggs, Henry L. "The Comic Humors: A New Interpretation." *PMLA* 62 (1947): 114–22.

Spingarn, J. E., ed. *Essays: "On Ancient and Modern Learning" and "On Poetry"*. By Sir William Temple. 1909. Reprint, Folcroft, PA: Folcroft, 1970.

Stedman's Medical Dictionary: A Vocabulary of Medicine and Its Allied Sciences with Pronunciations and Derivations. 23d ed. Edited by Thomas Lathrop Stedman. Baltimore: Williams, 1976.

Stephen, Sir Leslie. *English Literature and Society in the Eighteenth Century.* New York: Putnam; London: Duckworth, 1904.

Tave, Stuart. *The Amiable Humorist: A Study in the Comic Theory and Criticism of the Eighteenth and Early Nineteenth Centuries*. Chicago: University of Chicago Press, 1960.

Temple, Sir William. "Of Poetry." In *Five Miscellaneous Essays*, 173–203. Ann Arbor: University of Michigan Press, 1962.

Thackeray, William Makepeace. *The English Humorists; Charity and Humor; The Four Georges*. 1912. Reprint, London: Dent; New York: Dutton, 1968.

———. *Vanity Fair: A Novel Without a Hero*. Signet Classic. New York: NAL, 1962.

Thomas, Lewis. *Late Night Thoughts While Listening to Mahler's Ninth Symphony.* New York: Viking, 1983.

Valins, G[eorge] H[enry]. *The Making [and] Meaning of Words: A Companion to the Dictionary.* 1949. Reprint, Bristol: Arrowsmith, n.d.

Watt, Ian. *The Rise of the Novel: Studies in DeFoe, Richardson and Fielding.* 1957. Reprint, Berkeley: University of California Press; London: Chatto, 1967.

Wells, Carolyn, ed. *An Outline of Humor: Being a True Chronicle from Prehistoric Ages to the Twentieth Century.* New York: Putnam, 1923.

White, E.B. "Some Remarks on Humor." In *The Comic Vision*, edited by Peter J. Monahan, 78–83. New York McGraw-Webster, 1971.

Williams, Raymond. *Keywords: A Vocabulary of Culture and Society.* New York: Oxford, 1976.

Wimsatt, Williams K. and Cleanth Brooks. *Literary Criticism: A Short History.* New York: Knopf, 1957.

Wordsworth, William. "Lines Composed a Few Miles Above Tintern Abbey." *Wordsworth: Poetical Works*. Edited by Thomas Hutchinson. Rev. ed. edited by Ernest de Selincourt, 163–65. London: Oxford, 1969.

Faulkner and Male Agonism

Thomas J. Farrell

Introduction

In *FIGHTING FOR LIFE: CONTEST, SEXUALITY, AND CONSCIOUSNESS*, Walter J. Ong sets forth his carefully considered reflections on male contesting behavior, which he styles agonistic behavior. This book culminates reflections that go back at least to his 1959 article "Latin Language Study as a Renaissance Puberty Rite" (1971, 113–41). He advanced his reflections on agonistic behavior further in *The Presence of the Word* (192–222) and then in "Agonistic Structures in Academia: Past to Present" (1995, 112–37).

As Ong's references in passing to Faulkner suggest (*Fighting* 62–63, 84, 91–92), William Faulkner was studying male agonistic behavior long before Ong. By using Ong's *Fighting for Life* to call attention to certain aspects of male behavior portrayed by Faulkner, I wish to suggest that these two older students of male behavior still have much to offer men and women who wish to reflect more fully and deeply on how men establish a specifically masculine sense of identity through male contesting behavior.[1]

While a book-length study would be required to examine male contesting in all of Faulkner's male characters, this essay begins such an examination by focusing on a few selected works. First, though, I briefly set forth Ong's insights about how male-male contesting enables men to establish a specifically masculine sense of identity. Next, I draw on biographies of Faulkner by David Minter and Frederick R. Karl to suggest how the focus on male contesting most likely grew out of Faulkner's personal situation as well as out of his reflections on the culture of the Old South and American culture in general. Then I examine in some detail the key white male characters in *Flags in the Dust* and *Absalom, Absalom!* while discussing the white male characters in *The Unvanquished* and *The Sound and the Fury* in passing. I conclude with some brief reflections about how the cultural conditions under which Faulkner wrote have been

changed for the better as a result of the black civil rights movement and the women's movement, and I then suggest how men
in the twenty-first century might appropriate the psychodynamics of contesting to rise to new levels of human flourishing.

Identity Emerges from Identifications

As Ong explains in *Fighting for Life*, the Greek word *agon*
means contest (43). As he uses the term, agonistic behavior is
contest-oriented, oriented toward adversativeness, built around
a sense of being "up against it." Male agonism, according to Ong,
enables males to establish a specifically masculine identity. As
Ong sees things, the male has to prove that he is not what he
came from—the mother and the feminine lifeworld—and is
therefore independent, while the female has to acknowledge that
she is what she came from—female and part of the feminine
lifeworld—and yet realize her self-identity as an independent
person.[2] In his view, males need to disidentify with their mothers
to establish a specifically masculine identity. He believes males
establish a specifically masculine identity primarily through
male-male contesting (as distinct from contesting, say, with the
forces of nature). While such rivalry can obviously be overdone,
it nevertheless offers a male a way to work out a specifically
masculine identity by providing him with a role model with
whom he may compare and assess himself.

It should be noted in this connection that Ong's work may
help elucidate a troubling aspect of Faulkner's work. Albert J.
Guerard has called attention to "Faulkner's persistent misogyny"
(8). As his comment suggests, either Faulkner portrays males
who are acting out male antifeminism in ways that should not
be condoned, or Faulkner's own antifeminism is being expressed—or both. But if Ong's theory is correct, the male need
to establish a specifically masculine identity through male-male
contesting may also be involved. Ong's observations in *Fighting
for Life* and "Truth in Conrad's Darkness" (1995, 186–201) can
help us understand Faulkner's life as well as his portrayal of
male-male contesting and the misogyny and racism that historically have accompanied such contesting.

Faulkner's identity as a writer emerged as a result of his selective identification with his great-grandfather who had also been
a writer as well as a Civil War hero and owner of a railroad. In
his sympathetic treatment of Faulkner's life, Minter emphasizes

that young William's disappointment in his own inadequate father led him to appropriate his great-grandfather, Col. William
Clark Falkner, as a role model by accentuating that the Colonel
had been a writer. (However, William changed the spelling of the
family name.) From the age of nine, Minter reports, young William said, "I want to be a writer like my great-granddaddy" (18).
Minter adds that young William repeated this statement until it
became almost formulaic. When Faulkner later published his
first book, he dedicated it to his mother, and he wrote a sketch
of himself as the author, saying, "Great-grandson of Col. W. C.
Faulkner, C. S. A., author of 'The White Rose of Memphis,' 'Rapid
Ramblings in Europe,' etc." (qtd. in Minter 18). In any event,
Faulkner clearly set up his own emulative rivalry, to borrow a
term from Warwick Wadlington (53, 151, 199), with his male
ancestor who had been a writer.

In addition, young William Faulkner also had dreamed of at-
taining distinction in war as his great-grandfather had. His volun-
teering for the Royal Air Force clearly showed this, as did some
of the tales he told to various people about his war experiences.
Karl calls attention to Faulkner's desire for the glory of war and
comparable male risk-taking exploits:

> Faulkner desperately wanted to be a great writer, but he wanted just
> as desperately to be an epic hero. Faulkner needed, often compul-
> sively, the warrior's bout with death. The other side of this devotion
> [to becoming a great writer] was his intense need to identify with
> masculine pursuits—to put away for good implications of effeminacy
> which had been cast upon him in his youth. Faulkner threw himself
> into activities normally associated with maleness: not only drinking
> but flying (at a time when it was still dangerous), annual hunting
> trips in rain and cold, which he continued well after he had won
> the Nobel Prize, and, finally, horsemanship, which was a near obses-
> sion, and which he pursued even when not up to it physically. (3,
> 24, 14)

Considered against this personal background of the author, the
fourth-generation twin (John Sartoris) who died in World War I
in *Flags in the Dust* may be the part of William Faulkner that
wanted military glory. The surviving twin (the last Bayard Sartoris) may be another part of Faulkner that about that time had
come to love and seek death. Faulkner himself did not see action
in WWI, but his brother Jack did. Karl notes that "his [Faulkner's]
limp and skull plate, which he affected later in New Orleans,
precisely duplicated Jack's real wounds of knee and skull injury"

(116). Clearly Faulkner was not a stranger to the dynamics of male-male contesting.

Faulkner's identification with his great-grandfather was selective, however, because he used the legends about his great-grandfather to call into question the ruthlessness, recklessness, misogyny, and racism of his own heritage. By selecting an aspect of his great-grandfather to identify with, Faulkner enabled himself to engage in a form of male-male contesting with his legendary ancestor. But Faulkner does not portray such a happy identification in *Absalom, Absalom!* On the contrary, he portrays the acute difficulty Quentin Compson is having in working out his own specifically masculine identity. Quentin's fascination with Thomas Sutpen most likely mirrors Faulkner's fascination with his legendary ancestor. But Quentin is overwhelmed as he becomes aware of certain negative aspects of his cultural heritage, as we shall see. In this regard, Quentin is perhaps a portrait of Faulkner as a young man, before he had fully worked out his happy selective identification with his great-grandfather as a writer. In a letter to Malcolm Cowley, Faulkner said, "I am telling the same story over and over, which is myself and the world" (qtd. in Minter 34; Karl 714). Faulkner's remark suggests that each of his novels is in some sense a portrait of the author himself, and so the male-male contesting portrayed in the novels discussed below must have been a central concern in his life.

To sum up the theory outlined and illustrated in this section, Ong has suggested that males need to work out a specifically masculine identity in relation to other males. That is what male-male contesting is all about. Male antifeminism aims to promote identification with other males and thereby to contribute to the establishment of a specifically masculine identity. It does not follow from Ong's position that females play no role whatsoever in how males work out a specifically masculine identity. But his position asserts that masculine identity is established primarily through male-male identifications and interactions. As Bly puts it, "only men can initiate men, as only women can initiate women. Women can change the embryo to a boy, but only men can change the boy to a man" (16). However, Ong's theory in *Fighting for Life* implies that males should reach a point where they have established their specifically masculine identities firmly enough that their antifeminism ceases. Elsewhere Ong sums up Jungian thought about such a stage of development as involving the "liberation of the ego from endogamous kinship libido and [the] emergence of the higher femininity, with woman now as person, anima-sister, related positively to ego conscious-ness" (1971, 11). (In "Secondary Orality and Consciousness To-day," I discuss this stage of the development of consciousness more fully.) But Faulkner does not portray such a development in the novels under consideration here, and he most likely had not fully experienced such a development up to the time when he wrote these novels, if he ever did fully experience such a psychological development. However that may be, Faulkner surely did recognize what Aaron R. Kipnis and others connected with the emerging men's movement call heroic masculinity and its inherent limitations.

The Last Bayard Sartoris and Heroic Masculinity

In *Flags in the Dust*,[3] Old Man Falls calls attention to one form of overdoing male agonism:

> "Ever' now and then a feller has to walk up to and spit in deestruc-tion's face, sort of, fer his own good. He has to kind of put a aidge on hisself, like he'd hold his axe to the grindstone ... Ef a feller'll show his face to deestruction ever' now and then, deestruction'll leave 'im be 'twell his time comes. Deestruction likes to take a feller in the back."

> "Deestruction's like ary other coward," he roared. "Hit wont strike a feller that's a-lookin' hit in the face lessen he pushes hit too clost."
> (*FD* 262–63)

While Old Man Falls goes on to praise Colonel John Sartoris for such masculine daring, the novel as a whole concerns how the last two Sartorises, the then already dead John and young Bayard, push such masculine daring too far. Usually overdoing male ago-nism is deeply connected with antifeminism, as we shall note that it is in the case of young Bayard.

In *Flags in the Dust*, Horace Benbow and young Bayard as he is called (he turns out to be the last Bayard Sartoris) represent the extremes, respectively, of underdevelopment and over-development of the male agonistic orientation. Miss Jenny calls attention to Horace's underdevelopment when she refers to him as a child in speaking to his sister Narcissa (32). In another scene Narcissa tries to defend the wild behavior of the Sartoris boys when they were boys against the censure of Miss Sally Wyatt

(71–75), and so she apparently recognized their overdevelopment of the male agonistic orientation and found it excusable. However, in the scene with Miss Jenny, Narcissa does not try to defend her own brother's underdevelopment against the censure of Miss Jenny. Although Narcissa on other occasions speaks out against Miss Jenny's remarks, she accepts in silence Miss Jenny's comment about Horace: "Horace was born to have some woman making a doormat of herself for him, just as some men are born cuckolded" (FD 33).

In other words, Horace likes to be mothered, and as a matter of fact, Narcissa picks up after him as a mother might pick up after a child (FD 335). It is no surprise that Horace is attracted to seemingly strong, take-charge women such as Belle and her sister. All of these factors bespeak a certain underdevelopment of his sense of masculinity in terms of the culture of the South. In addition, Horace's glassblowing is "effeminate" in his own culture's terms (Karl 297). As Ong explains, the male needs to develop a sense of his own masculinity by, on the one hand, eschewing feminine sources of comfort and by, on the other hand, proving himself in adversative behavior, often involving another male. Horace does neither, while young Bayard does both.

Young Bayard's parents died while he and his twin brother John were young boys (FD 86), and the boys were raised by their grandfather, old Bayard as he is called (the son of Col. John Sartoris), and their great-great-aunt, Miss Jenny (the sister of Col. John and of the Bayard of Civil War fame). Old Bayard and Miss Jenny were probably too old to function well as father and mother surrogates for the boys. Moreover, the boys grew up hearing the legends of oral tradition about the daring exploits of their great-grandfather, Col. John Sartoris, and of their great-great-uncle, Bayard Sartoris, in the Civil War.

Perhaps it is not surprising under the circumstances that the boys grew up rivalling one another in daring exploits, with John usually getting the better of Bayard. As Ong notes, this kind of male rivalry can lead to a deep bond of affection between rivals. This male bond is undoubtedly part of Bayard's grief over his brother's death in World War I. But his grief is compounded by the fact that John's dying gesture to Bayard was clearly a challenge, and Bayard clearly understood it: "Then he thumbed his nose at me like he always was doing and flipped his hand at the Hun and kicked his machine out of the way and jumped," Bayard says (*FD* 280). The memory of his brother's "familiar gesture"(*FD* 368) haunts Bayard after the war. Although John is no longer present for Bayard to rival, Bayard feels a compulsive need to rival John and prove himself.

Since John's challenge to him came in a war, the absence of a war will make it nearly impossible for Bayard to answer that challenge, which he feels very deeply. But the absence of John from Bayard's life now means that Bayard will never again enjoy the thrill, satisfaction, or disappointment of rivalry with his brother. In the rivalry between the boys as they grew up, John and Bayard were establishing their masculine identities in relation to one another. Bayard's problem after the war is that he cannot maintain his own identity because the person against whom he has been establishing his identity is no longer there to offer him the foil he needs. But John's implicit challenge is there, haunting Bayard and driving him to prove over and over his own courage. While his daring and at times reckless actions show his as yet unsatisfied male agonism, his persistent antifeminism is most obvious in the essential coldness he shows in his marriage with Narcissa. Neither in his first marriage nor in his marriage with Narcissa does Bayard experience "woman now as person, anima-sister, related positively to ego consciousness" (Ong 1971, 11). Instead, young Bayard is cold and indifferent toward his wife and cold and bloodless in his reckless daring. Such coldness is surely a form of misogyny. But Bayard's coldness pales when compared with the cold calculation of Thomas Sutpen.

Out of the tales of oral tradition about the Civil War and his great-grandfather, Faulkner shaped the larger than life characters of Colonel John Sartoris in *The Unvanquished* and Thomas Sutpen in *Absalom, Absalom!* Like the Trojan-Greek conflict memorialized in the *Iliad*, the Civil War as remembered in oral tradition gave the male figures involved in that conflict a seemingly glorious opportunity to establish a specifically masculine identity. The last John and Bayard Sartoris in *Flags in the Dust*, growing up in the honor-shame culture of the South, as Wadlington (50–64) characterizes that culture, would think of the brave deeds done in war as virtually the only way to establish a specifically masculine identity through male-male contesting. No doubt young William Faulkner also thought that up to a certain point in his life, and so they can in this respect be seen as at least partial portraits of the author.

Thomas Sutpen and the Limits of Heroic Masculinity

Of course, war is not the only arena of endeavor in which male-male contesting is possible. Before the Civil War started, Thomas Sutpen started his male-male contesting or "emulative rivalry" with the plantation owner whose servant affronted him as a boy. When the Civil War was over, Charles Bon continued his male-male contesting with Thomas Sutpen, while Col. John Sartoris's son Bayard found a less violent way to assert himself through his confrontation with his father's killer. However, the problem with Quentin Compson in *The Sound and the Fury* is similar to the problem faced by Gail Hightower in *Light in August* and, in different ways, by both Horace Benbow and the last Bayard Sartoris: without appropriate male-male contesting a man cannot establish a specifically masculine identity, the acknowledgment and recognition of which identity enables him to feel that he has made a contribution to society. While Thomas Sutpen's behavior was self-defeating in many ways, his grand design clearly expressed a desire to feel that he had made such a contribution. But his misogyny and racism kept him from ever fulfilling the substance of that desire.

One of the most glaring examples of misogyny in Faulkner's works is the aging Sutpen's rejection of Milly Jones after she gives birth to a girl. If the child had been a boy, Sutpen presumably would have married her and thereby would have made the boy his heir apparent. Such calculation makes Sutpen seem colder than young Bayard. Of course, Sutpen's rejection of Milly is consistent with the terms of his "proposal" to Miss Rosa Coldfield and with his impersonal use of both his first and second wives. Surely Sutpen had engaged in male-male contesting aplenty. Consequently, he should have had an established sense of his own specifically masculine identity, if male-male contesting can yield such an identity. Why didn't Thomas Sutpen advance to having a firmly established sense of masculine identity? An examination of the origins of his contesting behavior will enable us to answer that question.

Dirk Kuyk, Jr., has called attention to the apparent idealism of Sutpen's design, which arises from an affront he suffered in his boyhood when he was turned away from the front door of a mansion by a slave. To avenge the affront, Sutpen thinks of killing the servant and then the master. "But since he desires vindication, shelter, and protection more than revenge," Minter notes

(154), "he determines to build a mansion of his own. . . . Since he wants to avoid the failure that marks his family, particularly his father, he adopts the plantation owner as a model: his goal is to match or even surpass that man's power and grandeur" (154).[4] Thus Minter has identified the male-male contesting that motivates Sutpen.

In effect Sutpen decides to avenge himself by becoming a big man with all the appropriate trappings. Since he knows only the outward trappings of a big man, he can count only such trappings as the sign that he has fulfilled the contest. However, because of unanticipated circumstances, these signs of success keep eluding him. Had he firmly grasped and held these trappings as he desired, though, he would not have experienced a sense of fulfillment because the grandiosity of his contesting signals its inner emptiness and inherent impossibility of fulfillment.

The plantation owner himself is not aware that he has been selected to participate in this male-male contesting. While this does not necessarily invalidate the contest from the standpoint of Thomas Sutpen, it certainly does mean that Sutpen's apparent rival will never provide Sutpen with the recognition that he (Sutpen) has fulfilled his part in the contest. However, the recognition of fulfillment of what he has been striving to achieve could presumably come from other people or even from Sutpen himself. Such recognition would presumably assure Sutpen that he had indeed established his own specific masculine identity. But Sutpen does not experience such recognition either from others or himself. Moreover, even as Kuyk describes Sutpen's design—as aimed to take in the nameless stranger—it is hard to imagine that Sutpen would have received recognition and therefore a sense of fulfillment even if he had managed to carry it out fully.

But Kuyk's analysis of Sutpen's words and imagery suggest that he believed that he needed to do the precise opposite of what the plantation owner did, whereas all Sutpen would need in the contesting pattern is to be the big plantation owner who knows he can deny anybody his door. In other words, the very idealism of his design, especially as Kuyk explicates it, seems to preclude satisfaction. Furthermore, acknowledging Bon as his son would deny him the possibility of fulfilling his idealistic design, not because of Bon's Negro blood but because Bon is presented as a social equal in terms of the class structure of the South. Sutpen's design according to Kuyk would require a nameless stranger who is as much in need of being taken in as

Sutpen as a boy was when he was turned away from the plantation owner's door.

But Sutpen's denial of his partly black son prevents Sutpen
from ever finding satisfaction within the design he has set for
himself. Although it is hard to imagine him putting aside his
design and recognizing Bon as his son, that in itself is a sobering
point to consider. Could a design that leads a father to deny his
son because he is partly black ever lead the father to a satisfying,
fulfilling life? Similarly, could a society that has been designed
to preserve certain caste lines ever foster the full development
of the humanity of the favored group?

These searching questions seem to have been on Faulkner's
mind as he wrote *Absalom, Absalom!* The story of Thomas Sutpen shows that agonism designed to establish one's superiority
or one group's superiority over others is empty, just as striving
for success after success as a means to compensate for an inner
sense that one is unlovable is empty. Misogyny, racism, and slavery do not give Sutpen a fulfilling life but an empty one. His
strivings are futile.

But the story of Thomas Sutpen needs to be considered not
only from the standpoint of the tragedy of Sutpen's life but also
from the standpoints of Quentin Compson and William Faulkner.
As we shall see, Quentin is apparently overwhelmed by his
awareness of the interconnection of male contesting with misogyny, racism, and slavery in the life of Sutpen. Faulkner was probably also overwhelmed by that awareness. But instead of
committing suicide as Quentin does, he directed his own male
agonism toward writing about these depressing aspects of our
cultural heritage.

Quentin Compson: The Plight of Awareness

In "Truth in Conrad's Darkness" (1995, 186–201), Ong observes that antifeminism, racism, and colonialism were interconnected phenomena in the consciousness of nineteenth-century
Europeans. Similarly, antifeminism, racism, and slavery are
interconnected in the life of Thomas Sutpen, and Quentin Compson in *Absalom, Absalom!* becomes aware of these connections.[5]
Quentin and Shreve are aware of Sutpen's crass misogyny in
putting aside his first wife because she did not fit into his idealistic design for his life, and they figure out that the reason he put
his wife aside is that she and therefore her child (Charles Bon)

had Negro blood. Thus while Quentin and Shreve are understandably intrigued by the male contesting that Sutpen embodies so spectacularly, they gradually piece together elements of Sutpen's story that enable them to become aware of the interconnection of misogyny, racism, and slavery in his life.

Cleanth Brooks raises the question of how Quentin and Shreve became aware of Bon's Negro blood: "If in fact Bon did have Negro blood, how did Shreve and Quentin come by that knowledge?" (315). Brooks notes on that same page that Quentin gave his father some information, and Brooks then considers the possibility that Quentin got that information from Henry, Sutpen's white son by Ellen Coldfield. However, another explanation is possible that enables us to see how Quentin's awareness of Sutpen's racism, as manifested in his denial of his son with Negro blood, registered on him.

General Compson and Mr. Compson had passed on to Quentin the story of Sutpen's visit with General Compson during the Civil War. Quentin says of that conversation: "and Grandfather [General Compson] not knowing [i.e., did not know] what choice he [Sutpen] was talking about even" (*AA* 340). Perhaps the two elder Compsons passed on things to Quentin without knowing what they meant, and perhaps Quentin simply figured out what they meant. Quentin clearly has the raw data from which to draw the conclusion that Charles Bon has Negro blood.

Sutpen is quoted as explaining his design to Quentin's grandfather (*AA* 341–42). Sutpen explains that his whole plan was conceived and carried forward as a vindication of that little boy who approached that door fifty years ago and was turned away. But his plan was threatened as the result of an agreement he had entered into in good faith. The one very factor which would destroy the entire plan had been concealed from him. Not until after the child was born did Sutpen discover that this factor existed, the factor which could render his plan a mockery and a betrayal.

And Quentin relates this information: "He [General Compson] just learned one morning that Sutpen had ridden up to Grandfather's old regiment's headquarters and asked and received permission to speak to Henry and did speak to him and rode away again before midnight" (*AA* 345). Obviously Sutpen made the choice to play his trump card. What was it? Earlier we learned that Sutpen said to Quentin's grandfather:

> yet they deliberately withheld from me the one fact which I have
> reason to know they were aware would have caused me to decline

the entire matter, otherwise they would not have withheld it from
me—a fact which I did not learn until after my son was born. (*AA*
329)

Sutpen's "last trump card" then is to inform Henry of this fact.
Given Henry's dogged fight as a Confederate soldier to defend
the caste system of the South, the information about Bon's Negro
blood would presumably be sufficient to move him to kill Bon
rather than allow Bon to marry Judith. For to allow a Negro to
marry his sister would be to make a mockery not only of the war
effort to preserve the caste system but also of his father's effort
to found a lily-white family dynasty.

The fact that neither Thomas Sutpen nor Henry tells Judith
about Charles Bon's biological relationship to her or about his
Negro blood can be seen as showing their misogyny. Brooks has
taken note of the odd facts about this situation:

> Even Judith evidently did not know why her marriage was forbidden
> nor did she know why her brother killed Charles Bon. After the
> murder and Henry's flight, Judith tells Mrs. Compson, the General's
> wife, that the war will soon be over now because "they [the Confeder-
> ate soldiers] have begun to shoot one another." The remark indicates
> her bafflement as well as her despair. (315)

The silence of her father and of her brother to Judith on these
matters clearly reduces her to the status of a negligible person,
one not to be consulted or considered when important family
decisions were made. Such a reduction of women is the essential
problem with misogyny.

One might wonder why Quentin figured out the true meaning
of Sutpen's statements when his grandfather and father had not.
Some might argue along with Brooks that Quentin received some
information directly from Henry (316). While that is a possibility,
it is not necessary to assume that. Meeting Henry was indeed a
major event in Quentin's life. He could not sleep afterward.
Clearly Quentin responded deeply to the meeting. Whatever one
calls it, Quentin's state of mind after his encounter with Henry
is a sufficient condition to explain why he figured out the meaning of Sutpen's statements when he did, for all we need to posit
is that the meeting served as a catalyst to his thought. Intellectual
breakthroughs can result from such profoundly moving experiences. Quentin in effect is clearly aware of how misogyny, racism,
and slavery are connected on the concrete level in Thomas Sut-

pen's life, although he certainly never used the terms "misogyny" or "racism."

Did Quentin's fascination with the story of Sutpen also make him aware of the troubling historical interconnection of misogyny, racism, and slavery in the culture of the South? Karl notes that "Quentin is the one to embrace the full racial dilemma: the knowledge that the Negro should be equal and yet the feeling that for the white Southerner things are more complicated than that" (555). The interconnection is plain enough in the words Sutpen is quoted as having said to Quentin's grandfather: "I had a design. To accomplish it I should require money, a house, a plantation, slaves, a family—incidentally, of course, a wife" (AA 329). Since Quentin's love for his sister Caddy is so acute in The Sound and the Fury, Sutpen's cavalier denigration of woman here—"incidentally, of course, a wife"—and elsewhere (as in his outrageous proposition to Miss Rosa) would have reminded Quentin of the denigration of his beloved sister, a denigration Caddy herself cooperated in because she had in effect introjected the antifeminine ethos of the culture of the South (which may have differed in degree only from the antifeminine ethos in Western culture in general at the time, as Ong's essay about Conrad suggests).

Thus Sutpen's manifold misogyny could not have escaped Quentin's notice, just as the role of slaves in Sutpen's idealistic design could not have escaped Quentin's notice. Kuyk points out that Quentin in effect became aware of the misogyny of Henry and Bon toward their own sister:

> Quentin cannot respond [to the tone of his father's letter, AA 469] because, in coming to understand the scene in the bedroom he has experienced a bitter, painful revelation: he has seen that Bon was selfish, that Henry was a racist who could accept incest but recoiled at miscegenation, and that both Bon and Henry had chosen to sacrifice their sister to their own ends. After that revelation Quentin believes that he will nevermore be at peace. (97)

Shreve apparently senses some revulsion of the South in Quentin's body language, as distinct from his words as such, when he asks Quentin why he hates the South (AA 471). Even though Quentin tells Shreve that he does not hate the South, Quentin subsequently commits suicide, which is the ultimate cancellation of male agonism.

In the novel many voices cry out about Sutpen's failure to acknowledge and recognize the distinctive personhood of others.

The very outcry of unaccommodation is designed to spur our opposing energies, says Wadlington. However, Quentin is unable to discover this on his own. If he had had this insight, it could have directed his agonistic striving accordingly. As Wadlington suggests, it should direct our agonistic strivings "to enact the cultural construction of human accommodation itself, in . . . opposition to the tragic devastation of humanity" (216). In his discussion of *As I Lay Dying*, Wadlington makes the following point: "In order to live, in order not to die in one's life, one must receive, or compel, recognition" (111–12). Thomas Sutpen set out to do just that through his male-male contesting with the plantation owner who through a slave had offended him. But Wadlington's discussion of Sutpen clearly indicates that one needs to reciprocate the recognition. Sutpen did not do that.

Awareness of the interconnection of misogyny, racism, and slavery is depressing, and so it is not hard to understand why Quentin Compson was not able to say "No" to death and fight for life. However, we also need to recognize that Quentin's death may represent a very positive step in Faulkner's psychological development. For just as Quentin was fascinated with the story of Sutpen, so, too, Faulkner was fascinated with the story of his legendary great-grandfather. The death of Quentin and of young Bayard in *Flags in the Dust* represent a psychic distancing of Faulkner from, a dying to, male antifeminism in its recklessness and ruthlessness—which is represented not only in Col. John Sartoris in *The Unvanquished*, young John Sartoris as well as young Bayard in *Flags in the Dust*, and Thomas Sutpen in *Absalom, Absalom!* but also in Faulkner's own great-grandfather, whom Faulkner appropriated as a role model. If Quentin's death arises from his awareness of the grim realities associated not only with Sutpen but also with the culture of the South, as I've suggested, then Quentin's death may also represent a further dying in Faulkner to his fascination with his violent ancestor, in which case he would be establishing for himself a firmer sense of his own masculine identity as arising from his own daring work of confronting in his writing the unfortunate and sad heritage of misogyny and racism in the specific culture of the South, which are also parts of the culture of the United States in general.

As young as Quentin was when he became aware of the grim realities of misogyny and racism in his culture, he could not figure out how to direct the energies of his male agonism to fight against them fruitfully. No doubt male agonism can be channelled into life-enhancing endeavors, despite the historical inter-

connection of male contesting with misogyny, racism, and slavery. William Faulkner himself elected to write stories about the recklessness and ruthlessness often associated with male contesting and about the overt misogyny and racism that historically have often accompanied male contesting in the United States. But while writing for Faulkner was a way of fighting for life and contributing to society, he does not portray in the novels under discussion here other socially constructive enterprises that white males such as Quentin Compson and the last Bayard Sartoris could devote their energies to as fully as he devoted himself to writing.[6]

Conclusion

Such life-enhancing possibilities are perhaps clearer to us today than they were to Faulkner because the black civil rights movement and the women's movement have made racism and misogyny socially unacceptable, thereby freeing white male agonism for more socially acceptable enterprises. Freed from the aim of asserting superiority over others simply to dominate them, white male agonism now can be directed to spurring males on to doing their own personal best in their chosen fields of endeavor and thereby making a contribution to the well-being of society, just as it spurred William Faulkner on to become the best writer he could be.

But the male writers whose works are ostensibly designed to help men develop a sense of masculine identity—Bly, Friel, Gilmore, Keen, Kipnis, Moore and Gillette, Osherson, Seidler, Vogt and Sirridge, Smalley and Trent, and Becker—have not studied Faulkner's portrayal of male agonism nor Ong's account of how male agonism enables men to establish a specifically masculine sense of identity. Faulkner and Ong have called attention to how identity emerges from identifications. For the alarming trend of violence against women to be stopped, the insights of Faulkner and Ong need to be put to use.

While the psychodynamics of male-male contesting can go tragically awry, men presumably will flourish when the process of identification is properly directed. For men to come to embody the archetypes of mature masculinity identified by Robert Moore and Douglas Gillette, they will need to discover aspects of those archetypes in men that they have known or know about and set out to emulate those aspects of their models that they find

admirable and praiseworthy. Such selective and self-conscious emulation is an example of what James G. Williams refers to as "good mimesis," as distinct from the model-obstacle kind that can lead to violence (222, 239). Good mimesis "calms human fear and conflict," Williams claims (222), and it "frees us from or drastically diminishes rivalry, conflict, and violence" (31).

While William Faulkner portrayed numerous examples of model-obstacle mimesis, most notably Thomas Sutpen, he himself practiced good mimesis to a certain degree by selectively emulating his great-grandfather who was a writer, regardless of whatever other shortcomings he (the elder Falkner) may have had. While we may be sad that Faulkner did not overcome his alcoholism and other personal limitations, we need to recognize how he did achieve the greatness that he did, because we may be able to emulate him at least partially to achieve our own personal greatness. In other words, the personal example he set may not be the smallest part of the legacy he has left us.[7]

Notes

1. For other views of male development, see the various books by Verne Becker, Robert Bly, John Friel, David D. Gilmore, Sam Keen, Aaron R. Kipnis, Eugene Monick, Robert Moore and Douglas Gillette, Samuel Osherson, Victor J. Seidler, Gary Smalley and John Trent, Gregory Max Vogt and Stephen T. Sirridge, and James Wyly. For other studies of gender in Faulkner's works, see the selections gathered together by Donald M. Kartiganer and Ann J. Abadie.

2. In "Discourse, Difference, and Gender: Walter Ong's Contributions to Feminist Language Studies," C. Jan Swearingen explores how Ong's work can be used to address concerns raised by feminist studies, and in the same volume the late Ruth El Saffar considers Ong's work in relation to other psychoanalytic theories in "The Body's Place: Language, Identity, Consciousness." In *Verbal Dueling in Heroic Narrative: The Homeric and Old English Traditions,* Ward Parks follows up Ong's work and explores the dynamics of male verbal contesting, especially flyting, in the *Iliad,* the *Odyssey, Beowulf, The Song of Roland, Sir Gawain and the Green Knight,* and the Sanskrit *Mahabharata.* His account of verbal dueling suggests that the whole history of Western rhetoric can be seen as a manifestation of male contesting. Ong's theory of male antifeminism, then, would help explain why females by and large (with a few notable exceptions) were excluded from training in and the practice of rhetoric. But his theory can help explain more than just those manifestations of the interconnection of male contesting with antifeminism. It helps explain (without condoning) virtually all manifestations of male dominance over females.

3. Subsequently referred to as *FD* in text citations.

4. Karl points out that "so much of this [sense of injury in Sutpen which leads to his actions] winds back to Faulkner himself—not in any definitive way, but in the way he was turned away from the Oldhams [as the prospective husband of young Estelle Oldham], in the way he spent all those years in

penury and oblivion while he honed his talents" (549). Karl fails to note, however, that early in life Faulkner apparently formulated his own design, however inchoately, which included being married to Estelle Oldham. Once Faulkner was married to her, he doggedly endured that marriage, as Sutpen doggedly pursued his idealistic design to the end. Faulkner also had to have a mansion—and did (Rowan Oak).

5. Subsequently referred to as *AA* in text citations.

6. Faulkner's concern for matters of race in "The Bear" and *Intruder in the Dust* grow out of awarenesses implicit in *Absalom, Absalom!*, just as Faulkner's concern about the myth of war in *The Fable* grows out of concerns implicit in *Flags in the Dust*, *Absalom, Absalom!*, and *The Unvanquished*. Given the degree to which Faulkner had died to the South's cultural conditioning with respect to race through writing such a searching exploration of this weighty issue in *Absalom, Absalom!*, his public opposition in the fifties to racism in the South is understandable (Karl 898–924). Moreover, given the degree to which Faulkner had died to the South's myth of war through writing various works about male enchantment with war heroics, his fear of the outbreak of another civil war over race is understandable, because Faulkner was dying to the myth of war, long before he wrote *The Fable*, through the deaths of the last Bayard Sartoris and his brother John in *Flags in the Dust*, Thomas Sutpen and Quentin Compson as freighted with and weighed down from the matters in *Absalom, Absalom!*, and Col. John Sartoris and his brother Bayard in *The Unvanquished*.

7. I wish to thank Martin Bock, the late Cleanth Brooks, Robert Hart, William J. Kennedy, John T. Matthews, Walter J. Ong, and Noël M. Valis for their comments on earlier drafts of this essay. Naturally I remain responsible for whatever shortcomings it still has.

Works Cited

Becker, Verne. *The Real Man Inside: How Men Can Recover Their Identity and Why Women Can't Help*. Grand Rapids, MI: Zondervan, 1992.

Bly, Robert. *Iron John: A Book About Men*. Reading, MA: Addison-Wesley, 1990.

Brooks, Cleanth. *William Faulkner: Toward Yoknapatawpha and Beyond*. New Haven: Yale University Press, 1978.

El Saffar, Ruth. "The Body's Place: Language, Identity, Consciousness." In *Media, Consciousness, and Culture: Walter Ong's Thoughts on Rhetoric, Communication, and Criticism*, edited by Bruce E. Gronbeck, Thomas J. Farrell, and Paul A. Soukup, 182–93. Newbury Park, CA: Sage, 1991.

Farrell, Thomas J. "Secondary Orality and Consciousness Today." In *Media, Consciousness, and Culture: Walter Ong's Thoughts on Rhetoric, Communication, and Criticism*, edited by Bruce E. Gronbeck, Thomas J. Farrell, and Paul A. Soukup, 194–209. Newbury Park, CA: Sage, 1991.

Faulkner, William. *Absalom, Absalom! The Corrected Text* Edited by Noel Polk. New York: Vintage, 1987.

———. *Flags in the Dust*. Edited by Douglas Day. New York: Vintage, 1974.

Friel, John. *The Grown-Up Man: Heroes, Healing, Honor, Hurt, Hope*. Deerfield Beach, FL: Health Communications, 1991.

Gilmore, David D. *Manhood in the Making: Cultural Concepts of Masculinity.* New Haven: Yale University Press, 1990.

Guerard, Albert J. *The Triumph of the Novel: Dickens, Dostoevsky, Faulkner.* New York: Oxford University Press, 1976.

Karl, Frederick R. *William Faulkner: American Writer.* New York: Weidenfeld and Nicolson, 1989.

Kartiganer, Donald M., and Ann J. Abadie, eds. *Faulkner and Gender: Faulkner and Yoknapatawpha, 1994.* Jackson: University Press of Mississippi, 1996.

Keen, Sam. *Fire in the Belly: On Being a Man.* New York: Bantam, 1991.

Kipnis, Aaron R. *Knights Without Armor: A Practical Guide for Men in Quest of Masculine Soul.* Los Angeles: Tarcher, 1991.

Kuyk, Dirk, Jr. *Sutpen's Design: Interpreting Faulkner's Absalom, Absalom!* Charlottesville: University Press of Virginia, 1990.

Minter, David. *William Faulkner: His Life and Work.* Baltimore: Johns Hopkins University Press, 1980.

Monick, Eugene. *Castration and Male Rage: The Phallic Wound.* Toronto: Inner City Books, 1991.

———. *Phallos: Sacred Image of the Masculine.* Toronto: Inner City Books, 1987.

Moore, Robert, and Douglas Gillette. *King, Warrior, Magician, Lover: Rediscovering the Archetypes on Mature Masculinity.* San Francisco: Harper, 1989.

———. *The King Within: Accessing the King in the Male Psyche.* New York: William Morrow, 1992.

———. *The Lover Within: Accessing the Lover in the Male Psyche.* New York: William Morrow, 1993.

———. *The Magician Within: Accessing the Shaman in the Male Psyche.* New York: William Morrow, 1993.

———. *The Warrior Within: Accessing the Knight in the Male Psyche.* New York: William Morrow, 1992.

Ong, Walter J. *Faith and Contexts: Volume Three: Further Essays, 1952–1990,* edited by Thomas J. Farrell and Paul A. Soukup. Atlanta: Scholars Press, 1995.

———. *Fighting for Life: Contest, Sexuality and Consciousness.* 1981. Reprint, Amherst: University of Massachusetts Press, 1989.

———. *The Presence of the Word: Some Prolegomena for Cultural and Religious History.* 1967. Reprint, Minneapolis: University of Minnesota Press, 1991.

———. *Rhetoric, Romance, and Technology: Studies in the Interaction of Expression and Culture.* Ithaca, NY: Cornell University Press, 1971.

Osherson, Samuel. *Wrestling with Love: How Men Struggle with Intimacy with Women, Children, Parents, and Each Other.* New York: Fawcett Columbine, 1992.

Parks, Ward. *Verbal Dueling in Heroic Narrative: The Homeric and Old English Traditions.* Princeton: Princeton University Press, 1990.

Seidler, Victor J. *Rediscovering Masculinity: Reason, Language, and Sexuality.* London: Routledge, 1989.

Smalley, Gary, and John Trent. *The Hidden Value of a Man: The Incredible Impact of a Man on His Family.* Colorado Springs: Focus on the Family Publishing, 1992.

Swearingen, C. Jan. "Discourse, Difference, and Gender: Walter Ong's Contributions to Feminist Language Studies." In *Media, Consciousness, and Culture: Walter Ong's Thoughts on Rhetoric, Communication, and Criticism,* edited by Bruce E. Gronbeck, Thomas J. Farrell, and Paul A. Soukup, 210–22. Newbury Park, CA: Sage, 1991.

Vogt, Gregory Max, and Stephen T. Sirridge. *Like Son, Like Father: Healing the Father-Son Wound in Men's Lives.* New York: Plenum, 1991.

Wadlington, Warwick. *Reading Faulknerian Tragedy.* Ithaca, NY: Cornell University Press, 1987.

Williams, James G. *The Bible, Violence, and the Sacred: Liberation from the Myth of Sanctioned Violence.* San Francisco: Harper Collins, 1991.

Wyly, James. *The Phallic Quest: Priapus and Masculine Inflation.* Toronto: Inner City Books, 1989.

The Crucial Antithesis: Orality/Literacy Interaction in the Poetry of Dylan Thomas

GEORGE P. WEICK

NEAR THE END OF *ORALITY AND LITERACY*, WALTER J. ONG WRITES, "THE interaction between the orality that all human beings are born into and the technology of writing, which no one is born into, touches the depths of the psyche" (178). Orality/literacy dynamics, Ong suggests, help clarify the development of human consciousness, from the individual's awaking through "articulate language" as a self engaged in participatory union with others,. through the "division and alienation" introduced by writing, to a "higher unity" consisting of "more conscious interaction between persons" (179). These ideas illuminate the poetry of Dylan Thomas, a writer whose work has inspired intense critical debate since his death in 1953. Thomas's early poetry, in particular, embodies a profound tension between oral and literate elements. Moreover, it chronicles the author's attempt to seek a fertile balance between the two, a balance designed to promote greater introspective awareness without losing contact altogether with the "magical" resources of the spoken word.

Thomas was born in Wales in 1914 to parents who were of quite different dispositions and backgrounds. According to one of Thomas's biographers, his mother Florence was a "gay, garrulous woman" with a deep devotion to the Welsh chapel (Fitzgibbon 16–17). Although she went to two schools as a child and had a respect for books, it is doubtful that "she ever read a book other than the Bible" (Fitzgibbon 17). Dylan's father, D. J. Thomas, a confirmed atheist, was from a different mold. A curmudgeonly schoolteacher who in his youth aspired to be both a university professor and a poet, he venerated English literature throughout his life (Fitzgibbon 10–25). Dylan loved and respected both his parents, and it is clear that D. J. Thomas's devotion to literature and his well-stocked library were important early influences on his son.

Thomas took to reading early. As he explained, "My first, and greatest, liberty was that of being able to read everything and anything I cared to. I read indiscriminately, and with my eyes hanging out" (qtd. in Fitzgibbon 325). His correspondence reveals that his early reading was indeed eclectic. He devoured children's comics, detective stories, and popular fiction alongside the Chaucer, Shakespeare, Dickens, Trollope, Hardy, Wordsworth, Byron, Shelley, Keats, and the many other literary "classics" found on his father's library shelves (Tremlett 25). The young Thomas began building a library of his own which included Yeats, Eliot, Aldous Huxley, Edith Sitwell, D. H. Lawrence, James Joyce, and Virginia Woolf, among others.

Alongside his love of reading, he developed an intense love of writing. He began with "imitations of anything I happened to be reading at the time: Sir Thomas Browne, de Quincy, Henry Newbolt, the Ballads, Blake, Baroness Orczy, Marlowe, Chums, the Imagists, the Bible, Poe, Keats, Lawrence, Anon., and Shakespeare" (Fitzgibbon 325). By the age of thirteen he had published poems in the Swansea Grammar School magazine. A few weeks after his fifteenth birthday, a precocious survey of modern poetry appeared under his name in the same publication. After finishing school at the age of sixteen-and-a-half, he took a job with a local newspaper, the South Wales Daily Post, with his first articles and reviews appearing shortly thereafter (Fitzgibbon 41–62). Of import to his future career, from 1930 to 1934 he wrote many poems in which he sought to find his own voice. More than two hundred of these poems have been preserved.[1] A few weeks after his twentieth birthday, his first book, 18 Poems, was published.

What all of this suggests, of course, is that Thomas achieved a high degree of literacy at an early age. Yet for him, then and throughout his life, what remained important was the beauty and power of the spoken word. When Thomas was a young child his father read nursery rhymes and short stories to him and his sister Nancy in the evenings in a voice that had the "timbre, pitch and resonance of a Shakespearian actor" (Tremlett 23). D. J. decided his son would benefit from exposure to more substantial literature and began reciting Shakespeare to him when Thomas was four (Tremlett 26). The thunderous sermons he heard as a youth also impressed upon him the power of the oral word, the "great rhythms . . . from the Welsh pulpits" as he characterized them later in life (Fitzgibbon 326). Words were, for Thomas, something far removed from the "quiescent visual phenomena" or "signs" of deeply interiorized literacy as described by Ong

(Ong, *Orality* 77). They were filled with the "evanescence, power, and freedom" characterized by "oral man's" experience of language (Ong, *Orality* 77). As Thomas explained in 1951 in a written answer to questions asked by a student about his work:

> I wanted to write poetry in the beginning because I had fallen in love with words. The first poems I knew were nursery rhymes, and before I could read them for myself I had come to love just the words of them, the words alone. What the words stood for, symbolised, or meant, was of very secondary importance; what mattered was the *sound* [Thomas's emphasis] of them as I heard them for the first time ... I did not care what the words said, overmuch, nor what happened to Jack & Jill & the Mother Goose rest of them; I cared for the shapes of sound that their names, and the words describing their actions, made in my ears; I cared for the colours the words cast on my eyes. (qtd. in Fitzgibbon 323–24)

Even in his mature work Thomas insisted upon the primacy of the spoken word. As with oral peoples for whom, as Ong says, "language is a mode of action and not simply a countersign of thought" (Ong 1982, 32), Thomas demanded that poetry be "moving" in a very real and immediate sense. In a 1949 radio broadcast on the work of fellow Welsh poet Edward Thomas, Dylan, then thirty-five, explained what he thought a poem was:

> Poetry is what makes me cry, what tingles my hair and scalp, what makes me want to do this, or that, or nothing. . . . All that matters about poetry is the enjoyment of it, however tragic it may be. All that matters is the eternal movement behind it, the vast undercurrent of human grief, folly, pretension, exaltation and ignorance . . . (Maud 1991, 210).

Ong notes that the Hebrew term *dabar* means both "word" and "event" (Ong 1982, 32), a connection that would be well understood by the twenty-three-year-old Thomas who criticized his friend and fellow poet Vernon Watkins for using words that made his work a "still-life or an experience *put down* [Thomas's emphasis], placed, regulated" and not "an event, a happening, an action" (Ferris 278). In an earlier letter he likened poetry to an experience of sexual intensity, saying that it should be "as orgiastic and organic as copulation" (Ferris 182). In a 1934 review appearing in the magazine *Adelphi*, Thomas, who was then only nineteen, charged the leading British and American poets of the day (a group which included Pound, Auden, Day-Lewis, and Wil-

liam Carlos Williams) with "debasing" poetry. "Too much poetry
to-day [sic] is flat on the page," he wrote, "a black and white
thing of words created by intelligences that no longer think it
necessary for a poem to be read and understood by anything but
eyes" (qtd. in Tremlett 46). Throughout his life he insisted that
poems were meant to be spoken, not merely read on the page.
When a friend, Bert Trick, asked to read the poems Thomas had
brought with him on the occasion of their first meeting, Thomas
replied: "Oh, no, poems shouldn't be read; they should be spoken," whereupon he proceeded to recite his work (Read 47). His
advice to Pamela Hansford Johnson was that "The speaking of
poetry should certainly be encouraged. I do hope you read aloud.
I myself chant aloud in a sonorous voice every poem I read. The
neighbors must know your poems by heart; they certainly know
my own" (Ferris 41).

Thomas's love of the spoken word was expressed in other ways
as well. In his youth, he joined a local theater group and acted in
a number of productions. An abbreviated list of his roles includes
Count Bellair in Farquhar's *The Beaux Stratagem*, Peter in H. F.
Rubenstein's *Peter and Paul*, and Witwoud in *The Way of the
World* (Fitzgibbon 65–68). In later life, he did extensive work in
the broadcasting and recording industries. From 1950 to 1953
Thomas made four lecture/reading tours of the United States.
One of his last major projects was the production of *Under Milk
Wood*, a "play for voices."

But for the young poet, in love with words, problems existed.
Although at an early age Thomas's "love for the real life of words
increased" until he "knew" that he "must live *with* them and
in them" [Thomas's emphases] (qtd. in Fitzgibbon 324), he was
nonetheless desirous of having them do his bidding. As he strug-
gled in writing his own poetry to make words say what he
wanted them to, he became interested more and more in control.
It would, in fact, be possible to make selections from Thomas's
correspondence and other prose writings on the subject of words
and language that would portray him quite differently from the
passages quoted above. He appears in this light as a meticulously
literate craftsman, prepared to sacrifice exuberance for precision.
A letter to Pamela Hansford Johnson says that the poet must
work at poetry "as a sculptor works at stone, chiselling, plotting,
rounding, edging & making perfect" (Ferris 114). Objecting to a
letter from Richard Rees, in which he was accused of automatic
writing, Thomas argued he was a painstaking composer whose
poetry was the product of "tremendously hard work." "I write

at the speed of two lines an hour," he claimed in the same letter (Ferris 51). In reviewing Thomas's second book, *Twenty-Five Poems*, Stephen Spender faulted his poetry for being "turned on like a tap; it is just poetic stuff with no beginning nor end, shape, or intelligent and intelligible control" (297). In rebuttal Thomas claimed "My poems *are* [Thomas's emphasis] formed; they are not turned on like a tap at all, they are 'watertight compartments'" (298). Using an even less felicitous metaphor in writing to Desmond Hawkins, Thomas refers to the poems published in his own first book as "coded blocks of feeling" and complains of his "policeman rhythms" (189).

The conflicting statements about language and poetry appearing in Thomas's correspondence and other prose writings imply an attitude that is fundamentally divided. One side seems to value participation, exuberance, and emotion; the other control, distance, and structure. Thomas's early poetry, too, embodies such a conflict, one which has been the subject of intense critical debate in the years since the poet's death.

Instances of this conflict appear throughout Thomas's poetry. Several poems are, in fact, devoted entirely to different aspects of the subject. A short poem, "The Spire Cranes," illustrates not only Thomas's treatment of one dimension of the core conflict, or crucial antithesis, appearing in his work, but also exemplifies the famous (or infamous) difficulty of his style. "The Spire Cranes" treats Thomas's double conception of poetry which, as the above passages from his correspondence indicate, was viewed by him at times as being "as orgiastic and organic as copulation" and at other times as being like "watertight compartments."[2]

The laconic opening sentence of "The Spire Cranes" (95) has proven baffling. Emery paraphrases it as "The church steeple stretches its neck away from earth, water, food" (154). Tindall cannot decide whether "cranes" is a noun or verb (158). "The spire's hook," from the eighth line, however, suggests a context in which the opening sentence can be properly understood. Apart from the connotations of "snare" or "trap" which the image raises (following through with the idea that the spire is a prison of sorts in which birds are kept), "hook" also suggests the hook of a derrick. "Cranes" is, therefore, a verb, and the sense of the line is that the spire acts like a "crane," or derrick, hoisting the "feathery/Carved birds" up to it.

These birds are the key to the poem's symbolism. "Striking throats" refers to their remarkable voices, making them songbirds, hence a metaphor for the poet's songs. The spire is a church spire, a symbol of order, control, and authority. The spire exercises its authority by drawing the birds up to it and then protectively imprisoning them. It does not allow them to "blunt their striking throats on the salt gravel" or "Pierce the spilt sky with diving." But, the bell chimes "cheat the prison spire" by sounding so loudly they scare away the birds. Some birds, however, return after a time while others plunge recklessly away, and herein lies the central point of the poem. Thomas appears to be suggesting that some birds, or metaphorically some poems, are content to be bound within a sphere of order such as that symbolized by the church spire and its statue. The bells, metaphorically poetic inspiration, send them flying off, but they wheel about in ordered paths, finally returning to their perch. No matter where they go they are bound within the "aviary" represented by the spire. They are "feathery" and "Carved" like pieces of statuary integral to a larger edifice, even when they are flying about in the skies. At no point do they leave their ordered paths to splash about in the puddles of rainwater "spilt" from the sky or to peck about for food in the "salt gravel." But, as the last four lines indicate, there is another, completely different type of bird which enjoys plunging away recklessly from its prison and indulging in all kinds of excesses.

The contrast Thomas draws in this poem is between one type of poetry which favors classical order and control, and another type which exults in prodigal exuberance. In the poem's conclusion, Thomas seems to mark a personal preference. Some songs, whether they "jump back/To the built voice" or "fly with winter to the bells," follow classical patterning and are choice for one type of poet. But Thomas would seem to prefer another type of poem, as the last line implies. The choice Thomas makes in his poem is strikingly similar to that which he makes in a letter written in March 1938 in which he distinguishes poems having a "concentric movement round a central image" and those which evidence conflict and contradiction in imagery and theme (Ferris 281). The former type of poetry, he argues, which develops a central idea through a logically constructed set of precise images would be, for Thomas, "a circular piece of experience placed neatly outside the living stream of time from which it came" (Ferris 282). The latter, with the contradictory, quarrelsome, and prodigal character of its imagery, approximates nearer to Thomas's perception of the true conditions of experience. It is this type of poetry he favors in both his letter and his poem.

"The Spire Cranes" argues for a fundamental "orality" that characterizes Thomas's orientation as a poet. Yet, as Ong explains, "orality" within the context of a dominant chirographic or typographic culture is essentially different from that experienced in a primarily oral society in which writing is unknown or little known. The "literate" individual can never experience what Ong has called, in *The Presence of the Word*, "total response to vocalization" (76). He may be "taken with" expressions of the power of language to enchant or influence known to the oral speaker or storyteller and may even study them "with real love," but "his psychological structures are different and he simply cannot respond as more directly oral persons do" (76). Thomas's responses to poetry, and his larger responses to experience itself, are clearly those of a literate person who is far removed from primary orality. Indeed, in the case of Thomas, other poems express distaste for the "oral" characteristics affirmed in "The Spire Cranes." In "Once It Was the Colour of Saying," for example, Thomas wishes to undo the "seaslides of saying" (98) of some of his more formless early work. "I Have Longed to Move Away," similarly, presents the poet as desiring to "move away" from "ghosts in the air / And ghostly echoes on paper, / And the thunder of calls and notes" (73). The structure and prosody of many of Thomas's early poems, in fact, argue for a "literate" rather than an "oral" bias. His poems, in general, are based upon lines having precise syllable counts and highly structured half-rhymes. Even "The Spire Cranes," whose argument favors a type of poetry associated more with "oral" traits, is based upon twelve-syllable lines with only two variants (the sixth and eighth lines each contain eleven syllables). Moreover, the poem has a strict A-A B-B half-rhyme scheme (aviary/feathery, gravel/heel and so on). The poetic form of "The Spire Cranes" thus contradicts the poem's argument. Within Thomas's poetry, as within his correspondence and other writings, there appears a fundamental conflict between "oral" and "literate" elements.

While no significant discussion exists within the criticism of orality/literacy distinctions in Thomas's poetry, the "conflict of opposites," as it is typically styled, has received extensive and often controversial treatment. I would suggest that viewing this subject through the lens of oral/literate polarities resolves many of the difficulties inherent in other approaches while being more consistent with Thomas's poetic interests and practices.

Critics are in agreement that the most obvious level of conflict appearing in Thomas's early poetry is presented in terms of the "war of opposites" present in nature and in natural forces. His poetry expresses what Ralph Maud, in *Entrances to Dylan Thomas's Poetry*, has called "his basic view of the universe as a war of conflicting forces" (39). Maud identifies more specific forms in which conflict is manifest. One aspect of this "war," for example, involves Thomas's vision of the physical processes of the universe poised against each other in Heraclitean strife (57–80). This perception is presented so extensively in the early poems that Jacob Korg has described them, pointedly, as "an arena of conflict between the forces of creation and destruction embodied in the processes of nature" (29). Since man is ineluctably a part of the natural world, he, too, experiences the conflict of physical processes. As Maud observes, "the two forces, growth and destruction, operate both in nature and in the individual" (68).

Many critics argue that conflict in Thomas's work goes far beyond purely formal characteristics of imagery, language, and style to touch the deepest structures of the author's sensibility. Conflict for them is more than a process the poet observes operating in the universe or in himself and faithfully records in his poetry. It is a core feature of his psychic disposition which determines comprehensively the framework of assumptions about reality upon which the poems themselves are based. Thus, David Holbrook argues that the many instances of contradictory imagery and paradoxical statement in the early poetry reflect a self that is essentially "divided" and therefore incapable of responding to experience in a more coherent and unified manner. Thomas suffered intense psychic stress originating in his inability to integrate the diverse fragments of his ego. His early poems evince the effects of an unresolved interior conflict between what Holbrook calls the "true Dylan self" and a "schizoid dissociated identity" (81). J. M. Kertzer, similarly, sees the "confusion" of the poetic imagery, syntax, and logic as evidence of Thomas's "divided state of mind" which is obsessively locked into a process of "striving but failing to come to terms with its own confusion, asserting itself yet lapsing back into lethargy and anguish" (309).

A totally different view of "foundational" or "core" conflict in the early poems emerges from the work of others. For them, Thomas's poetry is the product of a finely controlled poetic imagination that seeks, depending upon the critic, a form of spiritual, mystical, or psychological transcendence. Conflict is a condition of the unregenerate self and the transitory world it inhabits, one which the poet seeks to overcome. Robert K. Burdette, for example, sees Thomas as struggling through the confused motives and contradictory experiences that plague the individual to portray in mystic light "the rediscovery and reaffirmation of the wholeness of man" (154). Raymond Stevens claims that Thomas's artistic quest is "for that unifying poetic self which will resolve the tensions of 'intricate manhood'" (39). Martin Dodsworth describes Thomas's desire "to resolve the duality of mind and body on Blakean lines" (117). Rob Jackaman approaches the early work through a Jungian analysis of mandalla symbolism and finds that in them the author attempts "to heal the polar division implicit in man's state on the earth" (28).

These two views of the core conflict in Thomas proceed by different lines of argument and emphasize different values, both expressed and implied by the poems. One sees the poems as tending to disunity as a consequence of the poet's failure to develop an enduring self-image large and stable enough to incorporate authentically the diverse fragments into which his identity has split. Kertzer writes, "it is not surprising that his early poetry grows increasingly devious until it argues itself into confusion" (315). Thomas was unable to unite these fragmentary "selves" in his poetry chiefly because the issues it touched were so deep-rooted and complexly disturbing he did not himself fully understand what it was he was confronting. "Thomas could not know at times," Holbrook says, "even what kind of experience it was he was trying to write about" (90). The other view credits Thomas with achieving—or at least being engaged in a successfully developing struggle to achieve—a holistic, transcendent self in which are joined all conflicting elements and identities. The complexities and obscurities of the poetry are attributed to the difficulty of expressing such a profound synthesis in language that, by its nature, emphasizes contrasts and distinctions. Burdette writes, "The union of opposites, the visionary experience, requires this verbal paradox, though the experience itself may be profoundly simple" (24).

Obviously, these views are not only different, but mutually exclusive. The question becomes which of them, if either, accurately represents what occurs in Thomas's poetry. Is conflict evidence of the author's inability to integrate his experiences and express them in a coherent manner consistent with the development of a unified self? Is it the reflection of an effort to transcend the contradictions and paradoxes inherent in existence? Or is it a sign of something altogether different?

Orality/literacy studies show the nature of the core conflict in Thomas's poetry in light quite different from that of either of the above theories. The early poems in particular embody antitheses and conflicts that correspond to oral/literate polarities discussed by Ong. Two of these are especially illustrative.

First, as with an individual living in a oral culture removed from "elaborate analytic categories that depend on writing to structure knowledge at a distance from lived experience" (Ong 1982, 42), Thomas's poetry is close to the human lifeworld. It treats a world of elemental processes of birth, growth, decay, and death. Its imagery is intensely physical, emphasizing the human body. As Thomas explained to Pamela Hansford Johnson, "What you call ugly in my poetry is, in reality, nothing but the strong stressing of the physical. Nearly all my images, coming, as they do, from my solid and fluid world of flesh and blood, are set out in terms of their progenitors" (Ferris 38). Later in the same letter he writes:

> The body, its appearance, death, and disease, is a fact, sure as the fact of a tree. It has its roots in the same earth as the tree. . . . All thoughts and actions emanate from the body. Therefore the description of a thought or action—however abstruse it may be—can be beaten home by bringing it onto a physical level. . . . Through my small, bonebound island I have learnt all I know, experienced all, and sensed all. All I write is inseparable from the island. As much as possible, therefore, I employ the scenery of the island to describe the scenery of my thoughts, the earthquake of the body to describe the earthquake of the heart. (39)

As Thomas expresses the matter in the opening of one of his most famous early poems:

> The force that through the green fuse drives the flower
> Drives my green age; that blasts the roots of trees
> Is my destroyer. (10)

Yet, Thomas recognizes, as only someone who has developed the sophisticated structures of consciousness Ong associates with literacy is capable of doing, that there is great value in distance. In fact, without distance, knowledge of the lifeworld and its meaning for humanity would be impossible. Thomas's "boys of summer" know that "seasons must be challenged or they totter / Into a chiming quarter / Where, punctual as death, we ring the stars" (2). In "I Fellowed Sleep," the poet, in his

232 GEORGE P. WEICK

imagination, flees the earth to a "cloud coast" where he can gain perspective on his "fathers' globe" and achieve a "deep" waking "in the worlded clouds" (31–32). The poet, in "If I Were Tickled By the Rub of Love," distances himself from the sexual round of life in order to gain painful knowledge of the all-pervasive presence of death. He sits alongside the sea of life, removed from his fellow humans and their careless enjoyment of its waters, and watches "the worm beneath my nail / Wearing the quick away" (14).

A second "oral/literate" characteristic of Thomas's early poetry is that it is "agonistically toned" (Ong 1982, 43), often juxtaposing diametrically opposed views. Such is the case in "I See the Boys of Summer" which is organized as a three-part dialogue or debate.[3] Two groups are involved, the "boys" and a solitary figure called the "man of winter" who criticizes the boys and their behavior in the first part of the poem. In the second part, the boys defend themselves, arguing that what the man sees as damaging rebelliousness is, from their perspective, crucial to life. Part three consists of a single stanza—making it only one-fourth as long as either part one or part two—representing a summary of the two positions in which the antagonists speak alternating lines. "Find Meat on Bones," similarly, consists of a debate between two voices which speak in alternating stanzas. As in "I See the Boys of Summer," one voice advocates *carpe diem* while the other urges rebellion against "the flesh and bone, / The word of the blood, the wily skin" and against "Autocracy of night and day, / Dictatorship of sun" (74). Another manifestation of agonism is found in the riddles, puns, and questions present in many of Thomas's poems. Ong suggests such devices are used "to engage others in verbal and intellectual combat" (44). For Thomas they are meant to tease and engage the reader by "saying two things at once in one word, four in two and one in six" (Ferris 182). One example is given by the riddle from "How Soon the Servant Sun": "A claw I question from the mouse's bone" (65) which is, upon first (and perhaps upon second) inspection, perplexing. The answer is "a cat," and the sense of the line is that from the bones of the dead mouse before him the poet wonders metonymically about the "claw" or cat responsible for the killing. By extension, from the evidence of death present in the world, the poet questions the nature and motives of the entity responsible for causing death (making life and death into a sort of "cat and mouse" game).

Other poems, however, are far from agonistic. At one point in his correspondence Thomas styles the act of writing as an attempt to rise above conflict and agonism to achieve "the momentary peace which is a poem" (Ferris 282). "All All and All the Dry Worlds Lever," the last work appearing in 18 Poems, represents a harmonious affirmation of life in all its confusion, paradox, and uncertainty, as the final stanza suggests:

> Flower, flower the people's fusion,
> O light in zenith, the coupled bud,
> And the flame in the flesh's vision.
> Out of the sea, the drive of oil,
> Socket and grave, the brassy blood,
> Flower, flower, all all and all. (39)

"Altarwise By Owl Light" expresses the same sort of transcendence of agonism found in "All All and All." The poem ends with a sort of Edenic restoration in which the "garden," described as "Green as beginning," soars with its "two bark towers" intact to the Judgment Day (85).

Oral/literate antitheses abound in Thomas's poetry, the above representing only a sample. They are present in terms of theme, structure, imagery, sound, and symbolism. A thorough treatment of the subject would require a lengthy treatise. What is significant for understanding the main thrust of Thomas's early work is that he, as a poet, appears to have had keen insight into the conflicting presences of the "word" within him and the various forms in which these conflicts were manifest. He was, certainly in the period of his early poetry and arguably throughout his life, in the position of a person (or, in a larger context, a culture) who has acquired literacy but who has not yet lost completely the sense of the purity and magic of the oral word. This situation is described incisively by Ong in The Presence of the Word:

the word in a world of sound, has its limitations. It can overcome some of these—impermanence, inaccuracy—only by taking on others—objectivity, concern with things as things, quantification, impersonality.

The question is: Once the word has acquired these new limitations, can it retain its old purity? It can, but for it to do so we must reflectively recover that purity. . . . what earlier man possessed instinctively and confusedly, we must possess more explicitly and clearly. (92)

Thomas's formulation of this experience is expressed in several of his letters. As he saw it, the language-world in which he existed as a literate entity was corrupt. Finding words to express his experiences in a way that would move himself and others to greater awareness was difficult because of the debasement of language by centuries of literate usage. As he wrote at the age of nineteen to Trevor Hughes:

> no single word in all our poetical vocabulary is a virgin word, ready for our first love, willing to be what we make it. Each word has been wooed and gotten by a vast procession of dead litterateurs who put their coins in the plate of a procuring Muse, entered at the brothel doors of a divine language, and whored the syllables of Milton and the Bible. (Ferris 93)

For Thomas, the consequence of corrupted language was the corruption of consciousness. In the same letter to Hughes, Thomas writes:

> We look upon a thing a thousand times; perhaps we shall have to look upon it a million times before we see it for the first time. Centuries of problematical progress have blinded us to the literal world; each bright and naked object is shrouded around with a thick pea soup mist of associations. (Ferris 93)

Thomas saw his poetry as an attempt to purify language and by so doing to penetrate this "mist of associations." A letter from Pamela Hansford Johnson had objected to his use of the word "double-cross" in one of his poems, presumably as being a colloquial and pedestrian expression. He responded that if a word or expression the poet needs is trite, it is up to the poet to refurbish it, to "smooth away the lines of its dissipation, and to put it on the market again, fresh and virgin" (Ferris 25). He explained more fully to Hughes:

> But consciousness of such prostitution [of language] need not lead us, as it has led James Joyce, into the inventing of new words; it need not make us, as it has made Gertrude Stein, repeat our simplicities over and over again in intricate and abstract patterns so that the meaning shall be lost and only the bare and beautiful shells of the words remain. All we need do is to rid our minds of the humbug of words, to scorn the pre-arranged leaping together of words, to make by our own judicious and, let it be prayed for, artistic selection, new associations for each word. (Ferris 93–94)

As the product of a highly literate environment, Thomas realized there could be no return to the pristine orality of early childhood, to the "time of innocence," as he was to call it later in his life, when "words burst upon me, unencumbered by trivial or portentous association," when "words were their spring-like selves, fresh with Eden's dew, as they flew out of the air" (qtd. in Fitzgibbon 324). As he expresses it in "From Love's First Fever to Her Plague," the period in his very early life when "All world was one" is irrecoverable. From the point of view of the literate adult this may well be deservedly so, since that time, perhaps, was no more than "one windy nothing" (24). If he is to gain authentic appreciation of the reality of words and life itself, he must try other means. His goal of purifying language through the "literate" search for "new associations" is inextricably bound with his desire to elevate consciousness—that of his own and that of others. As he writes in another letter: "I do not want to express only what other people have felt; I want to rip something away and show what they have never seen" (25). Writing, for Thomas, is indubitably an act of "consciousness raising" as Ong describes it (Ong, *Orality* 179). In response to a set of questions asked of its contributors by the magazine *New Verse* in 1934, Thomas explained his purposes more formally. Answering the question "Do you intend your poetry to be useful to yourself or others?" he said:

> To both. Poetry is the rhythmetic, inevitably narrative, movement from an overclothed blindness to a naked vision that depends in its intensity on the strength of the labour put into the creation of the poetry. My poetry is, or should be, useful to me for one reason: it is the record of my individual struggle from darkness toward some measure of light, and what of the individual struggle is still to come benefits by the sight and knowledge of the faults and fewer merits in that concrete record. My poetry is, or should be, useful to others for its individual recording of that same struggle with which they are necessarily acquainted. (qtd. in Fitzgibbon 142)

In the context of Thomas's understanding of his own poetry and purposes, then, there can be no authentic transcendence or "healing" of the polarities within him. The interplay of oral and literate elements within his own consciousness represents an antithesis crucial to his identity, as crucial as Blake's necessary contraries were for him. This awareness is expressed powerfully in several early poems, including "I See the Boys of Summer." As the first poem appearing in the body of Thomas's *Collected*

Poems, "Boys" occupies a position of special importance. It was
one of the two poems Thomas thought "best in my book" (Ferris
208). One assumes Thomas intended it to provide an introduction to the themes, imagery, and style that "set the tone" for the
rest of his work. The basic dialogue structure of the poem has
already been discussed. It is clear that the boys of summer and
man of winter are, as their names indicate, polar opposites. While
oral/literate language contrasts are not explicitly a subject of this
poem, the two sides express conflicting views that are nonetheless associated with value differences based upon oral and literate perspectives as discussed by Ong.

From the man's perspective, stated in the first part of the poem,
the boys propose nothing less than absolute anarchy. They advo-
cate rebellion, struggle, resistance to the status quo, particularly
as represented by the cycles of nature. The man, on the contrary,
affirms the value of living in accord with nature. He cautions the
boys to enjoy their youth while they have it. He criticizes their
rebelliousness, claiming that it spoils the very sources that give
life joy and sweetness. When the harvest of life is waiting to be
gathered, they figuratively freeze the soil by their defiance, laying
barren the fields golden with grain. When the summer honey is
theirs for the asking, they poke into the hives like fingers of
wintry ice. The boys, in the second part, reply that what they do
is, in their eyes, indeed vital. They defy nature in order to affirm
and protect man's ability to assert himself against the forces in
life which urge mindless conformity. Were the seasons of nature
and life to go unchallenged, the boys suggest, man would become
totally submissive to the physical universe, his image of himself
formed by what he sees of nature at work about him. Man's will-
ing submission to natural law—which is precisely what they see
the man of winter proposing—deadens his intellectual, artistic,
and spiritual promise. Without the development of the individual's capacity to know and judge for himself, man becomes
merely a cog in the machinery of existence, blindly moving on
cue to the signaling "chiming quarters" of the seasons, from stage
to stage in the cycle of life and death. By denying what is, in
one sense, good for them, the boys affirm other values, ones more
appropriate to the "literate" values expressed through the human
intellect and the creative spirit.

Of crucial importance to understanding what the poem has to
say about conflict is the last stanza, particularly the final line,
"O see the poles are kissing as they cross" (3), which appears to
represent an authorial comment about all that has taken place.

Holbrook sees the stanza generally and the last line specifically as "an expression of black and petrified futility" the poet feels because he has failed to synthesize the schizoid "poles" of his identity (177). The crossing of the poles is, thus, a validation of the utterly debilitating incompatibility of the poet's divided selves which subverts his every attempt to gain psychic whole-ness. They "bring everything to cross purposes" and "cross him at every turn," Holbrook says (177). This is, it should be noted, the minority interpretation of the line. Most critics read it as an expression of an harmonious *conjuntio* of the conflicting poles. Olson says it "remarks that the two extremes are really one; that in the whole view North Pole and South Pole are the same" (92). Moynihan echoes this thought: "Then comes the poet's final ironic comment which seems to say that both points of view, views that appear to be poles apart, are actually in agreement, are saying the same thing finally" (185). Rushworth Kidder inter-prets the line as meaning that the boys "unite all sorts of oppo-sites" (95). Jackaman has the conflicting sides kissing "in a gesture of Love as they coincide" (31). William York Tindall says the line "unites all contraries" (31).

These comments represent a microcosm of the two different critical views on the nature of conflict in Thomas's early poetry as a whole. One side argues that the line represents unresolved conflict; the other sees it as depicting unity or identity.

Although the early poems as a group are both a far more coher-ent and well-ordered body of poetry than Holbrook would ac-knowledge and understandable in their own terms, his position here is in a significant way more tenable than the other. The structure, imagery, and rhetorical patterns ordering "I See the Boys of Summer" argue not for harmonious conciliation but un-resolved strife, disparity, and conflict. If Thomas wanted his reader to see that "the two extremes are really one" he needed to provide a more compelling reason than the single use of the word "kissing" in the final line of the poem. To say that the boys of summer and the man of winter are one is either to ignore or to dismiss the fact that Thomas has spent the entire poem up to this point delineating their differences. "Kissing," in light of all that takes place in the poem, would seem to indicate not that the poles are the same but that they are in some way attracted to each other like the authentic opposites they are. They meet, but meeting does not necessarily imply union. In fact, Thomas's language suggests the meeting itself is a temporary thing; they

"Kiss" in a demonstration of complementariness as they "cross" in conflict and in momentary juxtaposition.

This is not to say, as Holbrook and others would have it, that the unresolved conflict of boys and man is necessarily a sign of psychic dissociation. The two sides may be—as indeed Olson and Moynihan claim they are—complementary parts of a larger self. However, Thomas's purpose, at least at this stage of his career, would seem to be to describe the nature and the character of their conflict, not their "union" or "identity" at a higher level.

The fact that Thomas structured "I See the Boys of Summer" as he did to give both sides the opportunity for an equal hearing suggests he did not intend to portray the "unity" of the opposites or to favor one side over the other. Instead, he would appear to be saying that both are, in some way, right. The antithetical dispositions embodied by the man of winter and the boys of summer are both necessary to human life and by implication to the life of the poet himself. By virtue of his physical self, man is inextricably a part of the world of natural law and process, as the man of winter affirms. But, because of his intellect and creative spirit, he also participates in a different order. In the context of oral/literate polarities, "I See the Boys of Summer" represents Thomas's attempt to understand how the two sides can be related in a productive way, one that affirms contact with the lifeworld while at the same time maintaining the distance necessary to promote creative awareness. The tension created by the conflict of these two incompatible elements is essential to intelligent, spiritually creative life. It is a "crucial antithesis," or necessary conflict between two essentially different, but co-existing sides of human nature.

Other early poems amplify upon Thomas's understanding of his antithetical nature. In "I, in My Intricate Image," for example, Thomas sees himself as a creative entity that is complexly formed. One aspect is "forged in man's minerals," or, that is, made from the physical materials from which all life and all matter is made. This part of his "intricate image" represents his awareness of himself as a physical creature subject to the natural laws governing birth, growth, decay, and death to which all physical creatures are subject. The other component is itself twofold: the "brassy orator laying my ghost in metal" (40), an intriguing construction which combines both the oral side of Thomas's identity which "brassily" speaks the truths of its discoveries about reality; and the literate side, which "lays to rest" these truths in the enduring "metal" of poetry.

The balance between the oral and literate elements of his interior life that Thomas's portrays so potently in "I See the Boys of Summer" and "I, in My Intricate Image" shifted constantly throughout his career, although he always strove to keep the two juxtaposed in creative tension. Even in the later work this tension is evident. There one of his central concerns is the awaking within himself of powerful forces promising spiritual transformation. Oral/literate, ear/eye polarities remain prominent in these poems. In the poems treating this subject, the inner awaking typically is announced orally but only understood when the poet's vision of the interior landscape comes into sharp focus.

In "Poem in October" the "morning beckon" rouses the poet from the metaphoric "sleep" of his mundane life. The beckon, as he has it, "Woke to my hearing from harbour and neighbour wood" (113). Only later in the poem does he see "in the turning" that his experience is related to the reawaking of the "true / Joy of the long dead child" within him, a joy that is itself associated with oral elements—the "parables / Of sun light / And the legends of the green chapels / And the twice told fields of infancy" (114–15).

In "A Winter's Tale" the poet, who cries for deliverance from a "nameless need" that binds him "burning and lost" (133) to creation, must first listen to the true message of the "voice of the dust of water from the withered spring" (133) and the "wizened / Stream" that "with bells and baying water bounds" (134). Only after the poet has heard and assimilated this oral message is he able to look and see the miraculous rebirth of the "long ago she bird" of love which transforms the desolate world of "A Winter's Tale" into Thomas's version of what T. S. Eliot called "midwinter spring." In "Vision and Prayer" the visionary experience begins with the poet asking the question "Who / Are you / Who is born / In the next room / So loud to my own / That I can hear the womb / Opening and the dark run / Over the ghost and the dropped son" (154). As in the other poems expressing inner awaking, only after the poet is engaged at the auditory level is he able to "see" the subject fully. In this case, the awaking is redemptive and apocalyptic. As Thomas writes: "I shall waken / To the judge blown bedlam / Of the uncaged sea bottom / the cloud climb of the exhaling tomb / And the bidden dust upsailing / With his flame in every grain" (158).

Orality/literacy distinctions are fertile ground for the study of Dylan Thomas's poetry. Among other things, they illuminate the nature of conflict in his early work and clarify the powerful yet perplexing inner awaking portrayed in the *Deaths and Entrances* volume (1946) and in *Last Poems* (1953).

Notes

1. The single most significant collection of Thomas's youthful work is at the Lockwood Memorial Library in Buffalo. The library holds the four manuscript notebooks the poet kept from 1930 to 1934 (now referred to as the "Buffalo Notebooks"). Other early manuscript poems are housed in several locations, including the British Museum and the Humanities Research Center at the University of Texas, among others.

2. References to Thomas's poetry are to the 1953 American edition *The Collected Poems of Dylan Thomas*. Other editions are available, including some that are more recent. No edition of Thomas's poetry is without its flaws, but the 1953 edition is less suspect than others. My treatment of "The Spire Cranes" here is based upon my reading of the poem, which appeared in *The Explicator*, 37, no. 1 (Fall 1978).

3. My reading of "I See the Boys of Summer" is indebted to that of Elder Olson's, which appears in *The Poetry of Dylan Thomas* (91–93).

Works Cited

Burdette, Robert K. *The Saga of Prayer: The Poetry of Dylan Thomas*. The Hague: Mouton, 1972.

Dodsworth, Martin. "The Concept of Mind in the Poetry of Dylan Thomas." In *Dylan Thomas: New Critical Essays*. Edited by Walford Davies. London: J. M. Dent, 1972.

Emery, Clark. *The World of Dylan Thomas*. Miami: University of Miami Press, 1962.

Ferris, Paul ed. *Dylan Thomas: The Collected Letters*. London: J. M. Dent, 1985.

Fitzgibbon, Constantine. *The Life of Dylan Thomas*. Boston and Toronto: Little, Brown, 1965.

Holbrook, David. *The Code of the Night*. London: The Athlone Press, 1972.

Jackaman, Rob. "Man and Mandalla: Symbol as Structure in a Poem by Dylan Thomas." *Ariel: An International Review of English Literature*, 7, no. 4 (October 1976).

Kertzer, J. M. "'Argument of the Hewn Voice': The Early Poetry of Dylan Thomas." *Contemporary Literature*, 20, no. 3, (Summer 1979).

Kidder, Rushworth M. *Dylan Thomas: The Country of the Spirit*. Princeton: Princeton University Press, 1972.

Maud, Ralph. *Entrances to Dylan Thomas's Poetry*. Pittsburg: University of Pittsburg Press, 1963.

———. *On the Air with Dylan Thomas: The Broadcasts*. New York: New Directions, 1991.

Moynihan, William T. *The Craft and Art of Dylan Thomas*. Ithaca: Cornell University Press, 1966.

Olson, Elder. *The Poetry of Dylan Thomas*. Chicago: The University of Chicago Press, 1954.

Ong, Walter J. *Orality and Literacy: The Technologizing of the Word*. London and New York: Methuen, 1982.

──────. *The Presence of the Word*. New Haven and London: Yale University Press, 1967.

Read, Bill. *The Days of Dylan Thomas*. London: Weidenfield and Nicholson, 1964.

Stevens, Raymond. "Self and World: The Earlier Poems." In *Dylan Thomas: New Critical Essays*. Edited by Walford Davies. London: J. M. Dent, 1972.

Thomas, Dylan. *The Collected Poems of Dylan Thomas*. New York: New Directions, 1953.

Tindall, William York. *A Reader's Guide to Dylan Thomas*. New York: Noonday, 1962.

Tremlett, George. *Dylan Thomas: In the Mercy of His Means*. New York: Saint Martin's Press, 1991.

Contributors

JAMES R. ANDREAS is Professor of English at Clemson University and the Director of two annual events: the Festival of African American Literature and the Arts, and the Clemson Shakespeare Festival. He has published widely on Chaucer, Shakespeare, and African American Literature and for the past ten years has been the editor of *The Upstart Crow: A Shakespeare Journal*.

ANNE DENISE BRENNAN, SC is an associate professor of English at College of Mount Saint Vincent, Bronx, New York. Sr. Anne Denise received the Enright Award for Teaching Excellence in 1992. She has contributed to the Papers of the Centennial Symposium on Eugene O'Neill and T. S. Eliot and to various religious publications on both local and national levels.

VINCENT CASAREGOLA is an associate professor of English at Saint Louis University, St. Louis, Missouri, where he teaches a variety of writing and literature courses that concern the essay. He has authored a number of articles and papers on literary nonfiction and on issues in rhetorical theory and writing pedagogy.

THOMAS J. FARRELL of the University of Minnesota at Duluth has recently completed a comprehensive book-length study of Walter Ong's work. Dr. Farrell is the co-editor and co-author of *Communication and Lonergan; Faith and Contexts*, three volumes of Ong's essays with an introduction by Farrell; and *Media, Consciousness, and Culture: Explorations of Walter Ong's Thought*.

JOHN MILES FOLEY is William H. Byler Professor of English and Classical Studies at the University of Missouri, where he also directs the Center for Studies in Oral Tradition. He is the author of a series of books, among them *Traditional Oral Epic, Immanent Art*, and *The Singer of Tales in Performance*, and numerous articles. Dr. Foley has also presented more than two hundred lectures in Africa, Asia, Europe, and the United States.

PATRICK COLM HOGAN is an associate professor of English at the University of Connecticut. He is the author of *The Politics of Interpretation* and *Joyce, Milton, and the Theory of Influence,* and co-editor of *Criticism and Lacan* and *Literary India: Comparative Studies in Aesthetics, Colonialism, and Culture.*

JANE HOOGESTRAAT is an associate professor of English at Southwest Missouri State University in Springfield, Missouri. Her essays have appeared in *ELH* and in *Resources for American Literary Study;* her poetry has appeared in such journals as *Poetry, Southern Review,* and *High Plains Literary Review.*

WERNER H. KELBER is the Isala Carroll and Percey E. Turner Professor of Religious Studies at Rice University, Houston, Texas. He is the author of *The Oral and the Written Gospel* and has contributed to the areas of the communications history of early Christian texts, Jewish and Christian hermeneutics, orality-literacy, rhetoric, narrative criticism, media studies, and postmodern philosophy.

ALVIN KERNAN is Professor of Humanities Emeritus at Princeton. His most recent book is *The Death of Literature.* Presently he is senior advisor in the humanities at the Andrew W. Mellon Foundation and director of the Mellon Fellowships in humanistic studies.

JULIE STONE PETERS is an associate professor of English and Comparative Literature at Columbia University. She is the author of *Congreve, the Drama, and the Printed Word,* the co-editor of *Women and Human Rights,* and has written a number of articles on orality and literacy, print history, and dramatic theory. She is currently working on a book on theater and printing in Europe, 1500–1900.

DENNIS L. WEEKS is Professor of English at The University of Great Falls in Great Falls, Montana. He is the author of *Steps Toward Salvation: Coinherence and Substitution in the Seven Novels of Charles Williams,* editor of *Classical Rhetorical Thought: Selected Highlights,* editor of *"To Love The World So Well": A Festschrift in Honor of Robert Penn Warren,* and co-editor of *Time, Memory and the Verbal Arts: Essays on the Thought of Walter Ong.*

GEORGE WEICK is Director of the Institute for Liberal Studies and full professor in the Honors College at Kentucky State University in Frankfort, Kentucky. His research interests are in the field of modern British literature. His recent work includes articles on Dylan Thomas for *The Journal of Modern Literature* and *The Explicator*.

Index